How to use Word Bank

The entry word ——— **among** amongst
PREPOSITION
1 Among means surrounded by. ——— What the word means
EXAMPLE The bike lay among piles of chains and pedals.

2 Among means in the company of.
EXAMPLE He was among friends.

3 Among means between more than two.
EXAMPLE The money will be divided among seven
charities.

Usage note ———
gives more information
on how the word is
used, and on any
grammar points

> If there are more than two things, you should use
> 'among'. If there are only two things you should use
> 'between'. The form 'amongst' is a bit old-fashioned and
> 'among' is more often used.

amount amounts amounting amounted ——— Other forms of the word
NOUN
1 An amount of something is how much there is of
it.
EXAMPLE I still do a certain amount of work for them.

Similar words list ——— ▭ **Similar words:** extent, number, quantity
shows words or
phrases with a similar
meaning
▸ VERB
2 If something amounts to a total, all the parts of it
add up to that total.
EXAMPLE Her vocabulary amounted to only 50 words.

amp amps
NOUN   **SCIENCE** ——— **Subject label**
An amp is a unit of electric current.   shows which school
EXAMPLE The current measured 15 amps.   subject the word is
                                                     used in

ample
The word's part of ——— ADJECTIVE
speech
Ample means more than enough.
EXAMPLE There'll be ample opportunity to relax and
swim.

analyse analyses analysing
analysed   **EXAM TERM**
VERB
To analyse means to break down into parts so that
you can describe the main aspects.
EXAMPLE Analyse the reasons for Hitler's rise in Germany. ——— An example of the
                                                               word being used

analysis analyses
NOUN
Analysis is the process of investigating something.
EXAMPLE He proposed a full analysis of the problem.

ancient
How to say the word ——— ▭ **Said:** ayn-shent
ADJECTIVE   **HISTORY**
1 Ancient means existing or happening in the
distant past.
EXAMPLE She loved studying ancient Greece.

Definition number ——— ② Ancient means very old or having a very long
history.
EXAMPLE They visited an ancient monastery.

Introduction

Word Bank is an introductory dictionary for students. Text and layout have been designed so that it is easy to use. *Word Bank* includes several features to help you understand more about the English language, and feel more confident about your reading and writing. These features are listed below. You may find it useful to refer to the labelled extract on the previous page when reading these notes.

The entry word

Each entry begins with the entry word in large blue letters. This is the main form of the word. Next to this, in smaller letters, are listed any other forms of the word. For example, next to the entry word 'analyse' are listed 'analyses', 'analysing' and 'analysed'. These are the other forms that the verb 'analyse' can take. When the entry word is a noun, it is given in the singular (for example, 'amp'), with the plural listed next to it as the other form of the word ('amps').

Parts of speech

The part of speech is given immediately underneath the entry word, in capital letters. This tells you the job that the word does in any sentence. For example, *ADJECTIVE* is given underneath the entry word 'ample', which tells you that 'ample' is a describing word. Sometimes a word can do more than one job, in which case two or more parts of speech are listed, though each with their own meanings. In the entry 'amount', for example, the first meaning given relates to its use as a *NOUN*. Later in the entry, another meaning is given relating to its use as a *VERB*. A little arrow in the margin helps you to spot when more than one part of speech is listed in an entry.

Meanings and examples

The meaning of the word (what is often called its 'definition') is given immediately under the part of speech. Often, of course, a word will have more than one meaning. Although there isn't room to list all the meanings of all the words in *Word Bank*, the most important meanings have been given. These are clearly numbered throughout the entry. For example, three different meanings for 'among' have been given. Each meaning is followed by an example of the word being used in a sentence with exactly that meaning. These are clearly labelled EXAMPLE.

Pronunciation

Some words in English are more difficult to pronounce than others, or are said in a different way from what you would expect. These have been labelled with the symbol ◘ which is followed by a guide of how to say them. Underneath 'ancient', for example, you are told that the word is said 'ayn-shent'. The bit in italics (slanting letters) shows you which bit of the word you stress when you say it.

Similar words

Sometimes you may want to use another word instead of one you have used already. It is good to vary the words you use, and it helps to increase your vocabulary. So look for the symbol ▤, which shows you that there is a list of similar words. In the entry 'amount', for example, this list of similar words is given: 'extent, number, quantity'. Note that these similar words only relate to the meaning immediately above the list (meaning 1).

Subject labels

School subjects such as Geography, Science, English, RE and Drama all have specialist words, or ordinary words with specialist meanings. Many of these words and meanings have been included in *Word Bank*, to give extra help to those of you who are studying these subjects. They are labelled with a blue tag to the right of the entry word, or to the right of the particular meaning that relates to that subject. Several terms that are used in exam questions have also been labelled EXAM TERM in this way, such as 'analyse'.

Usage notes

Some entries end with a usage note within two thin blue lines. Usage notes give you more information about how a word can be used, its spelling or any other feature that will help you to use the word correctly in your writing. The usage note in the entry for 'among', for example, tells you that you should only use 'among' when there are more than two things. It also gives you more information about the two different forms of the word.

A
B
C
D
E
F
G
H
I
J
K
L
M
N
O
P
Q
R
S
T
U
V
W
X
Y
Z

abandon abandons abandoning abandoned
VERB
If you abandon something, you leave it or give it up for good.
EXAMPLE His parents had abandoned him.

▪ **Similar words:** desert, leave

abbreviation abbreviations **ENGLISH**
NOUN
An abbreviation is a short form of a word or phrase.
EXAMPLE **www** is an abbreviation for World Wide Web.

ability abilities
NOUN
Ability is the intelligence or skill needed to do something.
EXAMPLE She questioned his ability to do the job.

▪ **Similar words:** capability, skill

able
ADJECTIVE
If you are able to do something, you can do it.
EXAMPLE The frog is able to jump 3 metres.

abortion abortions
NOUN
If a woman has an abortion, the pregnancy is ended deliberately and the baby dies.
EXAMPLE She considered having an abortion.

about
PREPOSITION
1 About means of or to do with.
EXAMPLE This is a book about London.

▪ ADVERB
2 About means roughly.
EXAMPLE See you about 2 o'clock.

▪ ADVERB OR PREPOSITION
3 About means in different directions.

EXAMPLE The kids ran about in the garden.

▸ PHRASE
4 If you are 'about to' do something, you are just going to do it.
EXAMPLE He was about to leave.

above
PREPOSITION OR ADVERB
1 Above means directly over or higher than something.
EXAMPLE They flew above the clouds.

2 Above means greater than a level or amount.
EXAMPLE The temperature didn't rise above freezing point.

abroad
ADVERB
Abroad means in a foreign country.
EXAMPLE His job means that he often travels abroad.

absence
NOUN
Something's absence from a place is the fact that they are not there.
EXAMPLE Jane looked after the children during my absence.

absolute
ADJECTIVE
Absolute means total and complete.
EXAMPLE This plan is absolute madness.

absolutely
ADVERB
Absolutely means totally and completely.
EXAMPLE She is absolutely right.

abuse abuses abusing abused
NOUN
▢ **Said:** ab-*yoose*
1 Abuse is cruel treatment of someone.
EXAMPLE She suffered abuse as a child.

▪ **Similar words:** ill-treatment, injury
2 Abuse is rude and unkind remarks.
EXAMPLE All I got was a torrent of abuse.

3 The abuse of something is the wrong use of it.
EXAMPLE Alcohol abuse is a serious problem.

▸ VERB
▢ **Said:** ab-*yooze*
4 To abuse someone means to treat them cruelly.
EXAMPLE She had been abused by her father.

▪ **Similar word:** ill-treat
5 If you abuse someone, you speak insultingly to them.
EXAMPLE She abused the workmen in the foulest language.

6 If you abuse something, you use it wrongly or for a bad purpose.
EXAMPLE It is important not to abuse your position.

A
B
C
D
E
F
G
H
I
J
K
L
M
N
O
P
Q
R
S
T
U
V
W
X
Y
Z

academic
ADJECTIVE
Academic work is work done in a school, college or university.
EXAMPLE Their academic standards are high.

accent accents
NOUN
ENGLISH
1 An accent is a way of pronouncing a language.
EXAMPLE She had a strong northern accent.
2 An accent is a mark placed above or below a letter in some languages, which affects the way the letter is pronounced.
EXAMPLE In the French word 'café' the mark over the letter 'e' is an accent.

accept accepts accepting accepted
VERB
1 If you accept something, you say yes to it or take it from someone.
EXAMPLE Did she accept his offer of marriage?
2 If you accept a statement or story, you believe it is true.
EXAMPLE The board accepts his explanation.
3 If a group accepts you, they treat you as one of the group.
EXAMPLE The others don't really accept him.

access accesses accessing accessed
NOUN
1 Access is the right or opportunity to use something or to enter a place.
EXAMPLE The hotel offers easy access to central London.
VERB
ICT
2 If you access information from a computer, you get it.
EXAMPLE He was able to access the information on his computer after entering a password.

accident accidents
NOUN
An accident is an unexpected event in which something unfortunate happens.
EXAMPLE She had an accident at work and broke her arm.

accommodation
NOUN
Accommodation is a place provided for someone to live or work in.
EXAMPLE They found accommodation in the next street.

accompany accompanies accompanying accompanied
VERB
1 If you accompany someone, you go with them.
EXAMPLE He offered to accompany me to the airport.
MUSIC
2 If you accompany a singer or musician, you play an instrument while they sing or play the main tune.
EXAMPLE I accompany him on the guitar.

according to
PREPOSITION
If something is true according to a particular person, that person says that it is true.
EXAMPLE He stayed at the hotel, according to his brother.

account accounts accounting accounted
NOUN
1 An account is a written or spoken report of something.
EXAMPLE There is an account of it in the paper.
2 A bank account is a means of leaving money in the bank.
EXAMPLE I'd like to open an account.
▶ PLURAL NOUN
3 Accounts are records of money spent and received by a person or business.
EXAMPLE He kept detailed accounts.
▶ PHRASE
4 'On account of' means because of.
EXAMPLE He couldn't be present, on account of a sore throat.
▶ VERB
5 To account for something is to explain it.
EXAMPLE This might account for her strange behaviour.

accurate
ADJECTIVE
Accurate is completely correct or precise.
EXAMPLE They issued an accurate description of the killer.
▪ Similar words: correct, exact, precise

accuse accuses accusing accused
VERB
If you accuse someone of doing something wrong, you say they have done it.
EXAMPLE He accuses her of having an affair.

ache aches aching ached
VERB
1 If a part of your body aches, you feel a continuous dull pain there.
EXAMPLE My leg still aches when I sit down.
▶ NOUN
2 An ache is a continuous dull pain.
EXAMPLE I've got lots of aches and pains.

achieve achieves achieving achieved
VERB
If you achieve something, you successfully do it or cause it to happen.
EXAMPLE We have achieved what we set out to do.
▪ Similar word: fulfil

achievement achievements
NOUN
An achievement is something that you succeed in doing.
EXAMPLE Running that distance was a great achievement.

acid acids
SCIENCE
NOUN
An acid is a solution which turns litmus paper red.
EXAMPLE He used litmus paper to test whether the solution was an acid or an alkali.

A

acknowledge acknowledges acknowledging acknowledged
VERB
If you acknowledge a fact or situation, you agree or admit it is true.
EXAMPLE He acknowledges that he is responsible.

☰ **Similar words:** accept, admit

acquire acquires acquiring acquired
VERB
If you acquire something, you get it.
EXAMPLE He wanted to acquire a new computer.

acre acres
NOUN
An acre is a unit for measuring areas of land.
EXAMPLE The property is set in two acres of land.

across
PREPOSITION OR ADVERB
1 Across means from one side to the other.
EXAMPLE He walked across Hyde Park.

2 Across means to or on the other side.
EXAMPLE Look at the house across the street.

act acts acting acted
VERB
1 If you act, you do something.
EXAMPLE We have to act quickly.

2 If you act in a particular way, you behave in that way.
EXAMPLE Don't act like a lunatic.

3 If a person or thing acts as something else, it has the function or does the job of that thing.
EXAMPLE She was able to act as an interpreter.

DRAMA
4 If you act in a play or film, you play a role in it.
EXAMPLE She always wanted to act.

☰ **Similar word:** perform

▸ NOUN
5 An act is a single thing someone does.
EXAMPLE The accused is guilty of an act of brutality.

☰ **Similar words:** action, deed

CITIZENSHIP
6 An Act of Parliament is a law passed by the government.
EXAMPLE The great Education Act was passed in 1944.

☰ **Similar words:** bill, law

action actions
NOUN
An action is something you do.
EXAMPLE He had a reason for his action.

active
ADJECTIVE
Someone who is active moves around a lot or does a lot of things.
EXAMPLE How physically active are you?

activity activities
NOUN
1 Activity is a situation in which a lot of things are happening at the same time.
EXAMPLE There was a buzz of activity in the village.

2 An activity is something you do for pleasure.
EXAMPLE What is your favourite activity?

actor actors   **DRAMA**
NOUN
An actor is a man or woman whose job is performing in plays or films.
EXAMPLE You have to be a good actor to play that part.

actress actresses   **DRAMA**
NOUN
An actress is a woman whose job is performing in plays or films.
EXAMPLE She's a great dramatic actress.

actual
ADJECTIVE
Actual means real.
EXAMPLE That is the rough figure – the actual figure is much higher.

actually
ADVERB
1 Actually means really.
EXAMPLE No one actually saw the shark.

2 Actually means in fact.
EXAMPLE She's a friend of mine, actually.

acute
ADJECTIVE
1 Acute means severe or intense.
EXAMPLE She felt an acute pain in her side.

2 An acute angle is an angle which   **MATHS**
measures less than 90 degrees.
EXAMPLE The acute angle measured 68 degrees.

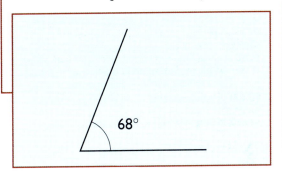

addition additions
NOUN
An addition is something that has been added to something else.
EXAMPLE This building is a fine addition to London's architecture.

additional
ADJECTIVE
Additional means extra or more.
EXAMPLE They took on additional staff for Christmas.

address addresses addressing addressed
NOUN
1 An address is exactly where you live.
EXAMPLE My address is 57 Castle Road, Whitstable.

▸ VERB
2 If a letter is addressed to you, it has your name and address written on it.
EXAMPLE The letter was addressed to Dr Jones.

3 If you address a group of people, you give a speech to them.
EXAMPLE He plans to address a mass meeting in Bristol.

A

B
C
D
E
F
G
H
I
J
K
L
M
N
O
P
Q
R
S
T
U
V
W
X
Y
Z

adequate
ADJECTIVE
Adequate means enough in amount, or good enough for a purpose.
EXAMPLE Eating only pasta is not an adequate diet.
Similar words: enough, sufficient

adjective adjectives
NOUN   ENGLISH
An adjective is a word which tells you something about a noun.
EXAMPLE 'Large' and 'white' are both adjectives.

adjust adjusts adjusting adjusted
VERB
1 If you adjust something, you alter it in some way.
EXAMPLE She adjusts the lamp so that it points at the ceiling.
2 If you adjust to a new situation, you get used to it.
EXAMPLE She has adjusted well to becoming a mother.

administration administrations
NOUN
1 Administration is the work of supervising an organization.
EXAMPLE Too much time is spent on administration.
2 The administration is the group of people that manages an organization or a country.
EXAMPLE He was part of the Clinton administration.

admire admires admiring admired
VERB
To admire means to respect and approve of.
EXAMPLE He admired the way she had coped with life.

admit admits admitting admitted
VERB
1 If you admit something, you agree that it is true.
EXAMPLE The president admitted taking bribes.
2 To admit someone to a place is to allow them to enter it.
EXAMPLE She was admitted to hospital with a fever.

adolescence
NOUN
Adolescence is the time between childhood and adulthood.
EXAMPLE Barry had a stormy adolescence.

adopt adopts adopting adopted
VERB
1 If you adopt a child, you take him or her into your family as your son or daughter.
EXAMPLE The couple wanted to adopt a child.
2 If you adopt an attitude, you start to have it.
EXAMPLE Please don't adopt that tone of voice.

adult adults
NOUN
An adult is a fully developed person or animal.
EXAMPLE All children must be accompanied by an adult.

advance advances advancing advanced
VERB
1 To advance is to move forward.
EXAMPLE Rebel forces are advancing on the capital.
▶ NOUN
2 An advance in something is progress in it.
EXAMPLE It was a period of great scientific advances.

Similar words: development, progress
▶ ADJECTIVE
3 Advance means happening before an event.
EXAMPLE The event received little advance publicity.
▶ PHRASE
4 If you do something 'in advance', you do it before something else happens.
EXAMPLE We booked up the room well in advance.

advanced
ADJECTIVE
Advanced means further along a scale.
EXAMPLE The course is suitable for both beginners and advanced students.

advantage advantages
NOUN
1 An advantage is a benefit or something that puts you in a better position.
EXAMPLE She explained the advantages of the new system.
▶ PHRASE
2 If you 'take advantage of' someone, you treat them unfairly for your own benefit.
EXAMPLE She took advantage of him even after they were divorced.
3 If you 'take advantage of' something, you make use of it.
EXAMPLE He took advantage of the time off to visit his mother.

adverb adverbs
NOUN   ENGLISH
An adverb is a word which tells you something about a verb.
EXAMPLE 'Quickly' and 'badly' are both adverbs.

advertise advertises advertising advertised
VERB
If you advertise something, you tell people about it.
EXAMPLE The house was advertised for sale at £149,000.

advertisement advertisements
Said: ad-ver-tiss-ment
NOUN
An advertisement is an announcement about something in a newspaper or poster, or on screen.
EXAMPLE The advertisements were eye-catching.

advice
NOUN
Advice is a suggestion from someone about what you should do.
EXAMPLE I gave him advice on how to build it.
Similar words: guidance, suggestion

advise advises advising advised
VERB
If you advise someone to do something, you tell them you think they should do it.
EXAMPLE She advised him to leave as soon as possible.

⬛ Similar words: recommend, suggest

affair affairs
NOUN
1 An affair is an event or series of events.
EXAMPLE The funeral was a sad affair.

2 To have an affair is to have a secret sexual or romantic relationship.
EXAMPLE No one knew of their affair.

▶ PLURAL NOUN
3 Your affairs are your private and personal life.
EXAMPLE Why had he interfered in her affairs?

affect affects affecting affected
VERB
To affect something is to cause it to change.
EXAMPLE Look at the ways in which computers affect our lives.

afford affords affording afforded
VERB
1 To afford something is to have enough money to pay for it.
EXAMPLE I can't afford a new car.

2 If you cannot afford something to happen, it would be harmful for you if it happened.
EXAMPLE We can't afford another scandal in the firm.

afraid
ADJECTIVE
1 Afraid means frightened or worried.
EXAMPLE I was afraid of the other boys.

⬛ Similar words: fearful, frightened, scared

Africa   GEOGRAPHY
NOUN
Africa is the second largest continent.
EXAMPLE They travelled through central Africa.

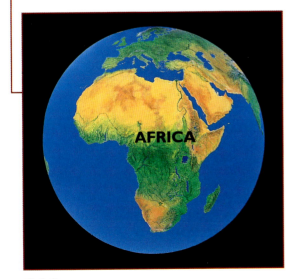

AFRICA

African Africans
ADJECTIVE
1 African means to do with Africa.
EXAMPLE He visited most African countries.

▶ NOUN
2 An African is someone who comes from Africa.
EXAMPLE Fish is important in the diet of many Africans.

after
PREPOSITION OR ADVERB
1 After means later than a particular time, date or event.
EXAMPLE She started work after breakfast.

⬛ Similar words: afterwards, following, later
2 After means behind and following.
EXAMPLE They ran after her.

▶ PREPOSITION
3 After means trying to get something.
EXAMPLE The police are after them.

afternoon afternoons
NOUN
The afternoon is the part of the day between 12 noon and about 6 o'clock.
EXAMPLE He's arriving in the afternoon.

afterwards
ADVERB
Afterwards means after an event or time.
EXAMPLE He was taken to hospital but died soon afterwards.

again
ADVERB
Again means happening one more time.
EXAMPLE He looked forward to becoming a father again.

against
PREPOSITION
1 Against means touching and leaning on.
EXAMPLE He leaned against the wall.

2 Against means in opposition to.
EXAMPLE The match was against England.

age ages ageing aging aged
NOUN
1 The age of someone is the number of years they have lived.
EXAMPLE Her nephew is ten years of age.

2 Age is the quality of being old.
EXAMPLE It's a wine capable of improving with age.

HISTORY
3 An age is a particular period in history.
EXAMPLE They are studying the Iron Age.

▶ VERB
4 To age is to grow old or to appear older.
EXAMPLE He has aged a lot in the last few months.

'Ageing' and 'aging' are both correct spellings.

agency agencies
NOUN
An agency is an organization which provides certain services.
EXAMPLE They ran a detective agency.

agenda agendas
NOUN
An agenda is a list of items to be discussed at a meeting.
EXAMPLE This issue wasn't on the agenda.

A

agent agents
NOUN

1 An agent is someone who arranges work for other people.
EXAMPLE He was a theatrical agent.

2 An agent is someone who works for their country's secret service.
EXAMPLE He suspected Charles was an enemy agent.

aggressive
ADJECTIVE

Aggressive means full of hostility and violence.
EXAMPLE He's an aggressive child.

agree agrees agreeing agreed
VERB

1 If you agree with someone, you have the same opinion as they do.
EXAMPLE I'm not sure I agree with you.

2 If you agree to something, you say you will do it.
EXAMPLE He agreed to pay me for the drawings.

agreement agreements
NOUN

An agreement is a decision.
EXAMPLE They took six hours to reach an agreement.

agriculture   GEOGRAPHY
NOUN

Agriculture is farming.
EXAMPLE The land in East Anglia is mostly used for agriculture.

ahead
ADVERB

1 Ahead means in front.
EXAMPLE He looked ahead.

2 Ahead means in the future.
EXAMPLE I haven't had time to think far ahead.

aid aids
NOUN

1 Aid is money, equipment or services provided for people in need.
EXAMPLE They sent food and medical aid to the region.

2 Aid is help or support.
EXAMPLE The report was compiled with the aid of experts.

3 An aid is something that makes a task easier.
EXAMPLE He bought an overhead projector and other teaching aids.

AIDS
NOUN

AIDS is a disease which destroys the body's natural system of immunity to diseases.
EXAMPLE He found out he had AIDS in February.

aim aims aiming aimed
VERB

1 To aim something is to point it in a direction.
EXAMPLE The missile was aimed at the arms factory.

■ **Similar word:** point

2 If you aim to do something, you are planning to do it.
EXAMPLE I aim to arrive early.

■ **Similar words:** intend, mean, plan

▸ *NOUN*

3 Your aim is what you intend to achieve.
EXAMPLE The aim of the festival is to encourage world peace.

■ **Similar words:** goal, intention, objective

air
NOUN   SCIENCE

1 Air is a mixture of oxygen and other gases which forms the earth's atmosphere.
EXAMPLE The window let in a blast of cold air.

2 The air is the space around things or above the ground.
EXAMPLE The troops fired their guns in the air.

aircraft
NOUN

An aircraft is any vehicle that can fly.
EXAMPLE Three military aircraft were destroyed.

air force air forces
NOUN

An air force is the part of a country's military organization that fights using aircraft.
EXAMPLE He joined the Royal Air Force at the outbreak of war.

airline airlines
NOUN

An airline is a company which provides air travel.
EXAMPLE They travelled on the Dutch airline, KLM.

airport airports
NOUN

An airport is a place where people go to catch planes.
EXAMPLE The flight goes from Heathrow Airport.

alarm alarms alarming alarmed
NOUN

1 Alarm is a feeling of fear and worry.
EXAMPLE The cat sprang back in alarm.

2 An alarm is an automatic device used to warn people of something.
EXAMPLE The car alarm suddenly went off.

▸ *VERB*

3 If something alarms you, it makes you worried and anxious.
EXAMPLE We couldn't see what had alarmed him.

album albums
NOUN   MUSIC

1 An album is a CD, cassette or record with songs on it.
EXAMPLE She loved the Beatles' final album.

2 An album is a book in which you keep a collection of things.
EXAMPLE She stuck my photo in her album.

alcohol
NOUN
Alcohol is any drink that can make people drunk.
EXAMPLE No alcohol is allowed on the premises.

alert alerts alerting alerted
ADJECTIVE
1 Alert means paying full attention.
EXAMPLE The cat was alert and watchful.

▰ Similar words: attentive, watchful

▸ VERB
2 If you alert someone you warn them.
EXAMPLE He alerted the police to the activities of the group.

alive
ADJECTIVE
Alive means living.
EXAMPLE She doesn't know if he is alive or dead.

▰ Similar word: living

alkali alkalis
SCIENCE
NOUN
An alkali is a solution which turns litmus paper blue.
EXAMPLE He added one drop of alkali to each test tube.

all
ADJECTIVE, PRONOUN OR ADVERB
1 All is used when referring to the whole of something.
EXAMPLE Why did he have to say all that?

▸ ADVERB
2 All is used when saying the two sides in a contest have the same score.
EXAMPLE The final score was six points all.

alley alleys
NOUN
An alley is a narrow passage between buildings.
EXAMPLE There was a fight going on in the alley.

alliteration
ENGLISH
NOUN
Alliteration is the use of several words together which begin with the same letter or letters.
EXAMPLE 'She shivers and shakes' is an example of alliteration.

allow allows allowing allowed
VERB
1 If you allow something, you say it is all right or let it happen.
EXAMPLE He allowed me to take the course.

2 If you allow a period of time or an amount of something, you set it aside for a particular purpose.
EXAMPLE Allow four hours for the paint to dry.

all right alright
ADJECTIVE
1 All right means satisfactory but not especially good.
EXAMPLE 'Do you like the meal?' 'It's all right.'

2 All right means safe and not harmed.
EXAMPLE Are you all right?

3 You say 'all right' to agree to something.
EXAMPLE 'Can you help?' 'All right.'

ally allies
HISTORY
▱ Said: al-lie
NOUN
An ally is a person or country that helps and supports another.
EXAMPLE France's allies included Denmark and Sweden.

▰ Similar words: friend, helper, partner

almost
ADVERB
Almost means very nearly.
EXAMPLE Over the past decade their wages have almost doubled.

▰ Similar words: just about, nearly

alone
ADJECTIVE OR ADVERB
Alone means not with other people or things.
EXAMPLE He just wanted to be alone.

along
PREPOSITION
1 Along means happening or existing from one end to the other of something.
EXAMPLE Metal filing cabinets stretched along each wall.

▸ ADVERB
2 Along means moving forward.
EXAMPLE We marched along wearily.

3 Along means with someone.
EXAMPLE Why don't you bring her along?

alongside
PREPOSITION OR ADVERB
Alongside means next to something.
EXAMPLE He worked alongside Robert De Niro.

Do not use 'of' after 'alongside'.

already
ADVERB
Already means having happened before the present time or earlier than expected.
EXAMPLE She has already gone to bed.

also
ADVERB
Also means in addition to something that has just been mentioned.
EXAMPLE Two other people were also injured.

altar altars
RE
NOUN
An altar is a holy table in a church or temple.
EXAMPLE The priest placed the prayer book on the altar.

B C D E F G H I J K L M N O P Q R S T U V W X Y Z

alter alters altering altered
VERB
To alter means to change.
EXAMPLE Little had altered in the village.

alternative alternatives
NOUN
1 An alternative is something you can do or have instead of something else.
EXAMPLE Are there alternatives to prison?

▶ ADJECTIVE
2 Alternative plans or actions can happen or be done instead of what is already happening or being done.
EXAMPLE There are alternative methods of travel.

Similar word: other

although
CONJUNCTION
Although means in spite of the fact that.
EXAMPLE He wasn't the winner, although he set a new British record.

altogether
ADVERB
1 Altogether means entirely.
EXAMPLE She wasn't altogether sorry to be leaving.

2 Altogether means in total.
EXAMPLE I get paid £1000 a month altogether.

always
ADVERB
Always means all the time or for ever.
EXAMPLE She's always moaning.

amateur amateurs
NOUN
An amateur is someone who does something as a hobby rather than as a job.
EXAMPLE He began playing football as an amateur.

amazing
ADJECTIVE
Amazing means very surprising or remarkable.
EXAMPLE New York is an amazing city.

Similar words: remarkable, surprising, wonderful

ambassador ambassadors
NOUN
An ambassador is a person sent to a foreign country to represent his or her own government.
EXAMPLE He was the German ambassador to Poland.

ambition ambitions
NOUN
An ambition is something that you want very much to achieve.
EXAMPLE Her lifelong ambition was to be a teacher.

amenity amenities
Said: am-*mee*-nit-ee
NOUN
Amenities are things that are available for the public to use.
EXAMPLE The hotel amenities include health clubs and a swimming pool.

America
NOUN
GEOGRAPHY
America refers to the United States, or to the whole of North, South and Central America.
EXAMPLE Have you been to America?

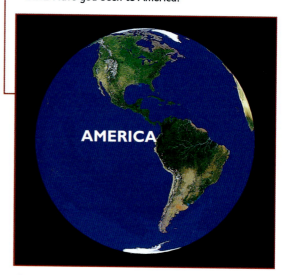

AMERICA

American Americans
ADJECTIVE
1 American means to do with the United States.
EXAMPLE He enjoyed watching American films.

▶ NOUN
2 An American is someone who comes from the United States.
EXAMPLE The prize was won by two Americans.

among amongst
PREPOSITION
1 Among means surrounded by.
EXAMPLE The bike lay among piles of chains and pedals.

2 Among means in the company of.
EXAMPLE He was among friends.

3 Among means between more than two.
EXAMPLE The money will be divided among seven charities.

If there are more than two things, you should use 'among'. If there are only two things you should use 'between'. The form 'amongst' is a bit old-fashioned and 'among' is more often used.

amount amounts amounting amounted
NOUN
1 An amount of something is how much there is of it.
EXAMPLE I still do a certain amount of work for them.

Similar words: extent, number, quantity

▶ VERB
2 If something amounts to a total, all the parts of it add up to that total.
EXAMPLE The collection amounted to only 50 pounds.

amp amps
NOUN
SCIENCE
An amp is a unit of electric current.
EXAMPLE The current measured 15 amps.

ample
ADJECTIVE
Ample means more than enough.
EXAMPLE There'll be ample opportunity to relax and swim.

analyse analyses analysing analysed

EXAM TERM

VERB

To analyse means to break down into parts so that you can describe the main aspects.

EXAMPLE Analyse the reasons for Hitler's rise to power in Germany.

analysis analyses

NOUN

Analysis is the process of investigating something.

EXAMPLE He proposed a full analysis of the problem.

ancient

📢 **Said:** *ayn*-shent

ADJECTIVE

HISTORY

1 Ancient means existing or happening in the distant past.

EXAMPLE She loved studying ancient Greece.

2 Ancient means very old or having a very long history.

EXAMPLE They visited an ancient monastery.

anger angers angering angered

NOUN

1 Anger is the strong feeling you get when you feel someone has behaved in an unfair or cruel way.

EXAMPLE There was anger at the bombing.

📗 **Similar words:** fury, rage

▶ *VERB*

2 If something angers you, it makes you feel angry.

EXAMPLE The decision has angered some residents.

angle angles

NOUN

MATHS

1 An angle is the space between two lines at the point where they join together, measured in degrees.

EXAMPLE The angle measured 45 degrees.

2 An angle is a direction from which you look at something.

EXAMPLE He had painted the vase from all angles.

angry angrier angriest

ADJECTIVE

Angry means very annoyed.

EXAMPLE Are you angry with me for some reason?

📗 **Similar words:** furious, mad

animal animals

NOUN

An animal is any living being except a plant.

EXAMPLE He was attacked by wild animals.

anniversary anniversaries

NOUN

An anniversary is a date which is remembered because something special happened on that date in a previous year.

EXAMPLE Today is our wedding anniversary.

announce announces announcing announced

VERB

If you announce something, you tell people about it publicly or officially.

EXAMPLE The team was announced on Friday morning.

📗 **Similar words:** broadcast, make known, proclaim

announcement announcements

NOUN

An announcement is an official statement about something.

EXAMPLE There will be further announcements later.

annual

ADJECTIVE

1 Annual means happening or done once a year.

EXAMPLE The annual conference was in July, as usual.

2 Annual means happening or calculated over a period of one year.

EXAMPLE The annual budget for defence is much lower.

another

ADJECTIVE OR PRONOUN

Another thing or person is one more thing or person.

EXAMPLE We're going to have another baby.

answer answers answering answered

📢 **Said:** *arn*-ser

VERB

1 To answer means to reply.

EXAMPLE Just answer the question.

📗 **Similar words:** reply, respond

▶ *NOUN*

2 An answer is a reply.

EXAMPLE I got their answer to my letter.

📗 **Similar words:** reply, response

3 An answer is a solution to a problem.

EXAMPLE There is no easy answer to this problem.

Antarctica

GEOGRAPHY

NOUN

Antarctica is the continent around the South Pole.

EXAMPLE They sailed south to Antarctica.

anthology anthologies

ENGLISH

NOUN

An anthology is a collection of writings by different authors.

EXAMPLE Get out your anthology of modern writers.

antique antiques

📢 **Said:** an-*teek*

NOUN

ART

1 An antique is an object from the past which is collected.

EXAMPLE He deals in antiques.

▶ *ADJECTIVE*

2 Antique means from or concerning the past.

EXAMPLE They loved antique furniture.

A

antonym antonyms

NOUN

An antonym is a word opposite in meaning to another word.

EXAMPLE 'Good' and 'bad' are antonyms.

anxiety anxieties

NOUN

Anxiety is nervousness or worry.

EXAMPLE They shared their anxieties about the journey.

anxious

⬛ **Said:** *ank*-shuss

ADJECTIVE

1 Anxious means nervous or worried.

EXAMPLE He was still anxious about the situation.

2 If you are anxious to do something, you very much want to do it.

EXAMPLE She was anxious to have children.

anybody

PRONOUN

Anybody means the same as anyone.

EXAMPLE Was anybody else there?

anyone

PRONOUN

Anyone means any person.

EXAMPLE I won't tell anyone.

anything

PRONOUN

Anything means any object, event, situation or action.

EXAMPLE Can you see anything?

anyway

ADVERB

Anyway means in any case.

EXAMPLE She doesn't want children – not yet, anyway.

anywhere

ADVERB

Anywhere means in, at or to any place.

EXAMPLE Can you see him anywhere?

apart

ADVERB OR ADJECTIVE

1 Apart means at some distance from something.

EXAMPLE The couple lived apart for four years.

2 When you take something apart, you separate it into pieces.

EXAMPLE Greg took the model glider apart.

▶ PHRASE

3 'Apart from' means except for, or in addition to.

EXAMPLE Apart from sport, my other interest is music.

apartment apartments

NOUN

An apartment is a set of rooms for living in.

EXAMPLE She has an apartment in New York.

apostrophe apostrophes

⬛ **Said:** a-*poss*-troff-ee

NOUN

An apostrophe is a punctuation mark which looks like this: '.

EXAMPLE There is an apostrophe in the word 'you're'.

1 An apostrophe with 's' at the end of a noun shows possession: 'Ian's books'. If the noun already has an 's' at the end, you just add the apostrophe: 'the fishes' gills'.
2 An apostrophe also shows where one or more letters have been missed out of a word: 'Who's next?'

apparatus

NOUN

The apparatus is the equipment used to carry out an experiment.

EXAMPLE The apparatus was a Bunsen burner and a flask.

apparent

ADJECTIVE

Apparent means clear and obvious.

EXAMPLE He left the room for no apparent reason.

apparently

ADVERB

You use 'apparently' to refer to something that seems to be true.

EXAMPLE Apparently the party was a great success.

appeal appeals appealing appealed

VERB

1 If you appeal for something, you make an urgent request for it.

EXAMPLE The police appealed for witnesses to come forward.

2 If something appeals to you, you find it attractive or interesting.

EXAMPLE The idea didn't appeal to me.

▶ NOUN

3 An appeal is a formal or serious request.

EXAMPLE The politician made an appeal for peace.

appear appears appearing appeared

VERB

1 When something appears, it moves so that it can be seen.

EXAMPLE Two men suddenly appeared from nowhere.

⬛ **Similar words:** come into view, emerge, show up

2 If something appears to be a certain way, it seems or looks that way

EXAMPLE He appeared to be searching for something.

appearance appearances

NOUN

1 An appearance is an arrival.

EXAMPLE The prompt appearance of the police saved him.

2 An appearance is the way something looks.

EXAMPLE She is so fussy about her appearance.

application applications

NOUN

An application is a formal request for something.

EXAMPLE His application to join the army was rejected.

apply applies applying applied
VERB
1 If you apply for something, you formally ask for it.
EXAMPLE I'm continuing to apply for jobs.

2 If something applies to a person or a situation, it is relevant to that person or situation.
EXAMPLE The law applies only to foreigners.

3 If you apply something to a surface, you put it on or rub it into the surface.
EXAMPLE She applied glue to the upper edge.

appoint appoints appointing appointed
VERB
To appoint is to choose formally.
EXAMPLE It made sense to appoint a banker to this job.

appointment appointments
NOUN
An appointment is an arrangement that you have with someone to meet them.
EXAMPLE I had an appointment with the doctor.

■ Similar words: date, engagement, meeting

appreciate appreciates appreciating appreciated
VERB
1 If you appreciate something, you like it because of its good qualities.
EXAMPLE He appreciates fine wines.

■ Similar words: prize, value

2 If you appreciate a situation or problem, you understand it.
EXAMPLE I appreciate the reasons for your anxiety.

3 If you appreciate something, you are grateful for it.
EXAMPLE I really appreciate you coming to visit me.

approach approaches approaching approached
VERB
1 To approach something is to come near or nearer to it.
EXAMPLE She approached the animal cautiously.

2 If you approach a situation or problem in a particular way, you think about it or deal with it in that way.
EXAMPLE The bank has approached the issue in a practical way.

▶ NOUN
3 An approach to a situation or problem is a way of thinking about it or dealing with it.
EXAMPLE He was very professional in his approach.

appropriate
ADJECTIVE
Appropriate means suitable or acceptable for a particular situation.
EXAMPLE It was not an appropriate film to show at that time.

approval
NOUN
1 Approval is agreement given to a plan or request.
EXAMPLE The plan will require the approval of the local authority.

■ Similar words: agreement, permission

2 Approval is admiration.
EXAMPLE She looked at James with approval.

approve approves approving approved
VERB
1 If you approve of something, you think it is acceptable or good.
EXAMPLE Not everyone approves of the festival.

■ Similar words: favour, like

2 To approve a plan or idea is formally to agree to it.
EXAMPLE Parliament approved the programme of economic reforms.

■ Similar words: agree to, permit

Arab Arabs
NOUN
An Arab is a member of a group of people who live in the Middle East and North Africa.
EXAMPLE He loved the Arabs and their culture.

Arabic
ADJECTIVE
Arabic is a language spoken in the Middle East and North Africa.
EXAMPLE The book was in Arabic.

arch arches arching arched
NOUN
1 An arch is a structure which has a curved top supported on pillars or a wall.
EXAMPLE They met beneath the railway arches.

▶ VERB
2 If something arches or if you arch it, it forms a curved line or shape.
EXAMPLE Don't arch your back; keep your spine straight.

archaeology   HISTORY
🔊 Said: ar-kee-*ol*-loj-ee
NOUN
Archaeology is the study of the past by digging up remains of buildings and other things.
EXAMPLE Archaeology has increased our knowledge of human history.

area areas   GEOGRAPHY
NOUN
1 An area is a particular part of a place, country or the world.
EXAMPLE It was a built-up area of the city.

■ Similar words: district, region, zone

2 An area of knowledge, interest or activity is a particular kind of subject or activity.
EXAMPLE Computers affect almost every area of our lives.

MATHS
3 The area is the amount of flat space that a piece of ground or a surface covers.
EXAMPLE The area of the pool was 49 square metres.

A

argue argues arguing argued
VERB

1 If you argue with someone, you disagree with them.
EXAMPLE He dislikes players who argue with referees.

2 If you argue that something is the case, you give reasons why you think it is so.
EXAMPLE She argued that her client had been wrongly accused.

argument arguments
NOUN

1 An argument is a disagreement between two people.
EXAMPLE We got into a big argument.

2 An argument is a point or a set of reasons you use to try to convince people about something.
EXAMPLE Do you accept this argument?

arm arms arming armed
NOUN

1 Your arms are the part of your body between your shoulder and your wrist.
EXAMPLE She stretched her arms out.

▶ PLURAL NOUN

2 Arms are weapons used in a war.
EXAMPLE They uncovered extensive supplies of arms.

▶ VERB

3 To arm someone is to provide them with weapons.
EXAMPLE He armed his men with guns.

army armies
NOUN

An army is a large group of soldiers who are trained to fight on land.
EXAMPLE He joined the army and fought in France.

around
PREPOSITION

1 Around means situated at various points in a place or area.
EXAMPLE There are many seats around the building.

2 Around means from place to place inside an area.
EXAMPLE We walked around the showroom.

3 Around means surrounding.
EXAMPLE We were sitting around a table.

4 Around means at approximately the time or place mentioned.
EXAMPLE The attacks began around noon.

▶ ADVERB

5 Around means here and there.
EXAMPLE His papers were scattered all around.

arrange arranges arranging arranged
VERB

1 If you arrange to do something, you make plans for it.
EXAMPLE Why don't you arrange to meet him later?

2 If you arrange something for someone, you make it possible for them to have it or do it.
EXAMPLE The bank has arranged a loan for her.

3 If you arrange objects, you set them out in a particular way.
EXAMPLE He started to arrange the books in piles.

arrangement arrangements
NOUN

1 An arrangement is an agreement that you make with someone to do something.
EXAMPLE The caves can be visited only by prior arrangement.

2 Arrangements are plans and preparations.
EXAMPLE I'm in charge of all the travel arrangements.

arrest arrests arresting arrested
VERB

CITIZENSHIP

1 If the police arrest someone, they take them to a police station because they believe the person may have committed a crime.
EXAMPLE Police arrested five men in connection with the attack.

▶ NOUN

2 An arrest is the act of arresting someone.
EXAMPLE An offer of a reward led to the arrest of the bombers.

arrival arrivals
NOUN

An arrival is the act or time of arriving.
EXAMPLE I apologize for my late arrival.

arrive arrives arriving arrived
VERB

1 When you arrive at a place or decision you reach it.
EXAMPLE A new group of guests had arrived.

arrow arrows
NOUN

An arrow is a weapon shot from a bow.
EXAMPLE The warriors were armed with bows and arrows.

art arts
NOUN

ART

1 Art is the creation of objects such as paintings and sculptures; also used to refer to the objects themselves.
EXAMPLE I've never been any good at art.

2 An activity is called an art when it requires special skill or ability.
EXAMPLE He was a master of the art of diplomacy.

article articles
NOUN

1 An article is a piece of writing in a newspaper or magazine.
EXAMPLE Have you read this article in *The Economist*?

2 An article is a particular item.
EXAMPLE The lost property included ten articles of clothing.

artist artists
NOUN

ART

An artist is a person who produces works of art.
EXAMPLE Van Gogh was a great artist.

Asia
NOUN

GEOGRAPHY

Asia is the largest continent.
EXAMPLE Asia is to the east of Europe.

ASIA

Asian Asians

ADJECTIVE

1 Asian means to do with Asia.
EXAMPLE They loved Asian food.

▶ NOUN

2 An Asian is someone who comes from Asia.
EXAMPLE Indians and Pakistanis are Asians.

aside

ADVERB

Aside means to one side.
EXAMPLE She closed the book and laid it aside.

aspect aspects

NOUN

An aspect of something is one of its features.
EXAMPLE This research highlights a new aspect of the disease.

assault assaults assaulting assaulted

NOUN

1 An assault is a violent attack on someone.
EXAMPLE I was later charged with assault.

▶ VERB

2 To assault someone is to attack them violently.
EXAMPLE She may have been sexually assaulted by her killer.

assembly assemblies   **RE**

NOUN

An assembly is a gathering of people for a religious purpose.
EXAMPLE School assembly takes place every day.

assess assesses assessing assessed   **EXAM TERM**

VERB

To assess means to look at the good and bad points of a subject and come to your own opinion about it.
EXAMPLE Assess the value of weight training to footballers.

asset assets

NOUN

1 An asset is a person or thing considered useful.
EXAMPLE He will be a great asset to the club.

▶ PLURAL NOUN

2 The assets of a person or company are all the things they own that could be sold to raise money.
EXAMPLE The company had assets of £3.5 million.

assist assists assisting assisted

VERB

To assist is to help.
EXAMPLE She assisted me with my chores.

assistance

NOUN

Assistance is help.
EXAMPLE He had the assistance of volunteers.

assistant assistants

NOUN

An assistant is someone who helps another person in their work.
EXAMPLE He called his assistant to take over.

associate associates associating associated

VERB

1 To associate two things is to connect them in your mind.
EXAMPLE Dignity is the quality that I associate mostly with her.

▣ Similar words: connect, link, relate

2 If you associate with a group of people, you spend a lot of time with them.
EXAMPLE She likes associating with criminals.

▣ Similar word: mix

▶ NOUN

3 Your associates are the people you work with.
EXAMPLE The owner's business associates arrived for a meeting.

association associations

NOUN

1 An association is an organization for people who have similar interests, jobs or aims.
EXAMPLE A housing association helped them find a home.

2 An association between things is a link you make in your mind between them.
EXAMPLE The place had associations for her.

assonance   **ENGLISH**

NOUN

Assonance is the use of similar sounds in words near to each other.
EXAMPLE 'The light of my life' is an example of assonance.

assume assumes assuming assumed

VERB

To assume is to suppose or accept.
EXAMPLE I assumed that he would come.

▣ Similar words: believe, presume, suppose

assumption assumptions

NOUN

An assumption is a belief.
EXAMPLE The general assumption was that I was guilty.

assure assures assuring assured

VERB

1 To assure someone is to tell them.
EXAMPLE I can assure you that the animals are well cared for.

2 If you assure yourself of something, you are certain to get it as a result.
EXAMPLE Their two victories assured them of a medal.

athlete athletes

NOUN

An athlete is someone who is good at sport.
EXAMPLE She was an Olympic athlete.

A

B
C
D
E
F
G
H
I
J
K
L
M
N
O
P
Q
R
S
T
U
V
W
X
Y
Z

atlas atlases `GEOGRAPHY`
NOUN
An atlas is a book of maps.
EXAMPLE Look in your atlas at a map of Europe.

atmosphere atmospheres `SCIENCE`
NOUN
1 The atmosphere is the air and other gases that surround a planet.
EXAMPLE Cigarettes pollute the atmosphere.

2 Atmosphere is the general mood of a place.
EXAMPLE The restaurant had a relaxed atmosphere.

atom atoms `SCIENCE`
NOUN
An atom is the smallest particle that can take part in a chemical reaction.
EXAMPLE Water is made from one atom of oxygen and two atoms of hydrogen.

attach attaches attaching attached
VERB
To attach is to join or fasten together.
EXAMPLE The gadget can be attached to any vertical surface.

attack attacks attacking attacked
VERB
1 To attack someone is to use violence against them.
EXAMPLE She attacked him with a knife.
▪ Similar words: assault, set upon

2 To attack someone or their ideas is to criticize them strongly.
EXAMPLE He attacked the government's economic policies.
▪ Similar word: criticize

▶ NOUN
3 An attack is violent physical action against someone.
EXAMPLE The soldiers launched their attack at dawn.
▪ Similar word: assault

4 An attack on someone or on their ideas is strong criticism of them.
EXAMPLE Repeated attacks on his work led to his suicide.

attempt attempts attempting attempted
VERB
1 To attempt is to try.
EXAMPLE They attempted to escape that very night.

▶ NOUN
2 An attempt is an act of trying to do something.
EXAMPLE He made no attempt to help.

attend attends attending attended
VERB
1 If you attend an event, you are present at it.
EXAMPLE Thousands of people attended the funeral.

2 To attend school or church is to go there regularly.
EXAMPLE She attended church twice on Sundays.

3 If you attend to something, you deal with it.
EXAMPLE We have business to attend to first.

attention
NOUN
1 If you give something your attention, you look at it, listen to it or think about it carefully.
EXAMPLE You have my complete attention.

2 If something is getting attention, it is being dealt with or cared for.
EXAMPLE The woman needed medical attention.

attitude attitudes
NOUN
Your attitude to something is the way you think about it and behave towards it.
EXAMPLE There is a change in attitude towards disabled people.

attract attracts attracting attracted
VERB
1 If something attracts people, it interests them.
EXAMPLE The trials have attracted many leading riders.

2 If someone attracts you, you like and admire them.
EXAMPLE He was attracted to her outgoing personality.

3 If something attracts support or publicity, it gets it.
EXAMPLE The march has attracted a lot of publicity.

`SCIENCE`

4 When two objects with opposite electrical or magnetic charges pull together they are said to attract.
EXAMPLE The north pole of one magnet attracts the south pole of another.

attractive
ADJECTIVE
Attractive means desirable or pleasant to look at or be with.
EXAMPLE It was an attractive prospect.
▪ Similar words: charming, lovely, pleasant

auction auctions auctioning auctioned
NOUN
1 An auction is a public sale in which goods are sold to the person who offers the highest price.
EXAMPLE He bought the picture at auction.

▶ VERB
2 To auction something is to sell it in an auction.
EXAMPLE We'll auction the goods for charity.

audience audiences `DRAMA`
NOUN
An audience is a group of people who are watching or listening to a performance.
EXAMPLE The audience broke into loud applause.

August
NOUN
August is the eighth month of the year.
EXAMPLE They went on holiday in August.

aunt aunts
NOUN
Your aunt is the sister of your mother or father, or the wife of your uncle.
EXAMPLE It was a present from my Aunt Vera.

Australia `GEOGRAPHY`
NOUN
Australia is a continent situated between the Indian Ocean and the Pacific.
EXAMPLE They travelled across Australia by motorbike.

AUSTRALIA

Australian Australians
ADJECTIVE
1 Australian means to do with Australia.
EXAMPLE The Australian rugby team toured the UK.

▶ NOUN
2 An Australian is someone who comes from Australia.
EXAMPLE Three of my friends are Australians.

author authors   ENGLISH
NOUN
The author of a book is the person who wrote it.
EXAMPLE The author of *Matilda* is Roald Dahl.

authority authorities
NOUN
1 Authority is the right to control other people.
EXAMPLE The judge had no authority to order a second trial.

2 Someone who is an authority on something knows a lot about it.
EXAMPLE She was a leading authority on fashion.

automatic
ADJECTIVE
Automatic means programmed to perform tasks on its own.
EXAMPLE Modern trains have automatic doors.

autonomy
🔲 **Said:** aw-*ton*-nom-ee
NOUN
Autonomy is making informed decisions for oneself.
EXAMPLE Tony showed his autonomy by disagreeing with his friends.

autumn autumns
NOUN
Autumn is the season between summer and winter.
EXAMPLE The leaves changed colour in autumn.

available
ADJECTIVE
1 Something that is available can be obtained.
EXAMPLE Artichokes are available in supermarkets.

2 Someone who is available is ready for work or free for people to talk to.
EXAMPLE She isn't available at weekends.

average averages
NOUN   **MATHS**
1 An average is a result obtained by adding several amounts together and then dividing the total by the number of different amounts.
EXAMPLE Here are ten measurements: work out the average.

▶ ADJECTIVE
2 Average means standard or normal.
EXAMPLE He's an average teenager.

🔲 **Similar words:** normal, ordinary, typical, usual

avoid avoids avoiding avoided
VERB
To avoid something means to get out of it or keep away from it.
EXAMPLE She managed to avoid him all day.

award awards awarding awarded
NOUN
1 An award is a prize or certificate.
EXAMPLE The new library has won an architectural award.

▶ VERB
2 If you award someone something, you give it to them formally or officially.
EXAMPLE She was awarded the prize for best film.

aware
ADJECTIVE
If you are aware of something, you know about it.
EXAMPLE Smokers are well aware of the dangers to their health.

🔲 **Similar words:** conscious of, knowing about

away
ADVERB
1 Away means moving from a place.
EXAMPLE I saw them walk away.

2 Away means at a distance from a place.
EXAMPLE Our nearest supermarket is 12 kilometres away.

3 Away means in its proper place.
EXAMPLE He put his cheque book away.

4 Away means not at home, school or work.
She had been away from home for years.

awful
ADJECTIVE
Awful means very unpleasant or very bad.
EXAMPLE Isn't the weather awful?

🔲 **Similar words:** dreadful, terrible

B C D E F G H I J K L M N O P Q R S T U V W X Y Z

Bb Bb Bb

baby babies
NOUN
A baby is a child in the first year or two of its life.
EXAMPLE She had another baby last year.

back backs backing backed
ADVERB
1 To move back is to move in the opposite direction.
EXAMPLE She stepped back from the door.

2 To go back is to return.
EXAMPLE I'll be back as soon as I can.

3 If you get something back, it is returned to you.
EXAMPLE You'll get your money back.

4 Back means in the past.
EXAMPLE It happened back in the early 1980s.

▶ NOUN
5 Your back is the rear part of your body.
EXAMPLE He was lying on his back looking up at the sky.

6 The back is the part of something that is behind the front.
EXAMPLE He read the back of the postcard.

▶ VERB
7 To back is to move backwards.
EXAMPLE He backed the car out of the driveway.

8 To back means to support or finance.
EXAMPLE A spokesman said the union would back him.

▶ PHRASE
9 If you 'back out' of something, you change your mind and decide not to do it.
EXAMPLE He backed out of the deal at the last minute.

background backgrounds
NOUN
1 The background of a picture or scene is the less noticeable things.
EXAMPLE She could hear voices in the background.

2 Your background is your home and education.
EXAMPLE She came from a working-class background.

3 The background is the things that help to explain an event or cause it to happen.
EXAMPLE They discussed the background to the crisis.

bacteria
SCIENCE
NOUN
Bacteria are tiny living things.
EXAMPLE Bacteria can cause food poisoning.

bake bakes baking baked
VERB
To bake food means to cook it in an oven.
EXAMPLE They had baked potatoes for lunch.

balance balances balancing balanced
VERB
1 To balance means to remain steady and not fall over.
EXAMPLE She stood balancing on one leg.

▶ NOUN
2 Balance is the state of being upright and steady.
EXAMPLE She lost her balance and fell.

ball balls
NOUN
1 A ball is a round object used in games.
EXAMPLE They took a tennis ball to the park.

2 A ball is a large formal social event at which people dance.
EXAMPLE The Christmas ball was the main social event of the year.

band bands
NOUN
MUSIC
1 A band is a group of musicians who play music together.
EXAMPLE He was a drummer in a rock band.

2 A band is a group of people who share a common purpose.
EXAMPLE He joined the band of rebels in the hills.

3 A band is a narrow strip of something used to hold things together.
EXAMPLE He put an elastic band around the papers.

bank banks
NOUN
1 A bank is a business that looks after people's money.
EXAMPLE I had £10,000 in the bank.

2 The bank is the raised ground along a river or lake.
EXAMPLE He followed the man along the river bank.

baptism baptisms
RE
NOUN
Baptism is the ceremony in which someone becomes a member of the Christian church.
EXAMPLE I attended the baptism of my nephew.

bare
ADJECTIVE
1 Bare means not covered by any clothing.
EXAMPLE Her feet were bare.

▪ Similar words: naked, nude, uncovered

2 Bare means not covered or decorated with anything.
EXAMPLE The flat had bare wooden floors.

▪ Similar word: plain

barely
ADVERB
Barely means only just.
EXAMPLE The girl was barely sixteen.

bargain bargains bargaining bargained
NOUN
1 A bargain is an agreement.
EXAMPLE You keep your part of the bargain and I'll keep mine.
2 A bargain is something sold at a low price.
EXAMPLE At this price the wine is a bargain.
▶ VERB
3 To bargain is to agree terms about what should be done or paid.
EXAMPLE The trade unions bargained with the employers.

barrel barrels
NOUN
1 A barrel is a wooden container with rounded sides.
EXAMPLE They rolled the beer barrels into the cellar.
2 The barrel of a gun is the long tube through which the bullet is fired.
EXAMPLE He looked down the barrel of the gun.

barrier barriers
NOUN
A barrier is a fence or wall that prevents people or animals getting from one area to another.
EXAMPLE The demonstrators broke through the police barriers.
■ Similar words: fence, wall

base bases basing based
NOUN
1 The base is the lowest part of something.
EXAMPLE The body was at the base of the cliffs.
■ Similar words: bottom, foot
2 A base is a place where military forces work from.
EXAMPLE The soldiers went back to base.
▶ VERB
3 If one thing is based on another thing, it is developed from it.
EXAMPLE The opera is based on a play by Shakespeare.
4 If you are based somewhere, you live there or work from there.
EXAMPLE I'm based in London but spend a lot of time abroad.

baseball
NOUN
Baseball is a team game played with a bat and a ball.
EXAMPLE Shall we watch the baseball on TV?

basic
ADJECTIVE
1 Basic means most important.
EXAMPLE The basic theme of these stories is love.
2 Basic means having only the necessary features.
EXAMPLE The accommodation is pretty basic.

basically
ADVERB
Basically is used to show that you are describing a situation in a simple way.
EXAMPLE Basically, you've got two choices.

basis bases
NOUN
The basis of something is the main principle from which it can be developed.
EXAMPLE This was the basis of the final design.
■ Similar word: base

bass basses | MUSIC
❑ Said: rhymes with *lace*
NOUN
1 A bass is a man with a very deep singing voice.
EXAMPLE The bass sang well.
▶ ADJECTIVE
2 A bass musical instrument is one that produces a deep sound.
EXAMPLE He played bass guitar.

bathroom bathrooms
NOUN
A bathroom is a room where you wash yourself.
EXAMPLE He phoned when I was in the bathroom.

battery batteries | SCIENCE
NOUN
A battery is a store of energy which can be used to operate electrical circuits.
EXAMPLE Sue replaced the battery in her torch.

battle battles | HISTORY
NOUN
A battle is a fight or a struggle.
EXAMPLE The Battle of Hastings was in 1066.

beach beaches
NOUN
A beach is an area of sand or pebbles beside the sea.
EXAMPLE The children love playing on the beach.
■ Similar words: seashore, seaside, shore

bean beans
NOUN
Beans are the seeds or pods of some plants.
EXAMPLE She opened a tin of baked beans.

bear bears bearing bore borne
NOUN
1 A bear is a large wild animal with thick fur.
EXAMPLE Bears roamed in the woods.
▶ VERB
2 To bear something means to carry it.
EXAMPLE The ice wasn't thick enough to bear their weight.
3 If something bears a mark or feature, it has it.
EXAMPLE The room bore all the signs of a violent struggle.

A B C D E F G H I J K L M N O P Q R S T U V W X Y Z

4 If you bear something difficult, you accept it and are able to deal with it.
EXAMPLE He can't bear to talk about it.

beat beats beating beat beaten
VERB

1 To beat is to hit hard and repeatedly.
EXAMPLE The rain was beating against the window.

⊟ **Similar words:** hit, strike

2 To beat is to defeat or do better than.
EXAMPLE Arsenal beat Oxford United 5-1.

⊟ **Similar words:** conquer, defeat

beautiful
ADJECTIVE

Beautiful means very attractive or pleasing.
EXAMPLE Listen to this beautiful music.

⊟ **Similar words:** attractive, gorgeous, lovely

beauty
NOUN

Beauty is the quality of being beautiful.
EXAMPLE Even a stupid person can appreciate beauty.

because
CONJUNCTION

'Because' is used with a clause that gives the reason for something.
EXAMPLE I went home because I was tired.

become becomes becoming became become
VERB

To become something means to start feeling or being that thing.
EXAMPLE I became very angry.

bedroom bedrooms
NOUN

A bedroom is a room used for sleeping in.
EXAMPLE She shut herself in the bedroom all night.

beer beers
NOUN

Beer is an alcoholic drink made from malt.
EXAMPLE He ordered a pint of beer at the bar.

before
ADVERB, PREPOSITION OR CONJUNCTION

'Before' is used to refer to a previous time.
EXAMPLE Can I see you before you go?

⊟ **Similar words:** earlier than, prior to

begin begins beginning began begun
VERB

To begin is to start.
EXAMPLE He stood up and began to move around the room.

⊟ **Similar word:** start

beginning beginnings
NOUN

The beginning of something is the first part of it or the time when it starts.
EXAMPLE This was the beginning of all her troubles.

behalf
PHRASE

'On behalf of' means for the benefit of, or as the representative of.
EXAMPLE Scientists are campaigning on behalf of local charities.

behave behaves behaving behaved
VERB

1 If you behave in a particular way, you act in that way.
EXAMPLE He apologized for behaving badly.

2 To behave yourself means to act correctly.
EXAMPLE They had to behave themselves at Granny's.

behaviour
NOUN

Your behaviour is the way in which you behave.
EXAMPLE She was unable to explain his behaviour.

behind
PREPOSITION

1 Behind means at the back of.
EXAMPLE The moon disappeared behind a cloud.

2 Behind means supporting.
EXAMPLE The whole country was behind him.

▶ *ADVERB*

3 If you leave something behind, you do not take it with you.
EXAMPLE The robbers escaped, leaving their guns behind.

being beings
NOUN

1 Being is the state or fact of existing.
EXAMPLE The party came into being in 1923.

2 A being is a living creature.
EXAMPLE She dreamed of beings from another planet.

belief beliefs
NOUN

A belief is a feeling that something exists or is true.
EXAMPLE He couldn't shake her belief in God.

believe believes believing believed
VERB

1 If you believe that something is true, you think that it is true.
EXAMPLE Experts believe the boom is over.

2 If you believe someone, you accept that they are telling the truth.
EXAMPLE He knew I didn't believe him.

3 To believe in things means to think that they exist or happen.
EXAMPLE I don't believe in ghosts.

4 To believe in an idea means to think it is good or right.
EXAMPLE I don't believe in fox hunting.

bell bells
NOUN

1 A bell is a hollow metal object which makes a sound.
EXAMPLE **They rang the church bells.**

2 A bell is a device that makes a ringing sound.
EXAMPLE **I've been ringing the door bell.**

belong belongs belonging belonged
VERB

1 If something belongs to you, it is yours.
EXAMPLE **That book belongs to me.**

2 To belong to a group means to be a member of it.
EXAMPLE **I used to belong to a youth club.**

below
PREPOSITION OR ADVERB

1 Below means in a lower position.
EXAMPLE **The sun slipped below the horizon.**

2 Below means less than.
EXAMPLE **Rainfall has been below average.**

belt belts
NOUN

A belt is a strip of leather or cloth that you fasten round your waist.
EXAMPLE **He wore a belt with a large brass buckle.**

bend bends bending bent
VERB

1 To bend something means to make it curved or angular.
EXAMPLE **The strong man bent the iron bar.**

■ **Similar words:** arch, curve

2 When you bend, you move your head and shoulders forwards and downwards.
EXAMPLE **I bent over and kissed her cheek.**

▸ *NOUN*
3 A bend is a curved part of something.
EXAMPLE **Watch the bend in the road!**

■ **Similar words:** arch, bow, curve

beneath
PREPOSITION OR ADVERB

Beneath means underneath.
EXAMPLE **She hid the bottle beneath her mattress.**

benefit benefits benefiting benefited
NOUN

1 The benefit of something is the advantage that it brings.
EXAMPLE **He had the benefit of a good education.**

■ **Similar words:** advantage, good, help

▸ *VERB*
2 If you benefit from something, it helps you.
EXAMPLE **He'll benefit from a few days on his own.**

■ **Similar words:** gain, profit

beside
PREPOSITION

Beside means next to.
EXAMPLE **I sat down beside my wife.**

■ **Similar words:** alongside, next to

besides
PREPOSITION OR ADVERB

1 Besides means in addition to.
EXAMPLE **What languages do you know besides English?**

2 Besides means anyway.
EXAMPLE **I don't need help. Besides, I've nearly finished.**

better
ADJECTIVE OR ADVERB

1 Better is the comparative of 'good' and 'well'.
EXAMPLE **He's better than I am at maths.**

■ **Similar words:** finer, greater, superior

▸ *ADJECTIVE*
2 Better means no longer ill.
EXAMPLE **Are you feeling better?**

between
PREPOSITION OR ADVERB

1 If something is between two other things, it is situated or happens in the space or time that separates them.
EXAMPLE **He was headmaster between 1955 and 1974.**

2 A relationship or difference between two people or things is one that involves them both.
EXAMPLE **What is the difference between the pictures?**

If there are two things you should use 'between'. If there are more than two things you should use 'among'.

beyond
PREPOSITION

1 Beyond means on the other side of.
EXAMPLE **Beyond the hills was the desert.**

2 Beyond means further than.
EXAMPLE **Don't push me beyond my limit.**

Bible Bibles   **RE**
NOUN

The Bible is the sacred book of the Christian religion.
EXAMPLE **She read from the Bible every day.**

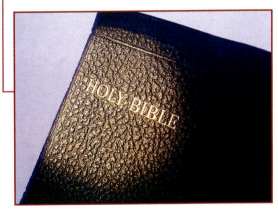

bill bills
NOUN

1 A bill is a written statement of how much is owed for goods or services.
EXAMPLE **Could I have the bill, please?**

CITIZENSHIP

2 A bill is a formal statement of a proposed new law.
EXAMPLE **This is the toughest crime bill for a decade.**

billion billions   **MATHS**
NOUN

A billion is a thousand million.
EXAMPLE **The company was worth 3 billion dollars.**

The meaning of 'billion' has changed: it used to mean one million million.

A
B
C
D
E
F
G
H
I
J
K
L
M
N
O
P
Q
R
S
T
U
V
W
X
Y
Z

biography biographies — ENGLISH
NOUN
A biography is the story of someone's life.
EXAMPLE This biography of Princess Diana is written by Andrew Morton.

bird birds
NOUN
A bird is an animal with feathers and wings.
EXAMPLE Birds were singing in the trees.

birth births
NOUN
A birth is when something is born.
EXAMPLE The twins were separated at birth.

birthday birthdays
NOUN
Your birthday is the anniversary of the date on which you were born.
EXAMPLE Happy Birthday!

bisect bisects bisecting bisected — MATHS
VERB
To bisect a line or area means to divide it in half.
EXAMPLE He bisected the line at its mid point.

bite bites biting bit bitten
VERB
1 To bite is to use your teeth to cut into or through something.
EXAMPLE I used to bite my nails as a child.

▸ *NOUN*
2 A bite is a small amount that you bite off something.
EXAMPLE She took a bite of her sandwich.

3 A bite is the injury you get when an animal or insect bites you.
EXAMPLE My face was covered with insect bites.

bitter bitterest
ADJECTIVE
1 Bitter means angry and resentful.
EXAMPLE She is very bitter about the way she was treated.

⊟ Similar words: resentful, sour

2 Bitter means having a sharp, unpleasant taste.
EXAMPLE The lemon juice tasted bitter.

⊟ Similar words: acid, sharp, sour

black blacker blackest; blacks
NOUN OR ADJECTIVE
1 Black is the darkest possible colour.
EXAMPLE He wore a black leather coat.

⊟ Similar words: dark, pitch-black

2 Someone who is black is a member of a dark-skinned race.
EXAMPLE He was the first black to be elected to Congress.

blame blames blaming blamed
VERB
1 If someone blames you for something, they believe you caused it.
EXAMPLE I was blamed for the theft.

⊟ Similar words: accuse, hold responsible

▸ *NOUN*
2 The blame for something bad that happens is the responsibility for letting it happen.
EXAMPLE The captain took the blame for the defeat.

blast blasts blasting blasted
VERB
1 To blast is to blow up with explosives.
EXAMPLE They're using dynamite to blast away rocks.

▸ *NOUN*
2 A blast is a big explosion.
EXAMPLE 250 people were killed in the blast.

blind blinds blinding blinded
ADJECTIVE
1 Blind means unable to see.
EXAMPLE He was blind from birth.

▸ *VERB*
2 To blind is to make someone unable to see.
EXAMPLE The strong sunlight blinded him.

▸ *NOUN*
3 A blind is a roll of cloth or paper that you pull down over a window.
EXAMPLE She pulled the blind down at dusk.

block blocks blocking blocked
NOUN
1 A block of flats or offices is a large building containing flats or offices.
EXAMPLE They lived in a block of council flats.

2 A block is an area of land with streets on all sides.
EXAMPLE He lives a few blocks down.

3 A block of something is a large rectangular piece of it.
EXAMPLE He bought a block of chocolate.

⊟ Similar words: bar, chunk, piece

▸ *VERB*
4 To block means to prevent access through.
EXAMPLE The police blocked the entrance to Westminster Bridge.

blood — SCIENCE
NOUN
Blood is the red liquid that is pumped by the heart round the body.
EXAMPLE He lost a lot of blood in the accident.

bloody bloodier bloodiest
ADJECTIVE
A bloody event is one in which a lot of people are killed.
EXAMPLE It was a bloody revolution.

blow blows blowing blew blown
VERB
1 When something blows it is moved by the wind.
EXAMPLE The snow blew into her face.

2 To blow is to make a sound by blowing.
EXAMPLE The referee blew his whistle.

▶ *NOUN*
3 A blow is a hit.
EXAMPLE He received a blow on the head.

4 A blow is something bad that happens.
EXAMPLE Mark's death was a terrible blow.

▶ *PHRASE*
5 To blow something up means to destroy it with an explosion.
EXAMPLE He threatened to blow the place up.

6 To blow up a balloon or a tyre means to fill it with air.
EXAMPLE I spent the afternoon blowing up balloons.

blue bluer bluest; blues
ADJECTIVE OR NOUN
Blue is the colour of the sky on a clear, sunny day.
EXAMPLE He had blue eyes and fair hair.

board boards boarding boarded
NOUN
1 A board is a flat piece of wood, plastic or cardboard.
EXAMPLE They put the pieces on the chess board.

2 A board is a group of people who control an organization.
EXAMPLE He put the suggestion to the board.

▶ *VERB*
3 If you board a ship or aircraft, you get on it or in it.
EXAMPLE The passengers were waiting to board the ship.

▶ *PHRASE*
4 If you are 'on board' a ship or aircraft, you are on it or in it.
EXAMPLE There were ten people on board the aircraft.

boat boats
NOUN
A boat is a small vehicle for travelling across water.
EXAMPLE They rowed the boat back to land.

body bodies
NOUN
1 Your body is all of you, from your head to your feet.
EXAMPLE My whole body hurt.

■ **Similar words:** build, figure, form

2 Your body is the main part of you, not including your head, arms or legs.
EXAMPLE Gently pull your leg towards your body.

3 A body is a person's dead body.
EXAMPLE Police later found a body in the lake.

boil boils boiling boiled
VERB
1 When a liquid boils, it starts to turn into steam.
EXAMPLE Boil the water in the saucepan.

2 When you boil food, you cook it in boiling water.
EXAMPLE She didn't know how to boil an egg.

bomb bombs bombing bombed
NOUN
1 A bomb is a container filled with explosives.
EXAMPLE The bomb killed sixteen people.

▶ *VERB*
2 When a place is bombed, it is attacked with bombs.
EXAMPLE The premises were bombed in the war.

bond bonds
NOUN
A bond is a close relationship between people.
EXAMPLE There is a strong bond between mothers and babies.

■ **Similar words:** connection, link, tie

bone bones   **SCIENCE**
NOUN
Bones are the hard parts of a person's or animal's body.
EXAMPLE Mary broke a bone in her back.

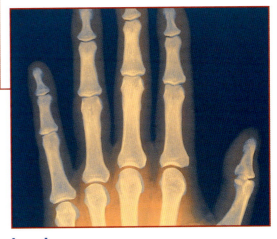

book books booking booked
NOUN
1 A book is a number of pages held together inside a cover.
EXAMPLE They read a book about witches.

▶ *VERB*
2 To book something is to arrange to have it or use it at a particular time.
EXAMPLE Can I book a table for two for tonight?

boost boosts boosting boosted
VERB
1 To boost something means to cause it to improve or increase.
EXAMPLE The campaign greatly boosted sales.

▶ *NOUN*
2 A boost is an improvement or increase.
EXAMPLE The new measure was a boost to the economy.

boot boots
NOUN
1 Boots are strong shoes.
EXAMPLE You need walking boots and a raincoat.

2 The boot is the covered space in a car for carrying things in.
EXAMPLE There's no more room in the boot.

border borders bordering bordered
NOUN
1 A border is the dividing line between two countries.
EXAMPLE They crossed the border into Mexico.

2 A border is a strip or band round the edge of something.
EXAMPLE The tiles were plain with a bright border.

▶ *VERB*
3 To border something means to form a boundary along the side of it.
EXAMPLE It was a sandy beach bordered by palm trees.

A B C D E F G H I J K L M N O P Q R S T U V W X Y Z

bore bores boring bored
VERB

1 If something bores you, you find it dull and uninteresting.
EXAMPLE I won't bore you with the details.

2 To bore is to make a hole in something with a tool.
EXAMPLE They had to bore a hole in the wall.

3 Bore is also the past tense of bear.
EXAMPLE She bore her illness with courage.

▸ NOUN

4 A bore is someone or something that bores you.
EXAMPLE He's such a bore.

born
VERB

Born is the past participle of bear.
EXAMPLE I was born in London.

borrow borrows borrowing borrowed
VERB

If you borrow something that belongs to someone else, they let you have it for a period of time.
EXAMPLE He borrowed £200 from his friend.

boss bosses bossing bossed
NOUN

1 A boss is the person in charge of a work place.
EXAMPLE You're not the boss around here.

▸ VERB

2 To boss someone around is to keep telling them what to do.
EXAMPLE They've bossed us around enough.

both
ADJECTIVE OR PRONOUN

Both refers to two things or people.
EXAMPLE He's fond of both of you.

You can use 'of' after 'both', but it is not essential. 'Both the boys' means the same as 'both of the boys'.

bother bothers bothering bothered
VERB

1 To bother to do something is to take time and effort to do it.
EXAMPLE The papers didn't even bother to report it.

2 If something bothers you, you are worried or concerned about it.
EXAMPLE Is something bothering you?

3 If you bother someone, you interrupt them when they are busy.
EXAMPLE I'm sorry to bother you.

▸ NOUN

4 Bother is trouble, fuss or difficulty.
EXAMPLE We're having a bit of bother with the children.

bottle bottles
NOUN

A bottle is a glass or plastic container for keeping liquids in.
EXAMPLE They opened another bottle of wine.

bottom bottoms
NOUN

1 The bottom of something is its lowest part.
EXAMPLE It sank to the bottom of the lake.

2 Your bottom is the part of your body that you sit on.
EXAMPLE Luckily he fell on his bottom.

▸ ADJECTIVE

3 The bottom thing in a series is the lowest one.
EXAMPLE Look in the bottom drawer.

bound bounds
ADJECTIVE

1 If something is bound to happen, it is certain to happen.
EXAMPLE He's bound to find out.

2 If a person or a vehicle is bound for a place, they are going there.
EXAMPLE The ship is bound for Italy.

▸ PLURAL NOUN

3 Bounds are limits which restrict or control something.
EXAMPLE Their enthusiasm knew no bounds.

▸ VERB

4 Bound is also the past tense and past participle of bind.
EXAMPLE The prisoner was bound and gagged.

bow bows bowing bowed
☐ **Said:** rhymes with *now*
VERB

When you bow, you bend your body or lower your head as a sign of respect or greeting.
EXAMPLE He bowed to her and left.

bow bows
☐ **Said:** rhymes with *low*
NOUN

1 A bow is a knot with two loops and two loose ends.
EXAMPLE The ribbon was tied in a bow.

2 A bow is a long piece of wood used for shooting arrows.
EXAMPLE Most of the warriors had bows and arrows.

bowl bowls bowling bowled
NOUN

1 A bowl is a round container with a wide uncovered top.
EXAMPLE Can I have a bowl of soup?

2 A bowl is the hollow, rounded part of something.
EXAMPLE He dropped his toothbrush in the toilet bowl.

▸ VERB

3 In cricket, to bowl means to throw the ball towards the batsman.
EXAMPLE He bowled so well that we won both matches.

brain brains
NOUN   **SCIENCE**

1 Your brain is the organ inside your head that controls your body and enables you to think and feel.
EXAMPLE The surgeons removed a tumour from his brain.

2 Your brain is your mind and the way that you think.
EXAMPLE I admired his legal brain.

branch branches branching branched
NOUN

1 The branches of a tree are the parts that grow out from its trunk.
EXAMPLE **There were no leaves on the branches.**

2 A branch of an organization is one of its offices or shops.
EXAMPLE **Go to the local branch of Marks and Spencer's.**

▶ *VERB*
3 To branch off is to split off and lead in a different direction.
EXAMPLE **A small road branches off to the right.**

brand brands
NOUN

A brand of something is a particular kind or make of it.
EXAMPLE **The firm made a popular brand of chocolate.**

brass
NOUN
MUSIC

1 Brass is a group of instruments made of brass which play in a band or orchestra.
EXAMPLE **The brass section included trumpets and trombones.**

SCIENCE

2 Brass is a yellow-coloured metal made from copper and zinc.
EXAMPLE **They investigated which objects were of brass, and which were of bronze.**

brave braver bravest; braves braving braved
ADJECTIVE

1 A brave person is willing to do dangerous things.
EXAMPLE **He made a brave attempt to prevent the hijack.**

☐ **Similar words:** courageous, daring, fearless

▶ *VERB*
2 If you brave an unpleasant or dangerous situation, you face up to it.
EXAMPLE **His fans braved the rain to hear him sing.**

bread
NOUN

Bread is a food made from flour which is baked in an oven.
EXAMPLE **He bought a loaf of bread at the baker's.**

break breaks breaking broke broken
VERB

1 When an object breaks or when you break it, it becomes damaged or separates into pieces.
EXAMPLE **She's broken her ankle.**

☐ **Similar words:** crack, snap

2 If you break a rule or promise you fail to keep it.
EXAMPLE **We didn't know we were breaking the law.**

☐ **Similar word:** disobey

3 To break a record means to do better than the previous recorded best.
EXAMPLE **He broke the world record by three seconds.**

▶ *NOUN*
4 A break is a short period during which you rest or do something different.
EXAMPLE **I'm taking a break because I'm tired.**

▶ *PHRASE*
5 When a machine 'breaks down', it stops working.
EXAMPLE **Their car broke down at the corner.**

6 If something 'breaks up', it ends.
EXAMPLE **The marriage broke up after a year.**

breakfast breakfasts
NOUN

Breakfast is the first meal of the day.
EXAMPLE **He likes two eggs for breakfast.**

breast breasts
NOUN
SCIENCE

A woman's breasts are the two fleshy parts on her chest that produce milk after she has had a baby.
EXAMPLE **The baby clung to its mother's breast.**

breath breaths
NOUN

Your breath is the air you take into your lungs when you breathe.
EXAMPLE **He took a deep breath.**

breathe breathes breathing breathed
VERB

When you breathe, you take air into your lungs and let it out again.
EXAMPLE **He seems to have stopped breathing.**

breed breeds breeding bred
NOUN

1 A breed of domestic animal is a particular type of it.
EXAMPLE **He kept rare breeds of cattle.**

▶ *VERB*
2 To breed animals or plants means to keep them in order to produce more of them.
EXAMPLE **He used to breed dogs for the police.**

3 When animals breed, they mate.
EXAMPLE **Frogs will breed in any convenient pond.**

bridge bridges
NOUN

A bridge is a structure built over a river, road or railway so that vehicles and people can cross.
EXAMPLE **The bridge collapsed into the river.**

brief briefer briefest; briefs briefing briefed
ADJECTIVE

1 Brief means lasting only a short time.
EXAMPLE **I have popped in for a brief visit.**

☐ **Similar words:** quick, short

▶ *VERB*
2 To brief someone means to give them the necessary information about a task.
EXAMPLE **A spokesman briefed reporters on the latest developments.**

▶ *NOUN*
DESIGN
3 A brief is a set of instructions describing the purpose of the task.
EXAMPLE **He read the brief carefully before beginning the project.**

bright *brighter brightest*
ADJECTIVE

1 Bright means strong and startling.
EXAMPLE **The painting was full of bright colours.**

📖 **Similar words:** brilliant, shining

2 Bright means clever.
EXAMPLE **He's very bright at maths.**

brilliant
ADJECTIVE

1 Brilliant means extremely clever.
EXAMPLE **She had a brilliant mind.**

2 Brilliant means extremely good or enjoyable.
EXAMPLE **This is a brilliant book.**

bring *brings bringing brought*
VERB

1 To bring something is to take it with you.
EXAMPLE **You can bring a friend to the party.**

▸ *PHRASE*
2 To bring something about means to cause it to happen.
EXAMPLE **We must try to bring about a better world.**

3 To bring up children means to look after them while they grow up.
EXAMPLE **She brought up her children alone.**

British
ADJECTIVE

British means belonging or relating to the United Kingdom.
EXAMPLE **He only listened to British music.**

broad *broader broadest*
ADJECTIVE

1 Broad means wide.
EXAMPLE **He gave her a broad smile.**

2 Broad means having many different aspects.
EXAMPLE **A broad range of issues was discussed.**

broadcast *broadcasts broadcasting broadcast*
NOUN

1 A broadcast is a programme or announcement on radio or television.
EXAMPLE **He was criticized for making these broadcasts.**

▸ *VERB*
2 To broadcast something means to make it public on television or radio.
EXAMPLE **The concert will be broadcast live on TV.**

brother *brothers*
NOUN

Your brother is a boy or man who has the same parents as you.
EXAMPLE **I love my younger brother.**

brown *browner brownest; browns*
ADJECTIVE OR NOUN

Brown is the colour of earth or wood.
EXAMPLE **She had deep brown eyes.**

brush *brushes brushing brushed*
NOUN

1 A brush is an object with bristles which you use for cleaning things, painting or tidying your hair.
EXAMPLE **The artist selected her brush carefully.**

▸ *VERB*
2 To brush is to clean or tidy with a brush.

EXAMPLE **You must brush your teeth after tea.**

3 If you brush something, you touch it while passing it.
EXAMPLE **Her lips brushed his cheek.**

Buddhist *Buddhists*   `RE`

🔊 **Said:** *Boo*-dist
NOUN

A Buddhist is someone who believes in Buddhism, a religion which teaches that the way to end suffering is by overcoming your desires.
EXAMPLE **There are many Buddhists in Nepal.**

budget *budgets budgeting budgeted*
NOUN

1 A budget is a plan showing how much money will be available and how it will be spent.
EXAMPLE **I'm on a tight budget this month.**

▸ *VERB*
2 If you budget for something, you plan your money carefully.
EXAMPLE **I've budgeted for food for six people.**

build *builds building built*
VERB

1 To build something means to make it from its parts.
EXAMPLE **John had built his own house.**

📖 **Similar word:** construct

2 To build something means to develop it gradually.
EXAMPLE **They want to build a fairer society.**

▸ *NOUN*
3 Your build is the shape and size of your body.
EXAMPLE **He had a lean, athletic build.**

building *buildings*
NOUN

A building is a structure with walls and a roof.
EXAMPLE **People were still trapped inside the building.**

bunch *bunches*
NOUN

A bunch is a group of people or things.
EXAMPLE **The players were a great bunch.**

burden *burdens*
NOUN

A burden is something that causes you a lot of worry or hard work.
EXAMPLE **This would relieve the burden on hospital staff.**

📖 **Similar words:** trouble, worry

burn burns burning burned burnt
VERB

1 To burn means to be on fire.
EXAMPLE One of the cars was still burning.

■ **Similar words:** be on fire, blaze

2 To burn something means to damage or destroy it with fire.
EXAMPLE Coal fell out of the fire and burned the carpet.

■ **Similar word:** set on fire

3 To burn is to be injured by something hot.
EXAMPLE Don't burn your fingers on the fire.

▶ *NOUN*

4 A burn is an injury caused by something hot.
EXAMPLE She suffered terrible burns in the blaze.

You can write either 'burned' or 'burnt' as the past form of 'burn'.

burst bursts bursting
VERB

1 When something bursts it splits open because of pressure from inside it.
EXAMPLE A tyre burst with a bang.

2 To burst means to happen suddenly and with force.
EXAMPLE The aircraft burst into flames.

▶ *NOUN*

3 A burst of something is a sudden short period of it.
EXAMPLE A burst of applause followed the announcement.

■ **Similar words:** outbreak, rush

bury buries burying buried
■ **Said:** berry
VERB

1 To bury someone means to put their body into a grave.
EXAMPLE Soldiers helped to bury the dead.

2 To bury something means to put it in the ground and cover it up.
EXAMPLE They want to discover buried treasure.

business businesses
■ **Said:** *biz*-niss
NOUN

1 Business is work relating to the buying and selling of goods and services.
EXAMPLE I'm here on business.

2 A business is an organization which sells goods or provides a service.
EXAMPLE He set up three businesses in a single year.

■ **Similar words:** company, firm, organization

3 A business is any event, situation or activity.
EXAMPLE This whole business has upset me.

busy busier busiest
■ **Said:** bizzy
ADJECTIVE

1 Busy means occupied in something.
EXAMPLE She was too busy to attend.

■ **Similar words:** employed, engaged, occupied

2 A busy place is full of people.
EXAMPLE The centre of town is too busy for me.

butter
NOUN

Butter is a fatty food which is spread on bread and used in cooking.
EXAMPLE They preferred butter to margarine.

button buttons
NOUN

1 A button is a small object used to fasten clothing.
EXAMPLE A button has come off my shirt.

2 A button is a small object on a piece of equipment that you press to make it work.
EXAMPLE The gate slid open at the push of a button.

byte bytes `ICT`
NOUN

A byte is a unit of storage in a computer.
EXAMPLE There are 1000 bytes in a megabyte.

A B C D E F G H I J K L M N O P Q R S T U V W X Y Z

A B C D E F G H I J K L M N O P Q R S T U V W X Y Z

cabin cabins
NOUN

1 A cabin is a room in a ship where a passenger sleeps.
EXAMPLE We had a first-class cabin on the cruise.

2 A cabin is a small wooden house in the country.
EXAMPLE We stayed in a log cabin by a lake.

cabinet cabinets
NOUN

1 A cabinet is a small cupboard.
EXAMPLE She kept her tablets in a medicine cabinet.

CITIZENSHIP

2 The cabinet in a government is a group of ministers who advise the leader and decide policies.
EXAMPLE The Prime Minister is the leader of the Cabinet.

cable cables
NOUN

1 A cable is a strong, thick rope or chain.
EXAMPLE He was lowered from the roof on a steel cable.

SCIENCE

2 A cable is a bundle of wires which carries electricity.
EXAMPLE The storm damaged the power cables.

calm calmer calmest; calms calming calmed
ADJECTIVE

1 Someone who is calm is quiet and unworried.
EXAMPLE In an emergency, you should try to keep calm.

☐ **Similar word:** cool

2 If water is calm, it is not moving very much.
EXAMPLE There was a clear blue sky and calm sea.

▶ *VERB*

3 If you calm someone, you make them less upset or excited.
EXAMPLE A cup of tea will help to calm you down.

camera cameras
NOUN

A camera is a piece of equipment used for taking photographs or for filming.
EXAMPLE I need some more film for my camera.

camp camps camping camped
NOUN

1 A camp is a place where people live or stay in tents or caravans.
EXAMPLE When I was young, I stayed in a holiday camp.

▶ *VERB*

2 If you camp or go camping, you stay in a tent.
EXAMPLE We camped near the beach.

cancel cancels cancelling cancelled
VERB

To cancel something is to stop it from happening.
EXAMPLE Many trains have been cancelled today.

cancer cancers
NOUN **SCIENCE**

Cancer is a serious disease which causes growths in the body.
EXAMPLE Smoking causes lung cancer.

candidate candidates
NOUN

A candidate is a person who is being considered for a job.
EXAMPLE The candidates chatted in the waiting room.

capable
ADJECTIVE

If you are capable of doing something, you are able to do it.
EXAMPLE He is easily capable of doing the work.

capacity capacities
☐ **Said:** kap-*pas*-sit-tee

NOUN

The capacity of something is the maximum amount that it can hold or produce.
EXAMPLE The stadium has a seating capacity of seventy thousand.

capital capitals
NOUN **GEOGRAPHY**

1 The capital of a country is the city where the government meets.
EXAMPLE Paris is the capital of France.

2 Capital is a sum of money owned, used or invested.
EXAMPLE Small companies are having difficulty in raising capital.

3 A capital or a capital letter is a larger letter used at the beginning of a sentence or a name.
EXAMPLE Please write your name in capitals.

captain captains
NOUN

1 The captain is an officer, especially one in charge of a ship or aeroplane.
EXAMPLE The captain apologized for the delay.

2 The captain is the leader of a team.

EXAMPLE He was the best captain the Scottish team had ever had.

capture captures capturing captured
VERB
To capture someone is to take them prisoner.
EXAMPLE The pilot was captured but managed to escape.

carbohydrate
carbohydrates   **SCIENCE**
NOUN
A carbohydrate is a food substance which gives you energy.
EXAMPLE Sugar and bread are good sources of carbohydrate.

care cares caring cared
VERB
1 If you care about something, you are concerned about it.
EXAMPLE I really don't care if he comes or not.

2 If you care about someone, you feel affection towards them.
EXAMPLE He still cared for me.

3 If you care for someone, you look after them.
EXAMPLE They hired a nurse to care for her.

▶ NOUN
4 Care of someone or something is treatment for them or looking after them.
EXAMPLE He argued for proper care of the elderly.

career careers
NOUN
A career is the series of jobs that someone has.
EXAMPLE He started his career in journalism at 16.

careful
ADJECTIVE
1 If you are careful, you pay attention to what you are doing.
EXAMPLE Be careful what you say to him.

■ Similar word: cautious

2 Something that is careful shows a concern for detail.
EXAMPLE It needs very careful planning.

cartridge cartridges   **ICT**
NOUN
A print cartridge stores the ink for the printer.
EXAMPLE His printer needs three colour cartridges.

case cases
NOUN
1 A case is a particular situation, event or example.
EXAMPLE A bad case of sunburn.

2 A case is a container for something.
EXAMPLE He could not find his camera case.

3 A case is a crime, or a trial that takes place after a crime.
EXAMPLE Police have re-opened the case.

4 In an argument, the case is the reasons used to support a point of view.
EXAMPLE There's a strong case for reform.

cash cashes cashing cashed
NOUN
1 Cash is money in the form of notes and coins.
EXAMPLE They each won two thousand pounds in cash.

▶ VERB
2 If you cash a cheque, you exchange it for money

at a bank.
EXAMPLE The cheque must be cashed within three months.

cast casts casting
NOUN
1 The cast is all the people who act in a play or film.
EXAMPLE The cast were amazed by the film's success.

▶ VERB
2 To cast actors is to choose them for roles in a play or film.
EXAMPLE He was cast as a college professor.

    CITIZENSHIP

3 To cast a vote is to vote.
EXAMPLE He cast his vote carefully.

castle castles   **HISTORY**
NOUN
A castle is a large defensive building.
EXAMPLE Bodiam Castle is in Sussex.

casual
ADJECTIVE
1 Casual means careless or without interest.
EXAMPLE He tried to appear casual when his mother walked in.

2 Casual clothes are suitable for informal occasions.
EXAMPLE He wore a casual shirt and chinos.

casualty casualties
NOUN
A casualty is a person killed or injured in an accident or war.
EXAMPLE The casualties of war are not just soldiers.

category categories
NOUN
A category is a set of things which have something in common.
EXAMPLE Most jobs can be divided into four categories.

Catholic Catholics   **RE**
NOUN
A Catholic is a member of the branch of the Christian church that accepts the Pope as its leader, called the Roman Catholic Church.
EXAMPLE There are many Roman Catholics in South America.

cause causes causing caused
NOUN
1 The cause of something is the thing that makes it happen.
EXAMPLE Nobody knew the cause of the explosion.

2 A cause is an aim or principle which a group of people are working for.
EXAMPLE He is sympathetic to our cause.

A
B
C
D
E
F
G
H
I
J
K
L
M
N
O
P
Q
R
S
T
U
V
W
X
Y
Z

▶ *VERB*
3 To cause something is to make it happen.
EXAMPLE **The weather can cause delays.**

cautious
ADJECTIVE
Cautious means acting carefully.
EXAMPLE **He was always cautious about crossing the road.**

CD-ROM CD-ROMs   ICT
NOUN
A CD-ROM is a compact disk where you can store video, sound, graphics and text.
EXAMPLE **The dictionary is available on CD-ROM.**

cease ceases ceasing ceased
VERB
If something ceases, it stops happening.
EXAMPLE **By 11 o'clock the rain had ceased.**

celebrate celebrates celebrating celebrated
VERB
If you celebrate, you do something special and enjoyable.
EXAMPLE **We held a party to celebrate the end of the exams.**

celebration celebrations
NOUN
A celebration is a special event to celebrate something.
EXAMPLE **Grandad enjoyed his birthday celebrations.**

cell cells
NOUN   SCIENCE
1 A cell is the basic unit from which all life is built.
EXAMPLE **Sophie looked at the onion cells using a microscope.**
SCIENCE
2 A cell is a chemical store of energy.
EXAMPLE **The cells in a battery are used to store energy.**
3 A cell is a small room where a prisoner is locked up.
EXAMPLE **He spent two years in a prison cell.**

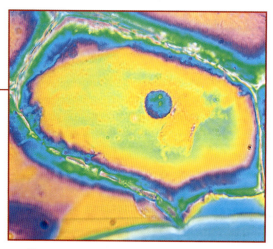

cello cellos   MUSIC
▪ **Said:** *chel-*loh
NOUN
A cello is a large stringed musical instrument.
EXAMPLE **She started playing the cello when she was eight.**

cement
NOUN
Cement is a grey powder which is mixed with sand and water to make concrete.

EXAMPLE **The builders used a large cement mixer.**

census censuses   HISTORY
NOUN
A census is an official survey of how many people there are in a country.
EXAMPLE **The census showed how the population grew.**

cent cents
NOUN
A cent is a coin in the USA and in some other countries.
EXAMPLE **He paid 2 dollars and 50 cents.**

central
ADJECTIVE
Central means in or near the centre.
EXAMPLE **We moved to central London.**

centre centres
NOUN
1 The centre of something is the middle.
EXAMPLE **He stood in the centre of the room.**
▪ **Similar words:** heart, middle
2 A centre is a building where people go for activities or help.
EXAMPLE **He was a member of the local leisure centre.**

century centuries   HISTORY
NOUN
A century is a period of 100 years.
EXAMPLE **There were two world wars in the twentieth century.**

ceremony ceremonies
NOUN
A ceremony is a formal event such as a wedding.
EXAMPLE **The funeral was a private ceremony.**

certain
ADJECTIVE
1 Certain means definite.
EXAMPLE **She is certain she's going to succeed.**
2 You use 'certain' to refer to a specific person or thing.
EXAMPLE **Certain aspects of the job appealed to me.**

certainly
ADVERB
Certainly means without doubt.
EXAMPLE **My boss was certainly interested in the idea.**

chain chains chaining chained
NOUN
1 A chain is a number of metal rings connected together.
EXAMPLE **He tried to fix his bicycle chain.**
2 A chain is a number of things in a series or connected to each other.
EXAMPLE **It was a strange chain of events.**
▶ *VERB*
3 To chain is to fasten with a chain.
EXAMPLE **The protesters had chained themselves to railings.**

chair chairs
NOUN
A chair is a seat for one person to sit on.
EXAMPLE **He got up from his chair.**

chairman chairmen
NOUN

1 A chairman is the person in charge of a meeting.
EXAMPLE **The chairman declared the meeting open.**

2 A chairman is the head of a company or committee.
EXAMPLE **He's the chairman of a big oil company.**

Some people don't like to use 'chairman' when talking about a woman. You can use 'chair' or 'chairperson' to talk about a man or a woman.

challenge challenges challenging challenged
NOUN

1 A challenge is something that is exciting but requires a lot of effort.
EXAMPLE **It's a new challenge for me.**

2 A challenge to something is a questioning of whether it is correct or true.
EXAMPLE **The demonstration was a challenge to the government.**

▶ *VERB*
3 If you challenge someone, you suggest that you compete with them.
EXAMPLE **He challenged anyone to enter the ring.**

4 If you challenge something, you question whether it is correct or true.
EXAMPLE **This idea has never been challenged.**

▪ Similar words: dispute, question

champion champions
NOUN

A champion is a person who wins a competition.
EXAMPLE **He became world champion at 110 metre hurdles.**

championship championships
NOUN

A championship is a competition to find the champion of a sport.
EXAMPLE **The chess championship was won by a Russian.**

chance chances
NOUN

1 A chance is a likelihood or possibility.
EXAMPLE **What chance have we got of winning?**

2 A chance is an opportunity.
EXAMPLE **He had the chance to visit his aunt in Canada.**

3 Chance is luck or the way things happen unexpectedly.
EXAMPLE **I only found out by chance.**

▪ Similar words: accident, luck

change changes changing changed
NOUN

1 A change in something is an alteration in it.
EXAMPLE **Steven soon noticed a change in Penny's attitude.**

2 A change is a replacement of one thing by something else.
EXAMPLE **She packed a change of clothes.**

3 Change is money you get back when you pay for something with more money than it costs.
EXAMPLE **She handed him his change.**

4 Change is coins rather than notes.
EXAMPLE **Have you any change for the phone?**

▶ *VERB*
5 To change is to become different or to make something different.
EXAMPLE **The accident changed my life.**

6 To change is to exchange.
EXAMPLE **I'm thinking of changing my job.**

channel channels channelling channelled
NOUN

1 A channel is a television or radio station.
EXAMPLE **I wanted to watch the other channel.**

GEOGRAPHY

2 The English Channel is the stretch of sea between England and France.
EXAMPLE **I crossed the Channel in only thirty minutes.**

▶ *VERB*
3 To channel something means to direct it.
EXAMPLE **We channel the children's energies into creative hobbies.**

chant chants chanting chanted
NOUN

1 A chant is a group of words repeated over and over again.
EXAMPLE **Fifty thousand fans joined in the chant.**

▶ *VERB*
2 To chant is to repeat the same words over and over again.
EXAMPLE **Crowds chanted his name.**

chaos

🔊 Said: *kay-*oss
NOUN

Chaos is complete disorder.
EXAMPLE **The band's concerts often ended in chaos.**

chapter chapters
ENGLISH
NOUN

A chapter is one of the parts into which a book is divided.
EXAMPLE **Turn to Chapter 1.**

character characters
NOUN

1 The character of a person or place is the qualities that it has.
EXAMPLE **There was a gentler side to his character.**

▪ Similar words: nature, personality, quality

ENGLISH

2 The characters in a film, play or book are the people in it.
EXAMPLE **The witch is an evil character.**

A
B
C
D
E
F
G
H
I
J
K
L
M
N
O
P
Q
R
S
T
U
V
W
X
Y
Z

characteristic characteristics
NOUN

1 A characteristic is a quality that is typical of something.
EXAMPLE He shares many characteristics with his father.

▶ ADJECTIVE

2 Characteristic means typical.
EXAMPLE That's very characteristic of him.

charge charges charging charged
VERB

1 To charge is to ask someone for money.
EXAMPLE They charge a small fee for their services.

CITIZENSHIP

2 To charge someone is to accuse them formally of having committed a crime.
EXAMPLE The police charged her with a number of offences.

SCIENCE

3 To charge a battery means to pass an electrical current through it to make it store electricity.
EXAMPLE Alex had forgotten to charge the battery.

4 To charge means to rush forward.
EXAMPLE She charged into the room, knocking over a chair.

▶ NOUN

5 A charge is the price that you have to pay for something.
EXAMPLE The museum makes a small charge for admission.

CITIZENSHIP

6 A charge is a formal accusation that a person is guilty of a crime.
EXAMPLE He may still face criminal charges.

charity charities
NOUN

1 A charity is an organization that raises money to help people.
EXAMPLE The RSPCA and Oxfam are both charities.

2 Charity is money or other help given to poor, disabled or ill people.
EXAMPLE She ran the marathon to raise money for charity.

chart charts
NOUN

A chart is a diagram or table showing information.
EXAMPLE He noted the score on his chart.

charter charters chartering chartered
ADJECTIVE

1 A charter flight or plane is one which is hired for use by a particular person or group.
EXAMPLE They were on a charter flight to Spain.

▶ VERB

2 To charter transport is to hire it for private use.
EXAMPLE He chartered a jet to fly her home.

chase chases chasing chased
VERB

If you chase something, you run after it.
EXAMPLE She chased the thief for 100 yards.

▤ Similar words: hunt, pursue

cheap cheaper cheapest
ADJECTIVE

1 Cheap means costing little money.
EXAMPLE Tickets are still unbelievably cheap.

▤ Similar word: reasonable

2 Cheap means unfair and unkind.
EXAMPLE Don't make cheap jokes at my expense.

check checks checking checked
VERB

1 To check something is to examine it.
EXAMPLE Always check your change before leaving the shop.

▶ PHRASE

2 When you check in at a hotel or airport, you arrive and sign your name or show your ticket.
EXAMPLE Let's check in first, then go for a coffee.

3 When you check out of a hotel, you pay your bill and leave.
EXAMPLE They packed and checked out.

4 If you check something out, you find out about it.
EXAMPLE Let's go to the library and check it out.

cheer cheers cheering cheered
VERB

1 To cheer is to shout with approval or to show support.
EXAMPLE The crowd cheered as he entered the stadium.

▶ NOUN

2 A cheer is a shout of approval or support.
EXAMPLE A great cheer went up when he finished his speech.

chemical chemicals
NOUN   **SCIENCE**

Chemicals are substances manufactured by chemistry.
EXAMPLE Are too many chemicals used in agriculture?

chest chests
NOUN

1 Your chest is the front part of your body between your shoulders and your waist.
EXAMPLE He was shot in the chest.

2 A chest is a large wooden box, used for storing things.
EXAMPLE My aunt keeps spare bedding in a chest.

chicken chickens
NOUN

A chicken is a bird kept on a farm; also the meat of this bird.
EXAMPLE We had roast chicken on Sunday.

chief
ADJECTIVE

Chief means most important.
EXAMPLE The North Sea is our chief source of oil.

child children
NOUN
1 A child is a young person who is not yet an adult.
EXAMPLE I lived in Durham when I was a child.

▪ **Similar words:** baby, kid, youngster

2 Someone's child is their son or daughter.
EXAMPLE Her children are all married.

childhood childhoods
NOUN
Someone's childhood is the time when he or she is a child.
EXAMPLE She had a happy childhood.

Chinese
ADJECTIVE
1 Chinese means to do with China.
EXAMPLE We went to a Chinese restaurant.

2 Chinese refers to any of the languages spoken in China.
EXAMPLE The book was in Chinese.

chip chips chipping chipped
NOUN
1 Chips are thin strips of fried potato.
EXAMPLE I like vinegar on my fish and chips.

ICT
2 A chip is a tiny piece of silicon inside a computer which is used to form electronic circuits.
EXAMPLE Many computer chips are made in the Far East.

▸ VERB
3 If you chip an object, you break a small piece off it.
EXAMPLE She chipped her tooth when she fell.

chocolate chocolates
NOUN
Chocolate is a sweet food made from cocoa beans.
EXAMPLE She bought a chocolate bar from the sweet shop.

choice choices
NOUN
Choice is the power or right to choose.
EXAMPLE I made the right choice.

choose chooses choosing chose chosen
VERB
To choose something means to decide to have it or do it.
EXAMPLE He chose to live in France.

▪ **Similar words:** pick, select

chord chords   MUSIC
NOUN
A chord is two or more notes played at the same time.
EXAMPLE Tim strummed a D chord on his guitar.

chorus choruses   DRAMA
NOUN
1 The chorus is the group of actors that gives a commentary on the play.
EXAMPLE The chorus began and ended the play in the same way.

2 The chorus is the body of singers or dancers that perform together.
EXAMPLE She sang in the chorus in the school musical.

Christian Christians   RE
NOUN
1 A Christian is someone who believes in Jesus Christ.
EXAMPLE Several of her friends were Christians.

▸ ADJECTIVE
2 Christian is to do with Jesus Christ and his teachings.
EXAMPLE They followed the Christian faith.

Christmas Christmases   RE
NOUN
Christmas is the festival when Christians celebrate the birth of Jesus Christ.
EXAMPLE Merry Christmas!

chronology chronologies   HISTORY
▪ **Said:** kron-*nol*-loj-jee
NOUN
Chronology is the order in which events happened.
EXAMPLE The chronology of the Second World War begins in 1939.

church churches   RE
NOUN
1 A church is a building where Christians go for religious services and worship.
EXAMPLE I didn't see you in church on Sunday.

2 A church is one of the groups in the Christian religion.
EXAMPLE She joined the Catholic church.

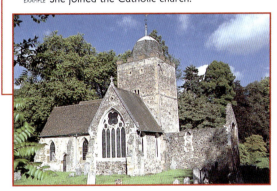

cigar cigars
NOUN
A cigar is a roll of dried tobacco leaves, which people smoke.
EXAMPLE He was sitting alone smoking a big cigar.

cigarette cigarettes
NOUN
A cigarette is a thin tube of paper containing tobacco, which people smoke.
EXAMPLE He bought a packet of cigarettes.

cinema cinemas
NOUN
A cinema is a place where people go to watch films.
EXAMPLE How often do you go to the cinema?

circle circles circling circled
NOUN
1 A circle is a round shape.
EXAMPLE The students sat in a circle on the floor.

2 The circle is an area of seats on an upper floor of a theatre.
EXAMPLE Shall we sit in the stalls or in the circle?

A B C D E F G H I J K L M N O P Q R S T U V W X Y Z

▸ *VERB*

3 To circle something means to move around it in a circle.

EXAMPLE **A police helicopter circled above.**

circuit circuits SCIENCE

◻ **Said:** *sir*-kit

NOUN

A circuit is the route around which an electric current flows.

EXAMPLE **Alison added a switch to the circuit.**

circumference circumferences MATHS

NOUN

The circumference is the outer line of a circle; also the length of this line.

EXAMPLE **They calculated the circumference of the circle.**

circumstance circumstances

NOUN

1 The circumstances of a situation or event are the conditions that affect what happens.

EXAMPLE **He did well under the circumstances.**

2 Someone's circumstances are their position and conditions in life.

EXAMPLE **Her circumstances changed when she began her new job.**

citizen citizens CITIZENSHIP

NOUN

A citizen of a country or city is a person who lives in it or belongs to it.

EXAMPLE **She is an American citizen.**

citizenship CITIZENSHIP

NOUN

1 Citizenship means belonging to and having the rights of a large community.

EXAMPLE **What are the benefits of citizenship?**

2 Citizenship means the qualities that make someone a good member of society.

EXAMPLE **Looking after the environment is good citizenship.**

city cities

NOUN

A city is a large town where many people live and work.

EXAMPLE **He visited the city of Oxford.**

civil CITIZENSHIP

ADJECTIVE

Civil is to do with the citizens of a country.

EXAMPLE **Martin Luther King fought for civil rights.**

civilian civilians HISTORY

NOUN

A civilian is a person who is not in the armed forces.

EXAMPLE **Many civilians were caught up in the fighting.**

civil war civil wars HISTORY

NOUN

A civil war is a war when people from the same country fight one another.

EXAMPLE **King Charles I was defeated in the English Civil War.**

claim claims claiming claimed

VERB

1 To claim is to state that something is the case.

EXAMPLE **He claimed to be a journalist.**

◼ **Similar word:** maintain

2 If you claim something, you ask for it because you believe you have a right to it.

EXAMPLE **The money will be given to charity if no one claims it.**

▸ *NOUN*

3 A claim is a statement that something is true, or that you have a right to something.

EXAMPLE **She will make a claim for compensation.**

clarify clarifies clarifying clarified EXAM TERM

VERB

To clarify means to make clearer by explaining.

EXAMPLE **Clarify the differences between Christian and Muslim views on marriage.**

clash clashes clashing clashed

VERB

1 If people clash with each other, they fight or argue.

EXAMPLE **Youths clashed with police in the streets.**

2 If colours or ideas clash, they are very different from each other.

EXAMPLE **The red door clashed with the green of the walls.**

3 If one event clashes with another, they happen at the same time.

EXAMPLE **His wedding clashed with the Cup Final.**

▸ *NOUN*

4 A clash is a fight or argument.

EXAMPLE **There were clashes between fans outside the stadium.**

class classes classing classed

NOUN

1 A class is a group of a particular type.

EXAMPLE **They came from different social classes.**

◼ **Similar words:** group, kind, type

2 A class is a group of students taught together.

EXAMPLE **If classes were smaller, children would learn more.**

▸ *VERB*

3 To class something is to put it in a group.

EXAMPLE **At 19 you're still classed as a teenager.**

classic

ADJECTIVE

1 Classic means typical.

EXAMPLE **It was a classic example of British fair play.**

2 If something is classic, it is of very high quality.

EXAMPLE **It is one of the classic films of all time.**

classical
ADJECTIVE
Classical means traditional in style, form or content.
EXAMPLE She enjoyed classical music.

clause clauses   **ENGLISH**
NOUN
A clause is a group of words which forms part of a sentence.
EXAMPLE 'After she had looked carefully' and 'Gita crossed the road' are both clauses.

clean cleaner cleanest; cleans cleaning cleaned
ADJECTIVE
1 Clean means free from dirt or unwanted marks.
EXAMPLE He wore a clean white shirt for work.

2 If humour is clean it is not rude.
EXAMPLE They show only clean, decent movies.

▶ VERB
3 To clean something is to remove dirt from it.
EXAMPLE It took half an hour to clean the bath.

clear clearer clearest; clears clearing cleared
ADJECTIVE
1 Clear means easy to understand, see or hear.
EXAMPLE I gave a clear account of the incident.

2 If something is clear, it is easy to see through.
EXAMPLE The water was beautifully clear.

3 If something is clear, it is free from obstructions.
EXAMPLE The runway is clear, so you may land.

▶ VERB
4 To clear unwanted things from a place is to remove them.
EXAMPLE Firemen were still clearing rubble from houses.
CITIZENSHIP

5 If someone is cleared of a crime, they are proved to be not guilty.
EXAMPLE He was cleared of all charges.

clever cleverer cleverest
ADJECTIVE
1 Clever means intelligent and quick to understand things.
EXAMPLE My sister was very clever at school.

Similar words: bright, intelligent, smart

client clients
NOUN
A client is someone who pays a professional person or company to receive a service.
EXAMPLE She is one of the firm's most valued clients.

climate climates   **GEOGRAPHY**
NOUN
The climate of a region is its average weather conditions.
EXAMPLE Southern Spain has a warm and dry climate.

climb climbs climbing climbed
VERB
To climb something is to move towards the top of it.
EXAMPLE He climbed the tree to reach the apples.

clinic clinics
NOUN
A clinic is a building where people go for medical treatment.
EXAMPLE The nurse worked at the local clinic.

close closes closing closed; closer closest
VERB
1 If you close something, or if it closes, you move it so that it is no longer open.
EXAMPLE He heard the door close behind him.

▶ PHRASE
2 If a business closes down, all work stops there permanently.
EXAMPLE Many small stores have been forced to close down.

▶ ADJECTIVE
3 Close means near.
EXAMPLE There is a pool close to their home.

Similar words: near, nearby

4 People who are close to each other are very friendly.
EXAMPLE She is a very close friend of mine.

5 If a competition is close, the competitors are nearly equal.
EXAMPLE It was close but we just managed to win.

close-up close-ups   **ART**
NOUN
A close-up is a detailed view of something.
EXAMPLE He drew a close-up of part of the body.

cloth cloths
NOUN
Cloth is fabric made by a process such as weaving.
EXAMPLE It was a coat of fine cloth.

clothes
PLURAL NOUN
Clothes are the things people wear.
EXAMPLE She went upstairs to change her clothes.

clothing
NOUN
Clothing is the same as clothes.
EXAMPLE What is your favourite item of clothing?

cloud clouds
NOUN   **GEOGRAPHY**
1 A cloud is a mass of water vapour in the sky.
EXAMPLE The sun went behind the clouds.

2 A cloud of smoke or dust is a lot of it floating in the air.
EXAMPLE The car pulled away, raising a cloud of dust.

club clubs clubbing clubbed
NOUN
1 A club is an organization of people with the same interest; also the place where they meet.
EXAMPLE He met his friends at the youth club.

Similar words: association, group, society

2 A club is a team which competes in competitions.
EXAMPLE **Barcelona football club plays in the Spanish league.**

3 A club is a thick, heavy stick used as a weapon.
EXAMPLE **The men were armed with knives and clubs.**

▶ VERB
4 To club someone is to hit them hard with a heavy object.
EXAMPLE **Riot police clubbed a student to death.**

coach coaches coaching coached
NOUN
1 A coach is a large bus that makes long journeys.
EXAMPLE **They travelled north by coach.**

2 A coach is a section of a train which carries passengers.
EXAMPLE **The front four coaches were for first-class travellers.**

3 A coach is someone who trains a person or sports team.
EXAMPLE **He was a famous football coach.**

▶ VERB
4 If someone coaches you, they help you to get better at a sport or a subject.
EXAMPLE **She had been coached by a former champion.**

⊟ Similar words: instruct, train

coast coasts   GEOGRAPHY
NOUN
The coast is the edge of the land where it meets the sea.
EXAMPLE **The west coast of Scotland is very beautiful.**

coat coats
NOUN
1 A coat is a piece of clothing which you wear over your other clothes.
EXAMPLE **He put on his coat and left.**

2 An animal's coat is the fur or hair on its body.
EXAMPLE **Her dog's coat was in a bad condition.**

3 A coat is a layer.
EXAMPLE **The front door needs a new coat of paint.**

▶ VERB
4 To coat something means to cover it with a thin layer of something.
EXAMPLE **I like nuts coated with chocolate.**

code codes
NOUN
1 A code is a secret system of communicating.
EXAMPLE **The message was in code.**

2 A code is a group of numbers and letters which is used to identify something.
EXAMPLE **I need the telephone code for Melbourne.**

coffee coffees
NOUN
Coffee is the roasted beans of the coffee plant; also a hot drink made from the beans.
EXAMPLE **I enjoy a cup of coffee after a meal.**

cold colder coldest; colds
ADJECTIVE
1 Something that is cold has a very low temperature.
EXAMPLE **It was windy and Jake felt cold.**

2 Cold means not showing much affection.
EXAMPLE **What a cold, unfeeling man you are!**

▶ NOUN
3 You can refer to cold weather as the cold.
EXAMPLE **She was complaining about the cold.**

4 A cold is an illness in which you sneeze.
EXAMPLE **I had a bad cold, so I stayed at home.**

collage collages   ART
⊡ Said: kol-lahj
NOUN
A collage is a picture made by sticking pieces of cloth or paper on to a surface.
EXAMPLE **She made a collage of an autumn scene.**

collapse collapses collapsing collapsed
VERB
1 To collapse is to fall down suddenly.
EXAMPLE **Jimmy collapsed on the floor.**

2 If a system or a business collapses, it suddenly stops working.
EXAMPLE **His business empire collapsed.**

colleague colleagues
NOUN
A person's colleagues are the people he or she works with.
EXAMPLE **He had lunch with a business colleague.**

collect collects collecting collected
VERB
1 To collect things is to gather them together.
EXAMPLE **They were collecting money for charity.**

2 To collect something from a place means to take it away.
EXAMPLE **We had to collect her from school.**

3 When things collect in a place, they gather there.
EXAMPLE **Food collects in holes in the teeth.**

collection collections
NOUN
1 A collection is a group of things brought together.
EXAMPLE **He had a huge collection of paintings.**

⊟ Similar word: set
2 A collection is the organized collecting of money, or the sum of money collected.
EXAMPLE **The church collection came to £53.50.**

college colleges
NOUN
A college is a place where students study after they have left school.
EXAMPLE **She went to the local technical college.**

colonel colonels
⊡ Said: kur-nl
NOUN
A colonel is a senior officer in the army.

EXAMPLE Colonel Edward Stanley was in charge of the parade.

colony colonies **HISTORY**
NOUN

1 A colony is a country or territory controlled by a more powerful country.
EXAMPLE India was a colony of Great Britain.

2 A colony is a group of people from the same country who settle in a foreign place.
EXAMPLE The Spanish formed colonies in America in the sixteenth century.

colour colours
NOUN

1 Colour is the appearance something has when light is reflected from its surface.
EXAMPLE They could see all the colours of the rainbow.

2 Someone's colour is the normal colour of their skin.
EXAMPLE She was proud of her colour.

column columns
NOUN

1 A column is a tall solid pillar.
EXAMPLE The columns of the temple were still in position.

2 A column is a line of people or vehicles.
EXAMPLE The column of tanks moved up the road.

3 In a newspaper or magazine, a column is a vertical section of writing.
EXAMPLE He writes a column for *The Evening News*.

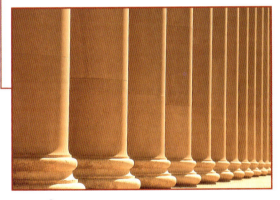

comb combs
NOUN

A comb is an object which you use for tidying your hair.
EXAMPLE He ran a comb through his hair.

combat combats
NOUN

Combat is fighting.
EXAMPLE It was his first experience of combat.

combination combinations
NOUN

A combination is a mixture of things.
EXAMPLE I did it for a combination of reasons.

combine combines combining combined
VERB

If someone combines two activities, they do them both at the same time.
EXAMPLE She combined a career with being a mother.

comedy comedies
NOUN

1 A comedy is a play, film or television programme that is intended to make people laugh.
EXAMPLE Did you watch that new comedy last night?

2 Comedy is something that amuses people.
EXAMPLE The book contains passages of great comedy.

comfort comforts comforting comforted
NOUN

1 Comfort is the state of being physically relaxed.
EXAMPLE Now you can shop from the comfort of your own home.

2 Comfort is a feeling of relief from worry or unhappiness.
EXAMPLE Your support is a great comfort to me.

▸ PLURAL NOUN

3 Comforts are things which make your life easier.
EXAMPLE The hotel had all the comforts of home.

▸ VERB

4 To comfort someone is to make them less worried or unhappy.
EXAMPLE Ned comforted his sister in her grief.

comfortable
ADJECTIVE

1 Comfortable means physically relaxed.
EXAMPLE Sit down and make yourself comfortable.

2 Something that is comfortable makes you feel relaxed.
EXAMPLE It was a comfortable bed.

3 If you feel comfortable, you are not anxious or embarrassed.
EXAMPLE I feel very comfortable with the idea.

comma commas **ENGLISH**
NOUN

A comma is a punctuation mark which looks like this: ,.
EXAMPLE Put a comma here, not a full stop.

1 A comma indicates a short pause in a sentence: 'In 1901, Queen Victoria died.'
2 A comma also separates items in a list: 'Red, blue, yellow and gold'.

command commands commanding commanded
VERB

1 To command is to order.
EXAMPLE The policeman commanded me to come out.

■ Similar words: direct, order

▸ NOUN

2 A command is an order.
EXAMPLE The soldiers waited for the command to advance.

3 Your command of something is ability in it.
EXAMPLE My father had a good command of German.

comment comments commenting commented
VERB

1 To comment is to remark.
EXAMPLE The president refused to comment on the rumours.

■ Similar word: remark

▸ NOUN

2 A comment is a remark.
EXAMPLE He received many comments about his appearance.

commentator commentators
NOUN
A commentator is someone who gives a description or explanation of something.
EXAMPLE Our commentator at the match is James Jones.

commercial commercials
ADJECTIVE
1 Commercial activities involve producing goods in order to make money.
EXAMPLE She preferred the commercial side of the business.

▶ NOUN
2 A commercial is an advertisement on television or radio.
EXAMPLE She switched channels during the commercials.

commit commits committing committed
VERB
1 To commit a crime or sin is to do it.
EXAMPLE They believe they know who committed the murder.

■ Similar words: do, perform

2 If you commit yourself to something, you accept it fully or state that you will do it.
EXAMPLE Mary was totally committed to her job.

3 If someone is committed to a hospital or prison, they are sent there.
EXAMPLE Eventually he was committed to a mental hospital.

commitment commitments
NOUN
1 Commitment is a strong belief in an idea or system.
EXAMPLE Her commitment to socialism was as strong as ever.

2 A commitment is something that regularly takes up some of your time.
EXAMPLE His business commitments grew and grew.

committee committees
NOUN
A committee is a group of people who make decisions on behalf of a larger group.
EXAMPLE She was on the fund-raising committee.

common commoner commonest; commons
ADJECTIVE
1 Something that is common exists in large numbers or happens often.
EXAMPLE McGregor is a common Scottish name.

■ Similar word: frequent

2 If something is common to two or more people, they all have it or use it.
EXAMPLE We had a common interest in music.

3 Common means lacking good taste or good manners.
EXAMPLE She was often common and rude.

▶ NOUN
4 A common is a public area of grassy land.
EXAMPLE He walked the dog on Clapham Common.

communicate communicates communicating communicated
VERB
1 To communicate is to exchange information, usually by talking or writing.
EXAMPLE They communicated regularly by e-mail.

2 If you communicate an idea or a feeling to someone, you make them aware of it.
EXAMPLE He was having trouble communicating his ideas.

communication communications
NOUN
1 Communication is the process by which people or animals exchange information.
EXAMPLE The telephone is an effective system of communication.

▶ PLURAL NOUN
2 Communications are the systems by which people communicate or broadcast information.
EXAMPLE After the storm, all communications were cut.

communism HISTORY
NOUN
Communism is the political belief that no one should own anything individually and that everything should belong to the state.
EXAMPLE He wrote about communism in China and Russia.

community communities
NOUN
1 A community is all the people living in a particular area.
EXAMPLE All sections of the community went to the meeting.

2 A community is a particular group within a society.
EXAMPLE Bradford has a large Asian community.

company companies
NOUN
1 A company is a business that sells goods or provides a service.
EXAMPLE She worked for a record company.

2 If you have company, you have a friend or visitor with you.
EXAMPLE I enjoyed her company.

compare compares comparing compared
VERB

EXAM TERM

1 To compare means to look at the similarities and differences between two things.
EXAMPLE Compare the ways the Eskimos and the Arabs adapt to the climates they live in.

2 If you compare one thing to another, you say it is like the other thing.
EXAMPLE His voice is often compared to Pavarotti's.

compass compasses GEOGRAPHY
NOUN
A compass is an instrument with a magnetic needle for finding directions.
EXAMPLE They used a compass to find north.

compete competes competing competed
VERB

1 When people or firms compete for something, they try to get it for themselves.
EXAMPLE Banks and building societies are competing for business.

2 If you compete in a contest or game, you take part in it.
EXAMPLE He competed in the 100 and 200 metres.

competition competitions
NOUN

1 Competition is the struggle between people or groups to get something.
EXAMPLE There's a lot of competition for places.

2 A competition is an event in which people take part to find who is best at something.
EXAMPLE He won the crossword competition.

competitive
ADJECTIVE

A competitive situation is one in which people or firms are competing with each other.
EXAMPLE Leisure wear is a very competitive market.

competitor competitors
NOUN

A competitor is a person or firm that is trying to become the most successful.
EXAMPLE The bank isn't performing as well as its competitors.

complain complains complaining complained
VERB

1 If you complain, you say that you are not satisfied with something.
EXAMPLE The neighbours complained to the police about the noise.

■ **Similar words:** find fault, grumble, moan

2 If you complain of pain or illness, you say that you have that pain or illness.
EXAMPLE He complained of a pain in the chest.

complaint complaints
NOUN

If you make a complaint, you complain about something.
EXAMPLE We've had a complaint from one of our customers.

complete completes completing completed
ADJECTIVE

1 If something is complete, none of it is missing.
EXAMPLE He read the complete works of Shakespeare.

■ **Similar words:** entire, full, whole

2 Complete means to the greatest degree possible.
EXAMPLE The party was a complete surprise.

■ **Similar words:** absolute, thorough, total

3 Complete means finished.
EXAMPLE The planning stage is now complete

▸ *VERB*

4 To complete is to finish.
EXAMPLE He has just completed his first novel.

5 If you complete a form, you fill it in.
EXAMPLE Complete the form below in black ink.

complex complexes
ADJECTIVE

1 Complex things have many different parts and are hard to understand.

EXAMPLE It was a very complex problem.

■ **Similar word:** complicated

▸ *NOUN*

2 A complex is a group of buildings used for a particular purpose.
EXAMPLE We stayed at a hotel and leisure complex.

complicated
ADJECTIVE

Something that is complicated has many parts and is difficult to understand.
EXAMPLE The form was extremely complicated.

component components `TECHNOLOGY`
NOUN

The components of something are the parts used to make it.
EXAMPLE He looked at all the components of the engine.

composer composers `MUSIC`
NOUN

A composer is someone who writes music.
EXAMPLE Sir Paul McCartney is a modern composer.

composition compositions `MUSIC`
NOUN

1 A composition is a piece of music.
EXAMPLE There were two compositions by Mozart on the CD.

`ART`

2 A composition is the arrangement of the parts of a work of art into a design.
EXAMPLE The composition was based on diagonal lines.

compound compounds `SCIENCE`
NOUN

A compound is a chemical made by joining two or more elements together.
EXAMPLE At the end of the experiment the scientist had made a new compound.

comprehensive comprehensives
ADJECTIVE

1 Something that is comprehensive includes everything necessary or relevant.
EXAMPLE We bought a comprehensive guide to the city.

▸ *NOUN*

2 A comprehensive is a school where children of all abilities are taught together.
EXAMPLE She taught at the local comprehensive.

compromise compromises compromising compromised
NOUN

1 A compromise is an agreement in which people accept less than they originally wanted.
EXAMPLE In the end they reached a compromise.

▶ *VERB*

2 When people compromise, they agree to accept less than they originally wanted.
EXAMPLE He simply refuses to compromise.

computer computers
ICT
NOUN

A computer is an electronic machine which can process and store information quickly.
EXAMPLE He used a computer to write his history homework.

concentrate concentrates concentrating concentrated
VERB

1 If you concentrate on something, you give it all your attention.
EXAMPLE He concentrated on his driving.

2 When something is concentrated in one place, it is all there.
EXAMPLE The cafés are concentrated in the city centre.

concentration
NOUN

Concentration on something involves giving it all your attention.
EXAMPLE Lynne's interruption broke my concentration.

concern concerns concerning concerned
NOUN

1 Concern is worry about something or someone.
EXAMPLE Her mother's health was a cause for concern.

2 Your concern is your duty or responsibility.
EXAMPLE That's not my concern.

▶ *VERB*

3 If something concerns you, it worries you.
EXAMPLE Security is the matter that most concerned me.

4 If something concerns you, it affects or involves you.
EXAMPLE These matters do not concern them.

▤ **Similar word:** involve

concert concerts
MUSIC
NOUN

A concert is a public performance by musicians.
EXAMPLE The concert included three woodwind pieces.

conclude concludes concluding concluded
VERB

1 If you conclude something, you finally decide that it is true.
EXAMPLE An inquiry concluded that the system was faulty.

2 When you conclude something, you finish it.
EXAMPLE At that point I concluded the interview.

conclusion conclusions
NOUN

1 A conclusion is what you finally decide.
EXAMPLE I've come to the conclusion that he was lying.

2 The conclusion of something is its ending or outcome.
EXAMPLE The conclusion was that we separated.

SCIENCE

3 A conclusion is what is learned from carrying out an experiment.
EXAMPLE His conclusion was that water boils at 100°C.

concrete
NOUN

1 Concrete is a building material made by mixing cement, sand and water.
EXAMPLE The posts had to be set in concrete.

▶ *ADJECTIVE*

2 Concrete means made of concrete.
EXAMPLE It was a delivery of concrete blocks.

3 Concrete means real and physical.
EXAMPLE He had no concrete evidence.

condemn condemns condemning condemned
VERB

1 If you condemn something, you say it is bad and unacceptable.
EXAMPLE Teachers condemned the new plans.

▤ **Similar word:** criticize

2 If someone is condemned to a punishment, they are given it.
EXAMPLE She was condemned to death.

▤ **Similar word:** sentence

condense condenses condensing condensed
VERB
SCIENCE

When a gas or vapour condenses, it changes into a liquid.
EXAMPLE He watched his hot breath condense on the window pane.

condition conditions
NOUN

1 A condition is the state something is in.
EXAMPLE The boat is in a good condition.

2 A condition is an illness.
EXAMPLE He was born with a mild heart condition.

▶ *PLURAL NOUN*

3 The conditions in which people live or do things are the factors that affect them.
EXAMPLE The living conditions were awful.

4 Conditions are things that must happen in order for something else to be possible.
EXAMPLE Our captors announced the conditions of our release.

▤ **Similar word:** requirement

conduct conducts conducting conducted
VERB

◻ **Said:** con-*duct*

1 When you conduct an activity, you do it.
EXAMPLE I decided to conduct an experiment.

2 The way you conduct yourself is the way you behave.
EXAMPLE He conducts himself well for someone so young.

▶ *NOUN*

📓 **Said:** *con-*duct

3 The conduct of an activity is the way it is done.
EXAMPLE The conduct of the trial was criticized.

4 Your conduct is your behaviour.
EXAMPLE The conduct of the fans has greatly improved.

conductor conductors
NOUN   **SCIENCE**

1 A conductor is any material that allows energy to flow through it easily.
EXAMPLE Copper wire is a good electrical conductor.

MUSIC

2 A conductor is someone who directs or guides an orchestra or choir.
EXAMPLE The conductor bowed at the end of the performance.

conference
NOUN

A conference is a meeting at which formal discussions take place.
EXAMPLE The union held its conference in Blackpool.

confidence
NOUN

1 Confidence is trust.
EXAMPLE I have complete confidence in you.

2 Someone who has confidence is sure of their own abilities or qualities.
EXAMPLE Working in a group gives you more confidence.

confident
ADJECTIVE

1 If you are confident about something, you are sure it will happen.
EXAMPLE I am confident that we will succeed.

📗 **Similar words:** certain, positive, sure

2 Someone who is confident is sure of their own abilities or qualities.
EXAMPLE He relaxed and became more confident.

confirm confirms confirming confirmed
VERB

1 To confirm something is to say or show that it is true.
EXAMPLE These new statistics confirm our fears.

📗 **Similar word:** prove

2 If you confirm an arrangement, you say it is definite.
EXAMPLE I'd like to confirm my booking.

conflict conflicts conflicting conflicted
NOUN

📓 **Said:** *con-*flict

1 Conflict is disagreement and argument.

EXAMPLE Conflict between workers and management was bitter.

📗 **Similar word:** disagreement

2 A conflict is a war or battle.
EXAMPLE The region has seen many military conflicts.

📗 **Similar words:** battle, clash

▶ *VERB*

📓 **Said:** con-*flict*

3 When ideas or interests conflict, they are different.
EXAMPLE The new findings conflicted with the old.

📗 **Similar words:** clash, disagree

confront confronts confronting confronted
VERB

1 If you are confronted with a problem or task, you have to deal with it.
EXAMPLE This is the task confronting us.

2 If you confront someone, you meet them face to face.
EXAMPLE The candidates confronted each other in a televised debate.

conjunction conjunctions
NOUN   **ENGLISH**

A conjunction is a word which links two other words or parts of a sentence.
EXAMPLE 'And', 'but', 'if' and 'while' are conjunctions.

connect connects connecting connected
VERB

1 To connect two things is to join them together.
EXAMPLE Connect the pipe to the tap.

2 If one thing or person is connected with another, there is a link between them.
EXAMPLE Police say she is not connected with the inquiry.

connection connections
NOUN

1 If there is a connection between things, there is a link between them.
EXAMPLE He had no connection with the police.

2 A connection is the point where two wires or pipes are joined together.
EXAMPLE A loose connection had caused the leak.

▶ *PLURAL NOUN*

3 Someone's connections are the people they know.
EXAMPLE He had powerful connections in the army.

conquer conquers conquering conquered
VERB   **HISTORY**

To conquer people is to take control of their country by force.
EXAMPLE Duke William conquered England in 1066.

conscious
📓 **Said:** *kon-*shus

ADJECTIVE

1 Conscious means aware.
EXAMPLE She was conscious of the time.

2 Conscious means deliberate.
EXAMPLE I made a conscious decision not to speak.

3 Conscious means awake.
EXAMPLE Still conscious, she was taken to hospital.

consciousness
NOUN

If you lose consciousness, you become unconscious.
EXAMPLE She banged her head and lost consciousness.

consequence consequences
NOUN
Consequences are results or effects.
EXAMPLE He didn't consider the consequences of his action.

conservative
ADJECTIVE   **CITIZENSHIP**
1 In Britain, Conservative refers to the views and policies of the Conservative Party.
EXAMPLE He was a member of a local Conservative group.
2 Conservative means unwilling to accept new ideas.
EXAMPLE You get more conservative as you get older.

consider considers considering considered   **EXAM TERM**
VERB
To consider means to think about and include your own opinions in your answer.
EXAMPLE Consider how the author makes us feel sorry for Billy Casper.

considerable
ADJECTIVE
Considerable means a lot of.
EXAMPLE His aunt left him a considerable sum of money.

consideration considerations
NOUN
1 Consideration is careful thought.
EXAMPLE It was a decision demanding careful consideration.
2 Consideration is attention to people's needs and feelings.
EXAMPLE He showed every consideration for his daughters.
3 A consideration is something that should be thought about.
EXAMPLE Money was also a consideration.

consist consists consisting consisted
VERB
Something that consists of particular things is formed from them.
EXAMPLE His diet consisted of bread, cheese and beer.

consistent
ADJECTIVE
1 If you are consistent, you keep doing something the same way.
EXAMPLE He was one of our most consistent players.
2 If things are consistent with another, they do not oppose each other.
EXAMPLE This result is consistent with earlier findings.

consonant consonants   **ENGLISH**
NOUN
A consonant is any letter other than the vowels.
EXAMPLE B, c, d and f are all consonants.

constant
ADJECTIVE
1 Something that is constant happens all the time or is always there.
EXAMPLE They suffered a constant stream of abuse.
2 Constant means staying the same.
EXAMPLE The tropical fish need a constant temperature.
■ **Similar words:** fixed, steady, unchanging

constitution constitutions   **CITIZENSHIP**
NOUN
The constitution of a country is the system of laws that formally states people's rights and duties.
EXAMPLE The French constitution was decided after the revolution.

construct constructs constructing constructed
VERB
To construct is to build or make.
EXAMPLE They constructed a series of fortresses.

consult consults consulting consulted
VERB
1 If you consult someone, you ask for their opinion.
EXAMPLE If the symptoms persist, consult your doctor.
2 If you consult a book or map, you look at it for information.
EXAMPLE Consult the chart on page 44.

consultant consultants
NOUN
1 A consultant is an experienced doctor.
EXAMPLE My sister is a consultant at Guy's Hospital.
2 A consultant is someone who gives expert advice.
EXAMPLE A management consultant was brought in to solve the problem.

consume consumes consuming consumed
VERB
1 To consume means to eat or drink.
EXAMPLE Martha consumed a pound of meat a day.
2 To consume fuel or energy is to use it up.
EXAMPLE The lamp consumes a tiny amount of electricity.

consumer consumers
NOUN
A consumer is someone who buys things or uses services.
EXAMPLE Consumers are more careful now about where they shop.

contact contacts contacting contacted
NOUN
1 Contact with someone is communication with them.
EXAMPLE He has kept in regular contact with his family.
2 When things are in contact, they are touching each other.
EXAMPLE There was no physical contact between them.
3 A contact is someone you know in a place or organization.
EXAMPLE He has contacts in government.
VERB
4 To contact someone is to communicate with them.
EXAMPLE I can be contacted at the following address.
■ **Similar words:** get or be in touch with, reach

contain contains containing contained
VERB

1 If a substance contains something, that thing is a part of it.
EXAMPLE Coke contains sugar.

2 The things a box or room contains are the things inside it.
EXAMPLE The bag contained three presents.

3 To contain something means to stop it increasing or spreading.
EXAMPLE The doctors tried to contain the disease.

contemporary contemporaries
ADJECTIVE

1 Contemporary means existing now or at the time you are talking about.
EXAMPLE This is a contemporary account of the war.

▸ *NOUN*

2 Someone's contemporaries are the people living at the same time as them.
EXAMPLE He was much criticized by his contemporaries.

content contents
NOUN

▣ **Said:** *con*-tent

1 The content or contents of something are what is contained in it
EXAMPLE The contents of the letter were never disclosed.

▸ *ADJECTIVE*

▣ **Said:** con-*tent*

2 Content means happy and satisfied.
EXAMPLE She is quite content with her life.

contest contests
NOUN

A contest is a competition or struggle for power.
EXAMPLE She entered an eating contest.

▣ **Similar words:** competition, game, match

context contexts
NOUN

The context of something is the background which helps to explain it.
EXAMPLE They studied the context of the war.

continent continents   **GEOGRAPHY**
NOUN

1 A continent is a very large area of land, such as Asia.
EXAMPLE They travelled across the continent of Africa.

2 In Britain, the mainland of Europe is sometimes called the Continent.
EXAMPLE They went to the Continent for a holiday.

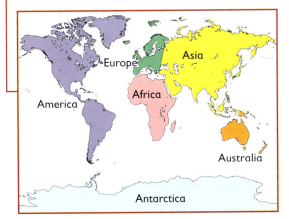

continue continues continuing continued
VERB

1 If you continue to do something, you keep doing it.
EXAMPLE She is determined to continue working.

2 If something continues, it does not stop.
EXAMPLE The war looks likely to continue.

▣ **Similar words:** carry on, go on, proceed

contract contracts contracting contracted
NOUN

▣ **Said:** *con*-tract

1 A contract is a legal agreement.
EXAMPLE He studied the contract of employment.

▸ *VERB*

▣ **Said:** con-*tract*

2 When something contracts, it gets smaller or shorter.
EXAMPLE When you are anxious, your muscles contract.

contrast contrasts contrasting contrasted
NOUN

▣ **Said:** *con*-trast

1 A contrast is a difference between things.
EXAMPLE The contrast between them was huge.

▸ *VERB*   **EXAM TERM**

▣ **Said:** con-*trast*

2 To contrast means to look at the differences between two things.
EXAMPLE Contrast the building methods of the northern and southern Africans.

contribute contributes contributing contributed
VERB

1 If you contribute to something, you do something to make it successful.
EXAMPLE The elderly have much to contribute to the community.

2 If you contribute money to something, you help to pay for it.
EXAMPLE The UK is contributing £4 million in loans.

▣ **Similar word:** give

contribution contributions
NOUN

1 If you make a contribution to something, you do something to make it successful.
EXAMPLE His contribution to world peace was immense.

2 A contribution is a sum of money that you give.
EXAMPLE Companies often make charitable contributions.

control controls controlling controlled
NOUN

1 Control of a country or organization is the power to run it.
EXAMPLE He was forced to give up control of the company.

2 Control over something is the ability to make it work.
EXAMPLE He lost control of the car on the icy road.

3 The controls on a machine are the devices used to work it.
EXAMPLE She explained the controls of the washing machine.

▸ *VERB*

4 To control a country or organization means to run it.
EXAMPLE He now controls the entire business.

5 To control a machine or system means to make it work.
EXAMPLE The computer system controlled the lighting.

6 To control yourself is to restrain your angry or

upset feelings.
EXAMPLE I managed to control myself.

convention conventions
NOUN
A convention is an accepted way of behaving or doing something.
EXAMPLE It's just a convention that men don't wear skirts.

conventional
ADJECTIVE
Someone who is conventional thinks or behaves in a normal way.
EXAMPLE He was a conventional man who was easily shocked.

conversation conversations
NOUN
A conversation is a talk between people.
EXAMPLE I had a conversation with Roger about fishing.

convert converts converting converted
VERB

☐ Said: con-*vert*

1 To convert one thing into another is to change it into the other thing.
EXAMPLE The body converts some foods into energy.

2 If someone converts you, they persuade you to change your religious or political beliefs.
EXAMPLE If you try to convert him, he'll just walk away.

▸ NOUN

☐ Said: *con*-vert

3 A convert is someone who has changed their religious or political beliefs.
EXAMPLE She was a convert to Roman Catholicism.

convict convicts convicting convicted
VERB
CITIZENSHIP

☐ Said: con-*vict*

1 If someone is convicted of a crime, they are found guilty of it in a law court.
EXAMPLE He was convicted of murder.

▸ NOUN

☐ Said: *con*-vict

2 A convict is someone serving a prison sentence.
EXAMPLE The convicts were shut in their cells at dusk.

conviction convictions
NOUN

1 A conviction is a strong belief or opinion.
EXAMPLE We had a conviction that we were right.

CITIZENSHIP

2 If someone has a conviction, they have been found guilty of a crime.
EXAMPLE He will appeal against his conviction.

convince convinces convincing convinced
VERB
To convince someone of something is to persuade them that it is true.
EXAMPLE I soon convinced him of my innocence.

☐ Similar word: persuade

co-operate co-operates co-operating co-operated
VERB

1 To co-operate means to work or act together.
EXAMPLE The French and British co-operated on the project.

2 To co-operate means to do what someone asks.
EXAMPLE He has agreed to co-operate with the police.

cope copes coping coped
VERB
If you cope with a problem or task, you deal with it successfully.
EXAMPLE She has had to cope with a lot in her life.

copy copies copying copied
NOUN

1 A copy is something made to look like something else.
EXAMPLE It's an exact copy of the painting.

2 A copy of a book, newspaper or record is one of many identical ones produced at the same time.
EXAMPLE That's my copy of the book.

▸ VERB

3 If you copy what someone does, you do the same thing.
EXAMPLE Just copy what I do.

4 If you copy something, you make a copy of it.
EXAMPLE He copied the information into a notebook.

core cores
NOUN

1 The core is the hard central part of a fruit.
EXAMPLE Peel the apple and remove the core.

2 The core is the central or most important part of something.
EXAMPLE The Earth's core is very hot.

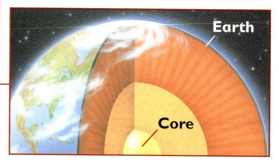
Earth
Core

correct corrects correcting corrected
ADJECTIVE

1 If something is correct, there are no mistakes in it.
EXAMPLE That's the correct answer.

2 The correct thing or method is the most suitable one.
EXAMPLE They took the correct course of action.

▸ VERB

3 If you correct something, you make it right.
EXAMPLE He asked her to correct his English.

correspond corresponds corresponding corresponded
VERB

1 If one thing corresponds to another, they are very similar or connected.
EXAMPLE The two maps of London correspond closely.

2 When people correspond, they write to each other.
EXAMPLE We corresponded regularly.

corrupt corrupts corrupting corrupted
ADJECTIVE

1 Corrupt means dishonest or immoral.
EXAMPLE We knew the policeman was corrupt.

▶ *VERB*

2 To corrupt someone means to make them dishonest or immoral.
EXAMPLE Power has totally corrupted him.

corruption

NOUN

Corruption is dishonesty and illegal behaviour by people in positions of power.
EXAMPLE The president faces serious charges of corruption.

cost costs costing

NOUN

1 The cost of something is the amount of money needed to buy it, do it or make it.
EXAMPLE The cost of the equipment is huge.

2 The cost of something is the loss or injury that it entails.
EXAMPLE The cost in human misery is enormous.

▶ *VERB*

3 To cost something is to be priced at that amount.
EXAMPLE How much does it cost?

costume costumes   **DRAMA**

NOUN

A costume is a set of clothes worn by an actor.
EXAMPLE The actor found it difficult to get into his costume.

cottage cottages

NOUN

A cottage is a small house in the country.
EXAMPLE They had a cottage in Scotland.

cotton

NOUN

1 Cotton is cloth made from the cotton plant.
EXAMPLE Is this shirt made of cotton or polyester?

2 Cotton is thread used for sewing.
EXAMPLE I need a needle and cotton.

cough coughs coughing coughed

☐ **Said:** koff

VERB

1 When you cough, you force air out of your throat with a sudden harsh noise.
EXAMPLE Graham began to cough violently.

▶ *NOUN*

2 A cough is the noise you make when you cough.
EXAMPLE She heard a polite cough behind her.

could

VERB

1 You use could to say that you are able to do something.
EXAMPLE She could leave if she wanted to.

2 You use could to say that something might happen or might be true.
EXAMPLE It could rain.

3 You use could when you are asking for something politely.
EXAMPLE Could you tell me how much this is?

council councils   **CITIZENSHIP**

NOUN

A council is a group of people elected to look after the affairs of a town, district or county.
EXAMPLE He was elected to Cheshire County Council.

count counts counting counted

VERB

1 When you count, you say all the numbers in order up to a particular number.
EXAMPLE He counted to twenty.

2 If you count, or count up, all the things in a group, you add them up.
EXAMPLE I counted the money to see if it was correct.

3 If something counts as a particular thing, it is regarded as being that thing.
EXAMPLE Does this count as a business expense?

4 To count on something means to rely on it.
EXAMPLE You can count on me.

▶ *NOUN*

5 A count is a European nobleman.
EXAMPLE Her father was a Polish count.

counter counters

NOUN

1 A counter is a surface over which goods are sold in a shop.
EXAMPLE The shop assistant stood behind the counter.

2 A counter is a small object used in board games.
EXAMPLE He moved his counter three spaces forward.

country countries   **GEOGRAPHY**

NOUN

1 A country is one of the political areas the world is divided into.
EXAMPLE Britain is a European country.

▤ **Similar words:** nation, state

2 The country is land away from towns and cities.
EXAMPLE I would like a house in the country.

countryside

NOUN

The countryside is land away from towns and cities.
EXAMPLE I've always loved the English countryside.

county counties   **GEOGRAPHY**

NOUN

A county is a region with its own local government.
EXAMPLE I was born in the county of Yorkshire.

couple couples coupling coupled

NOUN

1 A couple is two people who are married or having a sexual relationship.
EXAMPLE I live next door to an elderly couple.

2 A couple of things or people means two of them.

A
B
C
D
E
F
G
H
I
J
K
L
M
N
O
P
Q
R
S
T
U
V
W
X
Y
Z

EXAMPLE I went away for a couple of weeks.

▸ VERB

3 To couple two things is to combine them.
EXAMPLE They offered high quality coupled with low prices.

courage
NOUN
Courage is bravery.
EXAMPLE The rescue team showed a lot of courage.

course courses
NOUN
1 A course is a series of lessons or lectures.
EXAMPLE He liked the other students on his French course.

2 A course is a piece of land used for racing or golf.
EXAMPLE The hotel is next to a golf course.

3 A course is the route a ship or aircraft takes.
EXAMPLE The captain changed course to avoid the storm.

4 A course is one of the parts of a meal.
EXAMPLE The first course was soup.

5 A course is a series of medical treatments.
EXAMPLE We needed a course of injections.

▸ PHRASE

6 If you say 'of course', you are showing that something is expected or that you are sure about something.
EXAMPLE Of course she wouldn't do that.

court courts
NOUN   **CITIZENSHIP**
1 A court is a place where legal matters are decided by a judge and jury or a magistrate.
EXAMPLE He is due to appear in court next week.

2 A court is a place where certain games are played.
EXAMPLE The house has its own tennis court.

cousin cousins
NOUN
Your cousin is the child of your uncle or aunt.
EXAMPLE All my cousins were at the wedding.

cover covers covering covered
VERB
1 To cover something is to put something over it.
EXAMPLE She covered the table with a cloth.

2 To cover a distance is to travel that distance.
EXAMPLE They covered 20 kilometres a day.

3 To cover a subject means to discuss it.
EXAMPLE We've covered a wide range of subjects today.

▸ NOUN

4 A cover is something put over an object.
EXAMPLE She put the cover on her keyboard.

5 The cover of a book or magazine is its outside.
EXAMPLE The price is on the back cover.

6 Insurance cover is a guarantee that money will be paid if something is lost or damaged.
EXAMPLE The policy provides cover for hospital charges.

crack cracks cracking cracked
VERB
1 If something cracks or if something cracks it, it becomes damaged, with lines appearing on its surface.
EXAMPLE A stone had cracked the window.

2 If you crack a problem or code, you solve it.
EXAMPLE After years of thought he finally cracked the code.

▸ NOUN

3 A crack is one of the lines appearing on something when it is damaged.
EXAMPLE The plate had a crack in it.

4 A crack is a narrow gap.
EXAMPLE She saw him through a crack in the curtains.

▤ Similar words: break, gap

craft crafts
NOUN
1 A craft is an activity involving skill and handiwork.
EXAMPLE Weaving and pottery are both crafts.

2 A craft is a boat, plane or spacecraft.
EXAMPLE Dozens of small craft set out from the shore.

crash crashes crashing crashed
NOUN
1 A crash is an accident involving vehicles.
EXAMPLE The road was blocked by a car crash.

2 A crash is a sudden loud noise.
EXAMPLE The tray fell to the floor with a terrific crash.

▸ VERB

3 If a vehicle crashes, it hits something.
EXAMPLE His car crashed into the rear of a van.

cream creams
NOUN
1 Cream is a liquid taken from the top of milk.
EXAMPLE Strawberries and cream are a real treat.

2 Cream is a substance that you can rub into your skin.
EXAMPLE She always uses skin cream after a bath.

▸ ADJECTIVE OR NOUN

3 Cream is a yellowish-white colour.
EXAMPLE She bought a pair of cream silk stockings.

crease creases creasing creased
NOUN
1 A crease is an irregular line that appears on cloth or paper when it is crumpled.
EXAMPLE She smoothed down the creases in her dress.

2 A crease is a straight line on something that has been pressed or folded neatly.
EXAMPLE She made a crease in the paper.

▸ VERB

3 To crease something is to make lines appear on it.
EXAMPLE His clothes were very creased.

create creates creating created
VERB
To create something is to cause it to happen or exist.
EXAMPLE They hope to create more jobs in the area.

creative
ADJECTIVE
Creative means good at inventing and developing new ideas.
EXAMPLE He is a most creative film director.

A B **C** D E F G H I J K L M N O P Q R S T U V W X Y Z

credit
NOUN
1 Credit is a system where you pay for goods after you have received them.
EXAMPLE **It can be useful to buy goods on credit.**

2 Credit is praise and recognition.
EXAMPLE **Some of the credit for this should go to me.**

creed creeds
RE
NOUN
A creed is a statement of religious belief.
EXAMPLE **They said the creed in church every Sunday.**

cricket crickets
NOUN
1 Cricket is a game with bat and ball played by two teams.
EXAMPLE **We played cricket all day.**

2 A cricket is a small jumping insect.
EXAMPLE **You can often hear crickets during the summer.**

criminal criminals
NOUN
1 A criminal is someone who has committed a crime.
EXAMPLE **Most of his friends are criminals.**

■ Similar word: crook
▶ ADJECTIVE
2 If something is criminal, it involves crime.
EXAMPLE **It is a criminal offence to drive under the influence of alcohol.**

crisis crises
■ Said: kry-seez in the plural
NOUN
A crisis is a serious or dangerous situation.
EXAMPLE **The country's economic crisis worsened.**

critic critics
NOUN
ENGLISH
1 A critic is someone who writes reviews of books, films, plays or musical performances.
EXAMPLE **He earned his living as a film critic.**

2 A critic is someone who criticizes.
EXAMPLE **He was one of the government's biggest critics.**

critical
ADJECTIVE
1 A critical time or situation is a very important one.
EXAMPLE **This was a critical moment.**

2 To be critical of something is to criticize it.
EXAMPLE **My father is always so critical.**

criticism criticisms
NOUN
Criticism is the action of expressing disapproval of something.
EXAMPLE **The government came in for severe criticism.**

criticize criticizes criticizing criticized
VERB
If you criticize something, you say what you think is wrong with it.
EXAMPLE **He criticized the police for their handling of the case.**

Criticize is also spelt criticise.

crop crops
NOUN
1 Crops are plants that are grown for food.
EXAMPLE **The farmers here still harvest their crops by hand.**

2 A crop is the plants or produce collected at harvest time.
EXAMPLE **They get two crops of rice a year.**

cross crosses crossing crossed; crosser crossest
VERB
1 If you cross something, you go to the other side of it.
EXAMPLE **She was killed while crossing the road.**

2 Lines or roads that cross go across each other.
EXAMPLE **Stand where the two roads cross.**

▶ NOUN
3 A cross is the shape of a cross; also used to describe any object shaped like this.
EXAMPLE **She wears a cross on a silver chain.**

4 A cross is a written mark shaped like an X.
EXAMPLE **I put a cross on the map where my house was.**

▶ ADJECTIVE
5 Cross means rather angry.
EXAMPLE **She's very cross with you.**

▶ PHRASE
6 If you 'cross out' words, you draw a line through them.
EXAMPLE **He crossed out the answer and wrote it again.**

crowd crowds crowding crowded
NOUN
1 A crowd is a large group of people gathered together.
EXAMPLE **A huge crowd had gathered outside the court.**

■ Similar words: mass, mob
▶ VERB
2 When people crowd around something, they gather together around it.
EXAMPLE **The children crowded around him.**

crown crowns crowning crowned
NOUN
1 A crown is a circular ornament worn on the head by a king or queen.
EXAMPLE **It's a picture of the queen with her crown.**

▶ VERB
2 To crown someone is to make them king or queen.
EXAMPLE **The king was crowned on Christmas Day.**

crucial
■ Said: kroo-shl
ADJECTIVE
Crucial means very important.
EXAMPLE **He has a crucial role to play.**

■ Similar words: critical, vital

A B C D E F G H I J K L M N O P Q R S T U V W X Y Z

cruise cruises cruising cruised
NOUN

1 A cruise is a holiday in which you travel on a ship.
EXAMPLE **They were planning to go on a world cruise.**

▸ *VERB*

2 When a vehicle cruises, it moves at a constant speed.
EXAMPLE **A police car cruised past.**

crusade crusades
NOUN

HISTORY

1 A Crusade was an expedition made by Christian knights in the Middle Ages to recover the Holy Land from the Muslims.
EXAMPLE **The knights were killed while on a Crusade.**

2 A crusade is a long and determined attempt to achieve something.
EXAMPLE **Many people are involved in the crusade for human rights.**

cult cults
NOUN

RE

1 A cult is a small religious group.
EXAMPLE **She belongs to a cult which worships the Goddess.**

▸ *ADJECTIVE*

2 Cult describes something that is very popular or fashionable among a particular group of people.
EXAMPLE **Since her death she has become a cult figure.**

culture cultures
NOUN

1 Culture refers to the arts and to people's appreciation of them.
EXAMPLE **Popular culture today is dominated by TV.**

2 A culture is a particular society, with its own ideas, customs and art.
EXAMPLE **People from different cultures gathered for the festival.**

curious
ADJECTIVE

1 Someone who is curious wants to know more about something.
EXAMPLE **She was curious about all aspects of my past.**

▪ **Similar word:** nosy

2 Something that is curious is unusual or difficult to understand.
EXAMPLE **A curious thing happened the other day.**

currency currencies
NOUN

A country's currency is its coins and bank notes.
EXAMPLE **We changed our money into foreign currency.**

current currents
NOUN

1 A current is a steady flowing movement of water or air.
EXAMPLE **She was swept out to sea by the current.**

SCIENCE

2 An electric current is a flow of electricity through a wire or circuit.
EXAMPLE **An electric current is passed through the liquid.**

▸ *ADJECTIVE*

3 Something that is current is happening, being done or being used now.
EXAMPLE **The current situation is very different.**

cursor cursors
NOUN

ICT

1 A cursor is the pointer displayed on a computer screen and controlled by the mouse.
EXAMPLE **Use the mouse to move the cursor to the top of the screen.**

2 A cursor is the blinking line which shows where the next letter will appear when you type.
EXAMPLE **As I typed, the cursor moved on the screen.**

curtain curtains
NOUN

Curtains are pieces of material which can be pulled across a window.
EXAMPLE **Her bedroom curtains were drawn.**

custom customs
NOUN

1 A custom is a traditional activity.
EXAMPLE **The tea ceremony is an ancient Chinese custom.**

▪ **Similar words:** convention, tradition

2 A custom is something usually done at a particular time.
EXAMPLE **It was my custom to interview every applicant personally.**

▪ **Similar words:** habit, practice

3 Customs is the place at a border, airport or harbour where you have to declare any goods you are bringing into a country.
EXAMPLE **We went through customs without any problems.**

customer customers
NOUN

A shop's or firm's customers are the people who buy its goods.
EXAMPLE **The shop was full of customers.**

▪ **Similar words:** buyer, client, consumer

customize customizes customizing customized
VERB

DESIGN

To customize something is to make it meet the needs of a particular purpose or person.
EXAMPLE **She customized the kitchen for a disabled user.**

Customize is also spelt customise.

cycle cycles cycling cycled
VERB

1 When you cycle, you ride a bicycle.
EXAMPLE **I usually cycle to work.**

▸ *NOUN*

2 A cycle is another word for a bicycle.
EXAMPLE **The Tour de France is a great cycle race.**

3 A cycle of events is where they are continually repeated.
EXAMPLE **The cycle of drought and famine is worrying.**

Dd Dd Dd

daily
ADJECTIVE
Daily means occurring every day.
EXAMPLE I made my daily visit to the gym.

damage damages damaging damaged
VERB
1 To damage something means to harm or spoil it.
EXAMPLE A fire had severely damaged the school.

▸ *NOUN*
2 Damage is injury or harm done to something.
EXAMPLE The bomb caused lots of damage.

dance dances dancing danced
VERB
1 When you dance, you move around in time to music.
EXAMPLE Would you like to dance?

▸ *NOUN*
2 Dance is a series of movements which you do in time to music.
EXAMPLE The limbo is an energetic dance.

danger dangers
NOUN
Danger is the possibility that someone may be harmed or killed.
EXAMPLE Your life is in danger.

▪ Similar word: risk

dangerous
ADJECTIVE
Dangerous means likely to hurt or harm you.
EXAMPLE It's dangerous to drive when you're tired.

▪ Similar word: unsafe

dare dares daring dared
VERB
If you dare to do something, you have the courage to do it.
EXAMPLE No one dared to complain.

dark darker darkest
ADJECTIVE
1 When it is dark, there is not enough light to see properly.
EXAMPLE It was too dark to find the way.

▪ Similar word: dim
2 Something that is dark or a dark colour is black or a shade close to black.
EXAMPLE He wore a dark suit.

▸ *NOUN*
3 The dark is the lack of light in a place.
EXAMPLE I'm afraid of the dark.

data
NOUN
Data is information, usually in the form of facts or statistics.
EXAMPLE The study was based on data from 2,100 women.

'Data' is really a plural word, but it is usually used as a singular.

database databases   ICT
NOUN
A database is a collection of information stored in a computer.
EXAMPLE Look at the records on the school's database.

date dates dating dated
NOUN
1 A date is a particular day or year.
EXAMPLE What's the date today?

▸ *VERB*
2 If something dates from a particular time, that is when it happened or was made.
EXAMPLE The treasure dates from the sixth century BC.

daughter daughters
NOUN
Someone's daughter is their female child.
EXAMPLE I have two daughters and a son.

dead
ADJECTIVE
1 Dead means no longer living.
EXAMPLE Both her parents are dead.
2 Dead means no longer functioning.
EXAMPLE The phone went dead.

▸ *ADVERB*
3 Dead means precisely or exactly.
EXAMPLE The boat appeared, dead ahead.

deadline deadlines
NOUN
A deadline is a time or date by which something must be done.
EXAMPLE We missed the deadline because of all the delays.

deal deals dealing dealt
NOUN
1 A deal is an agreement or arrangement.
EXAMPLE It was the best business deal I ever did.

▸ *VERB*
2 If you deal with something, you do what is necessary to achieve the result you want.
EXAMPLE He must learn to deal with stress.

3 If someone deals in a particular type of goods, they buy and sell those goods.
EXAMPLE She deals in antiques.

▸ *PHRASE*
4 'A good deal' or 'a great deal' of something is a lot of it.
EXAMPLE They spent a great deal of money on the house.

dear dearer dearest
ADJECTIVE
1 Dear means much loved.
EXAMPLE He's a very dear friend.

2 Something that is dear costs a lot of money.
EXAMPLE They're far too dear.
▣ **Similar words:** costly, expensive

death deaths
NOUN
Death is the end of life.
EXAMPLE It's the anniversary of his death.

debate debates debating debated
NOUN
1 Debate is argument or discussion.
EXAMPLE There has been a lot of debate about this.

▸ *VERB*
2 When people debate something, they discuss it in a formal manner.
EXAMPLE The meeting will debate the death penalty today.

debt debts
▣ **Said:** det
NOUN
1 A debt is a sum of money that you owe someone.
EXAMPLE He is still paying off his debts.

2 Debt is the state of owing money.
EXAMPLE He got into debt as a student.

decade decades
NOUN
A decade is a period of ten years.
EXAMPLE His career spanned five decades.

decide decides deciding decided
VERB
1 If you decide to do something, you choose to do it.
EXAMPLE Why did you decide to get married?

2 If you decide that something is the case, you form that opinion about it.
EXAMPLE He decided that she must be right.

decimal decimals
MATHS
NOUN
1 A decimal is a fraction in which a decimal point is followed by numbers representing tenths, hundreds and thousandths.
EXAMPLE 0.25 and 0.5 are both decimals.

ADJECTIVE
2 Decimal refers to systems based on the number 10.
EXAMPLE Our number system is a decimal system.

decision decisions
NOUN
A decision is a choice or judgement which is made about something.
EXAMPLE I think you made the right decision.
▣ **Similar word:** judgement

deck decks
NOUN
1 A deck on a bus or ship is a downstairs or upstairs area.
EXAMPLE He sat on the top deck of the bus.

2 A tape deck or record deck is a piece of audio equipment.
EXAMPLE The cassette got stuck in the tape deck.

declare declares declaring declared
VERB
1 If you declare something, you say it firmly.
EXAMPLE She declared that she would fight on.
▣ **Similar words:** announce, state
2 To declare something means to announce it formally.
EXAMPLE He was declared insane.

decline declines declining declined
VERB
1 If something declines, it becomes smaller or weaker.
EXAMPLE The number of staff has declined in recent years.

2 If you decline something, you politely refuse to accept it or do it.
EXAMPLE I declined his offer of a drink.

▸ *NOUN*
3 A decline is a gradual weakening or decrease.
EXAMPLE There was a decline in the birth rate.

decorate decorates decorating decorated
VERB
1 If you decorate something, you make it more attractive.
EXAMPLE He decorated his office with pictures.

2 If you decorate a room or building, you paint or wallpaper it.
EXAMPLE He paid someone to decorate the bedroom.

deep deeper deepest
ADJECTIVE

1 If something is deep, it extends a long way down from the surface.
EXAMPLE She fell into a deep hole.

2 Deep is used when you measure something from the surface to the bottom.
EXAMPLE The water was only three feet deep.

3 Deep means great or intense.
EXAMPLE His letters showed his deep love of his family.

4 A deep sound is a low one.
EXAMPLE He had a deep voice.

defeat defeats defeating defeated
VERB

1 To defeat something is to win a victory over it.
EXAMPLE The team hasn't been defeated all year.

▸ *NOUN*

2 Defeat is the state or occasion of being beaten or of failing.
EXAMPLE He refused to admit defeat.

defence defences
NOUN

1 Defence is action that is taken to protect something.
EXAMPLE Weapons were to be used only in defence.

2 A defence is any argument used to support something.
EXAMPLE The lawyer put up a strong defence of his client.

defend defends defending defended
VERB

1 To defend means to protect from harm or danger.
EXAMPLE He tried to defend himself but was badly beaten.

2 If you defend a person or their ideas, you argue in support of them.
EXAMPLE The decision was hard to defend.

define defines defining defined **EXAM TERM**
VERB

To define means to give a clear meaning of something.
EXAMPLE Define the term 'soil erosion'.

definite
ADJECTIVE

Definite means clear and unlikely to be changed.
EXAMPLE It's too soon to give a definite answer.

definitely
ADVERB

You use definitely to emphasize that something is certain and will not change.
EXAMPLE I'm definitely going to contact her.

definition definitions
NOUN

A definition is a statement explaining the meaning of a word or idea.
EXAMPLE What's your definition of a good holiday?

degree degrees
NOUN

1 A degree is a unit of measurement for temperatures, angles and longitude and latitude.
EXAMPLE The temperature was 20 degrees in the shade.

2 A degree is a university qualification.
EXAMPLE She has a degree in English.

delay delays delaying delayed
VERB

1 If you delay doing something, you do not do it until a later time.
EXAMPLE They delayed getting married until they were older.

▬ Similar words: postpone, put off

2 If something delays you, it makes you late or slows you down.
EXAMPLE The flight was delayed for an hour.

▸ *NOUN*

3 If there is a delay, something does not happen until later than planned or expected.
EXAMPLE The fog caused serious delays.

deliberate
ADJECTIVE

If something that you do is deliberate, you intended to do it.
EXAMPLE It was a deliberate insult.

▬ Similar words: intentional, planned

delight delights delighting delighted
NOUN

1 Delight is great pleasure or joy.
EXAMPLE Andrew roared with delight.

▸ *VERB*

2 If something delights you, it gives you a lot of pleasure.
EXAMPLE Her music has delighted the audience.

deliver delivers delivering delivered
VERB

1 If you deliver something to someone, you take it and give it to them.
EXAMPLE The postman delivered the letter.

2 If you deliver a lecture or speech, you give it.
EXAMPLE He delivered an emotional speech.

3 If someone delivers a baby, they help the woman who is giving birth.
EXAMPLE The same midwife delivered three of her children.

delivery deliveries
NOUN

1 Delivery is the act of bringing letters or goods to someone's house or office.
EXAMPLE Please allow 28 days for delivery.

2 A delivery of letters or goods is an occasion when they are delivered.
EXAMPLE I got a delivery of fresh eggs this morning.

demand demands demanding demanded
VERB

1 If you demand something, you ask for it forcefully.
EXAMPLE I demanded an explanation from him.

A
B
C
D
E
F
G
H
I
J
K
L
M
N
O
P
Q
R
S
T
U
V
W
X
Y
Z

2 If a situation demands a particular quality, it needs it.
EXAMPLE What this demands is hard work.

▶ NOUN

3 A demand is a forceful request for something.
EXAMPLE My demand for a refund was successful.

democracy democracies   CITIZENSHIP
NOUN
Democracy is a system of government in which the people elect their leaders.
EXAMPLE Britain is a democracy.

democrat democrats
NOUN
A democrat is a person who believes in democracy.
EXAMPLE A true democrat believes in the right to vote.

democratic   CITIZENSHIP
ADJECTIVE
Democratic means governed by representatives who are elected by the people.
EXAMPLE We live in a democratic society.

demonstrate demonstrates demonstrating demonstrated
VERB   EXAM TERM
1 To demonstrate means to show or prove an idea or theory to be true.
EXAMPLE Demonstrate how farmers use crop rotation to improve their harvest.

2 If you demonstrate something to somebody, you show them how to do it.
EXAMPLE She demonstrated how to apply the make-up.

3 If people demonstrate, they march or gather together to show that they oppose or support something.
EXAMPLE They demonstrated against the new laws.

demonstration demonstrations
NOUN
1 A demonstration is a march or gathering in support of, or protesting against, something.
EXAMPLE Police broke up the demonstration.

2 A demonstration is a talk or explanation which shows how to do something.
EXAMPLE The first public demonstration of television amazed viewers.

denominator denominators   MATHS
NOUN
The denominator is the bottom part of a fraction.
EXAMPLE The denominator of $\frac{1}{2}$ is two.

deny denies denying denied
VERB
1 If you deny something, you say that it is not true.
EXAMPLE She denied all the accusations.

2 If you deny someone something, you refuse to give it to them.
EXAMPLE They were denied permission to attend.

depart departs departing departed
VERB
To depart from a place means to leave it.
EXAMPLE The train now departing from Platform 5 is going to London.

department departments
NOUN
A department is one of the sections into which an organization is divided.
EXAMPLE She worked in the marketing department.

departure departures
NOUN
Departure is the act of leaving a place or a job.
EXAMPLE Her departure for Helsinki was delayed.

depend depends depending depended
VERB
1 If one thing depends on another, it is influenced by it.
EXAMPLE The cooking time depends on the size of the potato.

2 If you depend on something, you trust and rely on it.
EXAMPLE You can depend on me.

☐ Similar words: count on, rely on, trust

deposit deposits
NOUN
A deposit is a sum of money given in part payment for goods or services.
EXAMPLE A £50 deposit is required with your order.

depression depressions
NOUN
Depression is a state of mind in which someone feels unhappy and has no energy or enthusiasm.
EXAMPLE He's been suffering from depression.

deputy deputies
NOUN
Someone's deputy is a person who acts on their behalf when they are away.
EXAMPLE The deputy chairman represented the council at the meeting.

describe describes describing described
VERB
If you describe something, you say what it is like.
EXAMPLE We asked her to describe his face.

description descriptions
NOUN
A description of something is an account which explains what it is like.
EXAMPLE The police have given a description of the man.

desert deserts deserting deserted
NOUN   GEOGRAPHY
☐ Said: des-ert
1 A desert is an area of land which has almost no water, rain, trees or plants.
EXAMPLE She crossed the Sahara Desert by jeep.

▶ VERB
☐ Said: des-ert
2 If someone deserts you, they leave you.
EXAMPLE His friends had deserted him.

deserve deserves deserving deserved
VERB
If you deserve something, you earn it or have a right to it.
EXAMPLE He deserves a rest.

design designs designing designed
VERB
1 If you design something, you plan what it should be like.
EXAMPLE Who designed the costumes?

▶ NOUN **DESIGN**
2 A design is a drawing from which something can be built or made.
EXAMPLE His design was for a new car.

3 A design is a decorative pattern of lines or shapes.
EXAMPLE They bought curtains and wallpaper with the same design.

desire desires desiring desired
VERB
1 If you desire something, you want it.
EXAMPLE He gave me everything I desired.

Similar words: long for, want, wish for

▶ NOUN
2 Desire is a strong feeling of wanting something.
EXAMPLE She had no desire to stay up all night.

Similar words: longing, want, wish

desk top publishing [ICT]
NOUN
Desk top publishing is the process of arranging text and pictures on a computer for printing on paper.
EXAMPLE She used desk top publishing to make her leaflet look more interesting.

desperate
ADJECTIVE
If you are desperate, you are in such a bad situation that you will try anything to change it.
EXAMPLE It was a desperate attempt to save their marriage.

despite
PREPOSITION
Despite means in spite of.
EXAMPLE He fell asleep despite all the coffee he'd drunk.

destroy destroys destroying destroyed
VERB
To destroy something means to ruin it.
EXAMPLE The building was completely destroyed by fire.

Similar words: ruin, wreck

destruction
NOUN
Destruction is the act of destroying something or the state of being destroyed.
EXAMPLE It was the destruction of all their hopes.

Similar word: ruin

detail details
NOUN
1 A detail of something is one of its facts or features.
EXAMPLE I remember every detail of the party.

2 Details about something are information about it.
EXAMPLE See the bottom of this page for details of how to enter the competition.

detect detects detecting detected
VERB
If you detect something, you notice or find it.
EXAMPLE Cancer can be detected by X-rays.

deter deters deterring deterred
VERB
To deter someone from doing something means to make them not want to do it.
EXAMPLE The alarm box deterred the burglar.

determine determines determining determined
VERB
1 If something determines what will happen, it controls it.
EXAMPLE Genes are responsible for determining your sex.

2 To determine something means to discover the facts about it.
EXAMPLE They are still trying to determine what happened.

determined
ADJECTIVE
If you are determined to do something, you will not let anything stop you from doing it.
EXAMPLE She was determined to succeed.

develop develops developing developed
VERB
1 To develop is to grow or become more advanced.
EXAMPLE As children develop, their needs change.

2 To develop photographs or film means to produce an image from them.
EXAMPLE I'd like to have this film developed.

development
NOUN
1 Development is gradual growth or progress.
EXAMPLE The development of children is fascinating.

GEOGRAPHY
2 Development is the level of economic growth of a country.
EXAMPLE Britain is at a late stage of development.

device devices
NOUN
A device is a machine or tool which is used for a particular purpose.
EXAMPLE The torch has a device to warn you when the batteries need changing.

A B C D E F G H I J K L M N O P Q R S T U V W X Y Z

A B C **D** E F G H I J K L M N O P Q R S T U V W X Y Z

diagram diagrams
NOUN
A diagram is a drawing which shows or explains something.
EXAMPLE Carol drew a diagram of a diesel engine.

dialect dialects — ENGLISH
NOUN
A dialect is a form of language spoken in a particular area.
EXAMPLE American English is a dialect of English.

dialogue dialogues — ENGLISH
NOUN
In a novel, play or film, dialogue is conversation.
EXAMPLE He writes great dialogue.

diameter diameters — MATHS
NOUN
The diameter of a circle is the length of a line drawn across it through its centre.
EXAMPLE He drew a circle with a diameter of ten centimetres.

dictator dictators — HISTORY
NOUN
A dictator is a ruler who has complete power, especially one who has taken power by force.
EXAMPLE The dictator had the rebel leader executed without a trial.

dictionary dictionaries — ENGLISH
NOUN
A dictionary is a book in which words are listed alphabetically and explained, or in which the same words are given in another language.
EXAMPLE He used a dictionary to check that he had spelt 'school' correctly.

diet diet — SCIENCE
NOUN
1 Diet is the contents of the food we eat.
EXAMPLE Poor diet is widespread in the Third World.

2 If you are on a diet, you eat only certain foods because you are trying to lose weight.
EXAMPLE No cake for me – I'm on a diet.

differ differs differing differed
VERB
1 If two or more things differ, they are unlike each other.
EXAMPLE The story differed from the one he told his wife.

2 If people differ, they disagree about something.
EXAMPLE This is where we differ.

difference differences
NOUN
1 The difference between things is the way in which they are unlike each other.
EXAMPLE There are many differences between the two societies.

MATHS
2 The difference between two amounts is the amount by which one is less than another.
EXAMPLE The difference between 5 and 3 is 2.

difficult
ADJECTIVE
1 Something that is difficult is not easy to do, understand or solve.

EXAMPLE I found it difficult to get out of bed.
■ Similar word: hard
2 Someone who is difficult behaves in an unreasonable way.
EXAMPLE She was a difficult child.

difficulty difficulties
NOUN
A difficulty is a problem.
EXAMPLE The main difficulty is lack of time.

digestion — SCIENCE
NOUN
Digestion is the process of breaking food down so that it can be used by the body.
EXAMPLE The process of digestion begins in the mouth.

digit digits — MATHS
NOUN
A digit is a written symbol for any of the numbers from 0 to 9.
EXAMPLE The number 1492 contains four digits.

digital camera digital cameras — ICT
NOUN
A digital camera is used to take pictures which can be put directly into a computer.
EXAMPLE He took pictures with his digital camera on sports day.

diploma diplomas
NOUN
A diploma is a qualification awarded by a college or university.
EXAMPLE She received a diploma in social work.

diplomat diplomats
NOUN
A diplomat is an official who represents his or her own country abroad.
EXAMPLE They were met at the embassy by a senior German diplomat.

direct directs directing directed
ADJECTIVE
1 Direct means going somewhere in a straight line or by the shortest route.
EXAMPLE There is a direct train service from Calais to Strasbourg.

2 If someone's behaviour is direct, they are honest and say what they mean.
EXAMPLE He gave a direct answer to the question.

■ Similar word: open

▶ *VERB*
3 To direct something means to aim or point it at something.
EXAMPLE **They directed their anger at the politicians.**

4 If you direct someone somewhere, you tell them how to get there.
EXAMPLE **Could you direct me to the station?**

DRAMA

5 Someone who directs a film or play organizes the way it is made and performed.
EXAMPLE **The play was directed by Peter Hall.**

direction directions
NOUN
1 A direction is the general line that something is moving or pointing in.
EXAMPLE **The town was ten miles away in the opposite direction.**

▶ *PLURAL NOUN*
2 Directions are instructions that tell you how to do something or how to get somewhere.
EXAMPLE **He gave Dan directions to the computer room.**

director directors
NOUN
1 The directors of a company are its senior managers.
EXAMPLE **The board of directors resigned two days later.**

DRAMA

2 The director of a film or play is the person who decides how it is made and performed.
EXAMPLE **The director asked the actors to learn their lines by Saturday.**

disappear disappears disappearing disappeared
VERB
If something disappears, it stops existing or goes where it cannot be seen.
EXAMPLE **The pain suddenly disappeared.**

⬛ **Similar words:** fade away, vanish

disappoint disappoints disappointing disappointed
VERB
If something disappoints you, it does not do what you had hoped.
EXAMPLE **I'm sorry if this reply disappoints you.**

disaster disasters
NOUN
1 A disaster is a very bad accident.
EXAMPLE **It was the second air disaster in the region.**

2 A disaster is a complete failure.
EXAMPLE **The party was a disaster.**

discipline disciplines disciplining disciplined
NOUN
1 Discipline is the practice of making people obey rules.
EXAMPLE **Discipline in the classroom was appalling.**

2 Discipline is the ability to behave and work in a controlled way.
EXAMPLE **The job requires discipline and dedication.**

▶ *VERB*
To discipline someone means to punish them.
EXAMPLE **The company is not going to discipline anybody.**

discount discounts
NOUN
A discount is a reduction in the price of something.
EXAMPLE **All staff get a 20 per cent discount on goods.**

discover discovers discovering discovered
VERB
If you discover something, you find it or learn about it for the first time.
EXAMPLE **She discovered that they had escaped.**

discovery discoveries
NOUN
The discovery of something is the act of finding it or learning about it for the first time.
EXAMPLE **The film was about the discovery of America.**

discuss discusses discussing discussed
VERB
1 To discuss is to talk about something in detail.
EXAMPLE **I shall discuss the situation with colleagues tomorrow.**

EXAM TERM

2 To discuss means to look at the arguments of both sides and try to reach your own opinion.
EXAMPLE **'Experiments on animals are unacceptable.' Discuss.**

discussion discussions
NOUN
A discussion is a conversation or piece of writing in which a subject is considered in detail.
EXAMPLE **We had a long discussion about the proposals.**

⬛ **Similar words:** conversation, talk

disk disks
ICT
NOUN
A disk is a storage device used in computers.
EXAMPLE **She saved her work on a floppy disk.**

Disk is also spelt disc.

disk drive disk drives
ICT
NOUN
A disk drive is part of a computer where a portable disk can be inserted.
EXAMPLE **She put the disk in the disk drive.**

dismiss dismisses dismissing dismissed
VERB
1 If you dismiss something, you decide that it is not important enough for you to think about.
EXAMPLE **I considered the idea, then dismissed it.**

2 If a boss dismisses an employee, they tell that person to leave their job.

A B C **D** E F G H I J K L M N O P Q R S T U V W X Y Z

EXAMPLE He was dismissed for incompetence.

3 If someone dismisses you, they tell you to leave.
EXAMPLE She dismissed the rest of the class.

display displays displaying displayed
VERB

1 If you display something, you show it.
EXAMPLE War veterans proudly displayed their medals.

▸ NOUN

2 A display is an arrangement of things designed to attract people's attention.
EXAMPLE They attended a firework display.

dispute disputes disputing disputed
☐ **Said:** *dis*-pute
NOUN

1 A dispute is an argument.
EXAMPLE A bitter dispute broke out with their neighbours.

☐ **Said:** dis-*pute*

▸ VERB

2 If you dispute a fact or theory, you say that it is incorrect.
EXAMPLE Nobody disputed that she was clever.

dissolve dissolves dissolved dissolving
VERB **SCIENCE**

If you dissolve something in a liquid, or if it dissolves, it becomes mixed with the liquid.
EXAMPLE The substance dissolved when they heated the liquid.

distance distances
NOUN

1 The distance between two points is the amount of space between them.
EXAMPLE The distance between the town and the sea is two miles.

2 Distance is the fact of being far away.
EXAMPLE Distance is not a problem.

district districts
NOUN

A district is an area of a town or country.
EXAMPLE They lived in a smart district of Paris.

divide divides dividing divided
VERB

1 When you divide something, you separate it into parts.
EXAMPLE She divided the apples into three groups.

MATHS

2 If you divide one number by another, you calculate how many times the first number contains the second.
EXAMPLE 35 divided by 7 is 5.

division divisions
NOUN

1 Division is the act of separating something into parts.
EXAMPLE That isn't a fair division of labour.

2 A division is any one of the parts into which something is divided.
EXAMPLE She ran the research division of the company.

divorce divorces divorcing divorced
NOUN

1 Divorce is the legal ending of a marriage.

EXAMPLE Too many marriages end in divorce.

▸ VERB

2 To divorce, or to get divorced, is to end a marriage legally.
EXAMPLE They got divorced two years ago.

document documents
NOUN

A document is an official record of something.
EXAMPLE Their travel documents arrived by post.

dome domes
NOUN

A dome is a round roof.
EXAMPLE The Millennium Dome was built to celebrate the year 2000.

domestic
ADJECTIVE

Domestic means involving or concerned with the home and family.
EXAMPLE Domestic peace was rare in Tommy's family.

dominate dominates dominating dominated
VERB

1 To dominate a situation means to be the most powerful or important thing or person in it.
EXAMPLE The news was dominated by the war.

2 If one person dominates another, they have power over them.
EXAMPLE The evil ruler dominated his people.

doubt doubts doubting doubted
☐ **Said:** rhymes with *out*
NOUN

1 Doubt is a feeling of uncertainty about whether something is true or possible.
EXAMPLE There is no doubt that he tries hard.

▸ VERB

2 If you doubt something, you think that it is probably not true or possible.
EXAMPLE He doubted whether he would learn anything new.

drama dramas
NOUN **DRAMA**

1 A drama is a serious play for the theatre, television or radio.
EXAMPLE They enjoyed watching the new TV drama.

DRAMA

2 Drama is plays and the theatre in general.
EXAMPLE The actors in ancient Greek drama wore masks.

3 Drama is the exciting aspects of a situation.
EXAMPLE The book was full of drama and suspense.

54

dramatic
ADJECTIVE

1 A dramatic event happens suddenly and is very noticeable.
EXAMPLE **There was a dramatic improvement in his health.**

DRAMA

2 Dramatic means to do with drama or acting.
EXAMPLE **It is a scene of great dramatic power.**

drift drifts drifting drifted
VERB

1 When something drifts, it is carried along by the wind or by water.
EXAMPLE **The boat drifted out to sea.**

2 When people drift somewhere, they move there slowly or without a plan.
EXAMPLE **She and her husband drifted apart.**

drive drives driving drove driven
VERB

1 To drive a vehicle means to operate it.
EXAMPLE **She was driving a small white car.**

2 If something drives a machine, it supplies the power that makes it work.
EXAMPLE **The wheels are driven by an electric motor.**

▶ *NOUN*

3 A drive is a journey in a vehicle.
EXAMPLE **It's a 30 mile drive to the lake.**

drug drugs drugging drugged
NOUN

1 A drug is a chemical given to people to treat illness or disease.
EXAMPLE **A new drug was used to treat her illness.**

2 Drugs are substances that some people take because of their stimulating effects.
EXAMPLE **She was sure Leo was taking drugs.**

▶ *VERB*

3 To drug someone means to give them a drug in order to make them unconscious.
EXAMPLE **They drugged the guard and made their escape.**

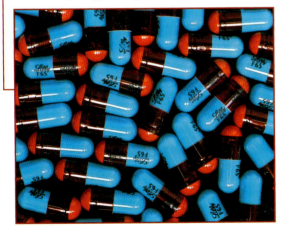

dual
ADJECTIVE

Dual means having two parts, functions or aspects.
EXAMPLE **He had a dual role in the team: as player and manager.**

duty duties
NOUN

1 Your duty is what you must do because it is your responsibility.
EXAMPLE **It is our duty to try to help.**

■ **Similar word:** responsibility

2 Duty is tax paid to the government on goods that you buy.
EXAMPLE **The government raised the duty on petrol.**

▶ *PLURAL NOUN*

3 Your duties are the tasks that you do as part of your job.
EXAMPLE **They helped nurses with their basic duties.**

dynasty dynasties

HISTORY

☐ **Said:** *din*-us-tee

NOUN

A dynasty is a series of leaders belonging to the same family.
EXAMPLE **The Tudor dynasty ruled England in the sixteenth century.**

A B C D **E** F G H I J K L M N O P Q R S T U V W X Y Z

Ee Ee Ee

eager
ADJECTIVE
If you are eager, you want very much to do or have something.
EXAMPLE He's eager to earn some money.

earn earns earning earned
VERB
1 If you earn money, you get it in return for work that you do.
EXAMPLE She earns £35,000 a year.
2 If you earn something such as praise, you receive it because you deserve it.
EXAMPLE He has earned my respect.

earnings
PLURAL NOUN
Your earnings are the money that you earn.
EXAMPLE He put his earnings into the bank.

earth   **GEOGRAPHY**
NOUN
1 The Earth is the planet on which we live.
EXAMPLE The Earth moves around the sun.
2 The earth is the surface of the Earth.
EXAMPLE The earth shook during the storm.
3 Earth is the substance in which plants grow.
EXAMPLE The tractor moved a huge pile of earth.

ease
NOUN
If you do something with ease, you do it without difficulty or effort.
EXAMPLE She passed her exams with ease.

easily
ADVERB
Easily means without difficulty.
EXAMPLE She won the race easily.

echo echoes echoing echoed
NOUN
1 An echo is a sound caused by a noise being reflected off a surface.
EXAMPLE He heard the echo of his footsteps along the corridor.

▶ *VERB*
2 If a sound echoes, it is reflected off a surface.
EXAMPLE His cry echoed back from the mountain.

economic
ADJECTIVE
Anything described as economic is about the money, industry and trade of a country.
EXAMPLE The government introduced economic reforms to help the poor.

economics
NOUN
Economics is the study of the way in which money, industry and trade are organized in a country.
EXAMPLE She was awarded a degree in economics.

economy economies
NOUN
The economy of a country is the system by which money, industry and trade are organized.
EXAMPLE The changes in the economy only helped the rich.

ecosystem ecosystems   **SCIENCE**
NOUN
An ecosystem is the plants, animals, weather and landscape of one area.
EXAMPLE The Amazon rainforest is a very large ecosystem.

edit edits editing edited
VERB
1 If you edit something, you make changes to it.
EXAMPLE We heard an edited version of the speech.
2 To edit a film or television programme means to select different parts of it and arrange them in a particular order.
EXAMPLE He taught me how to edit film.

edition editions
NOUN
1 An edition of a book or magazine is a particular version of it that is printed at one time.
EXAMPLE A paperback edition of the dictionary is now available.
2 An edition of a television or radio programme is a single programme which is one of a series.
EXAMPLE Tonight's edition of *Panorama* deals with homelessness.

editor editors
NOUN
1 An editor is a person who is in charge of a newspaper or magazine.

EXAMPLE He was editor of *The Times* for ten years.

2 An editor is a person who checks and corrects texts before they are published.
EXAMPLE He worked closely with his editor on his second book.

3 An editor is a person who edits a film or television programme.
EXAMPLE He worked as a film editor at the BBC.

editorial editorials
ADJECTIVE
1 Editorial refers to the work done in preparing a newspaper, book or magazine for publication.
EXAMPLE Thanks to the editorial staff, the book was published on time.

▶ *NOUN*
2 An editorial is an article in a newspaper or magazine which gives the opinion of the editor on a particular subject.
EXAMPLE A front-page editorial on the war appeared next day.

education
NOUN
Education means learning and teaching.
EXAMPLE A child's education begins at home.

effect effects
NOUN
1 The effect of one thing on another is the change or reaction that it causes.
EXAMPLE Eating too many sweets had an effect on his teeth.

2 An effect is the overall impression that something creates.
EXAMPLE The moonlight created a wonderful effect on the water.

▶ *PHRASE*
3 If something 'takes effect' at a particular time, it starts to happen or to have results at that time.
EXAMPLE The law will take effect next year.

effective
ADJECTIVE
Something that is effective does the job well that it is meant to do.
EXAMPLE One of the most effective ways of teaching a foreign language is through talk.

efficient
ADJECTIVE
Efficient means able to do something without wasting time or energy.
EXAMPLE Cycling is the most efficient form of transport.

🔲 Similar word: capable

effort efforts
NOUN
1 Effort is the physical or mental energy needed to do something.
EXAMPLE He stood up slowly and with great effort.

🔲 Similar word: work

2 An effort is an attempt to do something.
EXAMPLE I went to keep-fit classes in an effort to lose weight.

either
ADJECTIVE, PRONOUN OR CONJUNCTION
1 Either refers to each of two possible alternatives.
EXAMPLE You can either come with me or stay here.

▶ *ADJECTIVE*
2 Either refers to both of two things.
EXAMPLE There are houses on either side of the road.

elder eldest
ADJECTIVE
The elder of two people is the one who was born first.
EXAMPLE His elder brother is called Christopher.

elderly
ADJECTIVE
Someone who is elderly is old.
EXAMPLE An elderly couple won the lottery this week.

elect elects electing elected   **CITIZENSHIP**
VERB
If you elect someone, you choose them to hold a position of responsibility.
EXAMPLE America elects a new president every four years.

election elections   **CITIZENSHIP**
NOUN
An election is a process in which people are chosen to hold a position of responsibility.
EXAMPLE Who did you vote for at the election?

electric
ADJECTIVE
Electric refers to something which is powered or produced by electricity.
EXAMPLE She bought an electric guitar and an amplifier.

electricity   **SCIENCE**
NOUN
Electricity is a form of energy which is carried by wires.
EXAMPLE The machine was powered by electricity.

electronic   **SCIENCE**
ADJECTIVE
An electronic device has transistors or silicon chips which control an electric current.
EXAMPLE Computers are expensive electronic equipment.

elegant
ADJECTIVE
Elegant means attractive and graceful.
EXAMPLE She wore an elegant dress.

element elements
NOUN
1 An element is a part of something which combines with others to make a whole.
EXAMPLE Timing was one of the key elements of the plan.

2 An element is a substance made up of one kind of atom only.
EXAMPLE Hydrogen, oxygen and sulphur are all elements.

SCIENCE

eliminate eliminates eliminating eliminated
VERB
If you eliminate something, you remove it completely.
EXAMPLE The police eliminated him from their inquiries.

elsewhere
ADVERB
Elsewhere means in or to another place.
EXAMPLE The song is popular in Europe and elsewhere.

e-mail e-mails
ICT
NOUN
E-mail is an electric message sent from one computer to another.
EXAMPLE She sent him an e-mail.

embassy embassies
NOUN
An embassy is a building in which an ambassador works.
EXAMPLE They demonstrated outside the US embassy.

emerge emerges emerging emerged
VERB
To emerge from a place is to come out of it.
EXAMPLE I saw the woman emerge from a shop.

emergency emergencies
NOUN
An emergency is an unexpected and serious situation which must be dealt with quickly.
EXAMPLE In an emergency, contact your doctor.

■ **Similar word:** crisis

emotion emotions
NOUN
An emotion is a strong feeling, such as love or fear.
EXAMPLE Jealousy is a destructive emotion.

emotional
ADJECTIVE
1 Emotional means relating to feelings and emotions.
EXAMPLE He suffered from emotional problems.
2 If someone is emotional, they show their feelings openly.
EXAMPLE He became quite emotional when I said goodbye.

emphasis emphases
NOUN
Emphasis is special importance that is given to something.
EXAMPLE Too much emphasis is placed on research.

emphasize emphasizes emphasizing emphasized
VERB
If you emphasize something, you show that it is very important.
EXAMPLE He emphasized the differences between the two methods.

Emphasize is also spelt emphasise.

empire empires
HISTORY
NOUN
An empire is a group of countries controlled by one country.
EXAMPLE Britain was at the edge of the Roman empire.

employ employs employing employed
VERB
If you employ someone, you pay them to work for you.
EXAMPLE 500 people are employed in the industry.

■ **Similar words:** hire, take on

employee employees
NOUN
An employee is a person who is paid to work for a company.
EXAMPLE Most of the company's employees are women.

employer employers
NOUN
Someone's employer is the person or organization that they work for.
EXAMPLE He was sent to Rome by his employer.

employment
NOUN
Employment is a paid job.
EXAMPLE She was unable to find employment.

enable enables enabling enabled
VERB
To enable something to happen means to make it possible.
EXAMPLE The test enables doctors to detect the disease earlier.

encounter encounters encountering encountered
VERB
1 To encounter is to meet.
EXAMPLE Did you encounter any problems?

▶ NOUN
2 An encounter is a meeting.
EXAMPLE Her encounter with her mother-in-law was a difficult occasion.

encourage encourages encouraging encouraged
VERB
If you encourage someone, you give them the confidence to do something.
EXAMPLE He always encourages me to do better.

A B C D E F G H I J K L M N O P Q R S T U V W X Y Z

enemy enemies
NOUN
Your enemy is someone who intends to harm you.
ᴇxᴀᴍᴘʟᴇ He has many enemies as well as friends.

energy energies
NOUN
1 Energy is the physical strength needed to do active things.
ᴇxᴀᴍᴘʟᴇ He was saving his energy for next week's race.

2 Energy is the power that drives machinery.
ᴇxᴀᴍᴘʟᴇ The power station uses nuclear energy.

engage engages engaging engaged
VERB
If you engage in an activity, you do it.
ᴇxᴀᴍᴘʟᴇ I have never engaged in such activities.

engine engines　　TECHNOLOGY
NOUN
The engine of a vehicle is the part that produces the power to make it move.
ᴇxᴀᴍᴘʟᴇ He got in the car and started the engine.

engineer engineers　　TECHNOLOGY
NOUN
An engineer is a person trained to design and build machinery, roads and bridges.
ᴇxᴀᴍᴘʟᴇ His mother was an electrical engineer.

English
ADJECTIVE
1 English means belonging to or relating to England.
ᴇxᴀᴍᴘʟᴇ The English team toured Australia.

▶ *NOUN*　　ENGLISH
2 English is the main language spoken in the United Kingdom, the USA and many other countries.
ᴇxᴀᴍᴘʟᴇ English is spoken throughout the world.

enormous
ADJECTIVE
Enormous means very large in size or amount.
ᴇxᴀᴍᴘʟᴇ His bedroom is enormous.

enough
ADJECTIVE OR ADVERB
1 Enough is as much or as many as required.
ᴇxᴀᴍᴘʟᴇ He did not have enough money for a coffee.

▶ *NOUN*
2 Enough is the quantity necessary for something.
ᴇxᴀᴍᴘʟᴇ There's not enough to go round.

▶ *ADVERB*
3 Enough means very or fairly.
ᴇxᴀᴍᴘʟᴇ The evening passed pleasantly enough.

ensure ensures ensuring ensured
VERB
To ensure that something happens means to make certain that it happens.
ᴇxᴀᴍᴘʟᴇ Please ensure that the door is locked when you leave.

entertain entertains entertaining entertained
VERB
If you entertain people, you keep them amused.
ᴇxᴀᴍᴘʟᴇ This game entertained the children for hours.

entertainment
NOUN
Entertainment is anything that people watch for pleasure.
ᴇxᴀᴍᴘʟᴇ The entertainment was provided by a dance group.

enthusiasm
NOUN
Enthusiasm is great eagerness to do something or to be involved in something.
ᴇxᴀᴍᴘʟᴇ Her enthusiasm for the theatre was obvious.

entire
ADJECTIVE
You use entire to emphasize that you are speaking about the whole of something.
ᴇxᴀᴍᴘʟᴇ He had spent his entire life in the village.

entirely
ADVERB
Entirely means wholly and completely.
ᴇxᴀᴍᴘʟᴇ An entirely new approach is needed.

entitle entitles entitling entitled
VERB
If you are entitled to something, you have the right to have it or do it.
ᴇxᴀᴍᴘʟᴇ Children are entitled to a discount.

entrance entrances
NOUN
1 The entrance of a building or area is its doorway or gate.
ᴇxᴀᴍᴘʟᴇ She was waiting at the entrance to the church.

2 A person's entrance is their arrival in a place.
ᴇxᴀᴍᴘʟᴇ He wanted to make a dramatic entrance.

entry entries
NOUN
1 Entry is the act of entering a place.
ᴇxᴀᴍᴘʟᴇ No entry after 11 pm.

2 An entry is something that you write in order to take part in a competition.
EXAMPLE Send your entry to the address below.

3 An entry is something written in a diary or list.
EXAMPLE The entry in her diary for 23 March said 'Mum's birthday'.

environment environments
NOUN
1 Your environment is your surroundings.
EXAMPLE The countryside is a healthy environment to grow up in.

SCIENCE

2 The environment is the natural world around us.
EXAMPLE Pollution damages the environment.

environmental
ADJECTIVE
Environmental means concerned with the protection of the natural world.
EXAMPLE Environmental groups campaign against pollution.

enzyme enzymes
SCIENCE
NOUN
An enzyme is a chemical which speeds up the digestion of food in the body.
EXAMPLE An enzyme in the mouth starts the process of digestion.

equation equations
MATHS
NOUN
An equation is a statement that two amounts or values are the same.
EXAMPLE She wrote down the equation $3 + y = 7$.

equator
GEOGRAPHY
NOUN
The equator is an imaginary line drawn around the middle of the earth.
EXAMPLE They crossed the equator on the fourth day.

equip equips equipping equipped
VERB
To equip someone with something is to provide them with it.
EXAMPLE The boat was equipped with all the latest technology.

■ Similar words: provide, supply

equipment
NOUN
Equipment is all the things such as tools or machines that are used for a particular purpose.
EXAMPLE The band needed new equipment.

■ Similar words: apparatus, gear, tools

equivalent equivalents
ADJECTIVE
1 Equivalent means of the same size, weight or value.
EXAMPLE He was given a sum equivalent to six months' wages.

▶ NOUN
2 If one thing is the equivalent of another, it has the same use, value or effect.
EXAMPLE One glass of wine is the equivalent of half a pint of beer.

■ Similar words: equal, match

erosion
GEOGRAPHY
NOUN
Erosion is the wearing away of the earth's surface by water, ice and wind.
EXAMPLE The erosion of the coastline is obvious at several points.

error errors
NOUN
An error is a mistake.
EXAMPLE There was an error in the calculations.

escape escapes escaping escaped
VERB
1 To escape means to get away from or avoid something.
EXAMPLE She was lucky to escape serious injury.

▶ NOUN
2 An escape is an act of escaping from a place.
EXAMPLE They planned their escape carefully.

especially
ADVERB
You say especially to show that something applies more to one thing than to any other.
EXAMPLE Regular eye tests are important, especially for the elderly.

essential essentials
ADJECTIVE
1 Something that is essential is absolutely necessary.
EXAMPLE Play is an essential part of a child's development.

▶ PLURAL NOUN
2 The essentials are things that are absolutely necessary.
EXAMPLE The flat contained the basic essentials.

establish establishes establishing established
VERB
1 To establish an organization or system is to create it.
EXAMPLE The school was established in 1989 by an Italian professor.

■ Similar words: create, set up

2 To establish a fact is to discover that it is definitely true.
EXAMPLE Our first task is to establish the cause of death.

establishment establishments
NOUN
An establishment is a business or other organization or institution.
EXAMPLE A scientific research establishment was set up in Manchester.

estate estates
NOUN

1 An estate is a large area of land in the country owned by one person or organization.
EXAMPLE They visited Lord Wyville's estate in Yorkshire.

GEOGRAPHY

2 An estate is an area of land which has been developed for housing or industry.
EXAMPLE They lived on a housing estate in Newcastle.

estimate estimates estimating estimated
VERB

1 If you estimate an amount or quantity, you calculate it roughly.
EXAMPLE The damage is estimated at £3000.

▶ *NOUN*
2 An estimate is a rough calculation of an amount or quantity.
EXAMPLE The final cost was twice the original estimate.

ethnic
ADJECTIVE

1 Ethnic means relating to different racial groups of people.
EXAMPLE Ethnic minorities make a huge contribution to British life.

2 Ethnic refers to a particular racial or cultural group, especially non-Western.
EXAMPLE Most people enjoy ethnic foods such as curry.

Europe
GEOGRAPHY
NOUN

Europe is the continent which is to the west of Asia.
EXAMPLE England is a major country in western Europe.

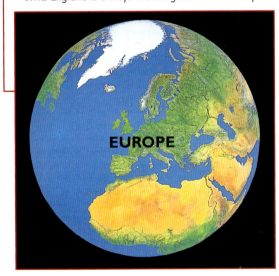

EUROPE

European Europeans
ADJECTIVE

1 European means to do with Europe.
EXAMPLE Belgium and France are European countries.

NOUN
2 A European is someone who comes from Europe.
EXAMPLE I'm a Briton first, a European second.

evaluate evaluates evaluating evaluated
EXAM TERM
VERB

To evaluate means to write about the strengths and weaknesses of a subject.
EXAMPLE Evaluate the practical work you have completed.

eventually
ADVERB

Eventually means in the end.
EXAMPLE I eventually arrived three hours late.

evidence
NOUN

1 Evidence is anything that causes you to believe that something is true or exists.
EXAMPLE There is no evidence to support this theory.

CITIZENSHIP

2 Evidence is the information used in a court of law to try to prove something.
EXAMPLE The evidence against the accused convinced the jury that he was guilty.

exact
ADJECTIVE

Exact means correct and complete in every detail.
EXAMPLE It was an exact replica of the ship.

exactly
ADVERB

1 Exactly means precisely.
EXAMPLE They're exactly the same.

2 You say exactly when you are agreeing with someone.
EXAMPLE 'I suppose he was late as usual.' 'Exactly.'

examination examinations
NOUN

1 An examination is a test.
EXAMPLE It was a three-hour written examination.

2 An examination is a careful inspection.
EXAMPLE I carried out an examination of the house.

examine examines examining examined
VERB

1 If you examine something, you look at it carefully.
EXAMPLE He examined her passport.

EXAM TERM

2 To examine means to look closely at the issues and form your own opinion on a subject.
EXAMPLE Examine the role played by France in the conflict.

example examples
NOUN

1 An example is something which is typical of a particular group of things.
EXAMPLE The Beatles are an example of a 1960s pop group.

2 If you say someone is an example to people, you mean that people should copy him or her.
EXAMPLE He is an example to us all.

▶ *PHRASE*
3 You use 'for example' to give an example of something you are talking about.
EXAMPLE Take my own situation, for example.

excellent
ADJECTIVE

Excellent means very good indeed.
EXAMPLE She did an excellent job.

▣ Similar words: first-rate, outstanding, superb

except
PREPOSITION

You use 'except' or 'except for' to introduce the only thing that a statement does not apply to.
EXAMPLE There was nobody there except for the police.

A
B
C
D
E
F
G
H
I
J
K
L
M
N
O
P
Q
R
S
T
U
V
W
X
Y
Z

exception exceptions
NOUN
An exception is something that is not included in a general statement.
EXAMPLE **Normally I don't drink, but tonight is an exception.**

excess
ADJECTIVE
1 Excess means more than is needed or allowed.
EXAMPLE **You have to pay for excess baggage on an aeroplane.**

▸ *PHRASE*
2 'In excess of' means more than.
EXAMPLE **She inherited in excess of £150,000.**

exchange exchanges exchanging exchanged
VERB
1 If people exchange things, they give them to each other at the same time.
EXAMPLE **We exchanged addresses and left.**

2 To exchange something is to replace it with something else.
EXAMPLE **I exchanged the shoes for another pair.**

▸ *NOUN*
3 An exchange is the act of giving or receiving something in return for something else.
EXAMPLE **There was an angry exchange of words between them.**

exclamation mark
exclamation marks   ENGLISH
NOUN
An exclamation mark is a punctuation mark used at the end of a sentence to express a strong feeling.
EXAMPLE **'What a great goal!' ends in an exclamation mark.**

excuse excuses excusing excused
NOUN
1 An excuse is a reason.
EXAMPLE **He kept finding excuses not to go home.**

▸ *VERB*
2 To excuse something is to find good reasons for it.
EXAMPLE **That doesn't excuse my mother's behaviour.**

3 To excuse somebody is to forgive them.
EXAMPLE **I simply couldn't excuse him for what he'd said.**

execute executes executing executed
VERB
1 To execute somebody means to kill them as a punishment for a crime.
EXAMPLE **The following month the king was executed.**

2 If you execute something such as a plan, you carry it out.
EXAMPLE **The crime was executed with great care.**

executive executives
NOUN
An executive is a person who works for a company at a senior level.
EXAMPLE **She was an advertising executive.**

exercise exercises exercising exercised
NOUN
1 Exercise is any activity that you do in order to be healthy.
EXAMPLE **Lack of exercise can lead to depression.**

2 Exercises are a series of movements which you do in order to get fit.

EXAMPLE **These exercises strengthen my stomach.**

▸ *VERB*
3 When you exercise, you do activities which help you to get fit and remain healthy.
EXAMPLE **How often do you exercise?**

exhaust exhausts exhausting exhausted
VERB
1 If something exhausts you, it makes you very tired.
EXAMPLE **The journey had exhausted her.**

▪ **Similar words:** tire out, wear out

2 If you exhaust a supply of something, you use it up completely.
EXAMPLE **They soon exhausted their supply of water.**

▸ *NOUN*
3 The exhaust is the pipe which carries the gas or steam out of the engine of a vehicle.
EXAMPLE **Black smoke was pouring from the exhaust.**

exhibit exhibits exhibiting exhibited
VERB
1 To exhibit is to show.
EXAMPLE **He still exhibited signs of stress.**

▸ *NOUN*   ART
2 An exhibit is something which is displayed in a museum or art gallery.
EXAMPLE **Our local museum has over a thousand exhibits.**

exhibition exhibitions   ART
NOUN
An exhibition is a public display of works of art.
EXAMPLE **Her exhibition of paintings was a great success.**

exist exists existing existed
VERB
If something exists, it is present in the world.
EXAMPLE **She tried to pretend the problem didn't exist.**

existence
NOUN
1 The existence of something is the fact that it is present in the world.
EXAMPLE **They had a discussion about the existence of God.**

2 An existence is a way of life.
EXAMPLE **He leads a comfortable enough existence.**

expand expands expanding expanded
VERB
If something expands, or if you expand it, it becomes larger.
EXAMPLE **He wanted to expand the business.**

expect expects expecting expected
VERB
If you are expecting something, you believe that it will arrive or happen.
EXAMPLE I'm expecting an important letter.

expectation expectations
NOUN
Your expectations are your beliefs that something will happen.
EXAMPLE Their success is far beyond our expectations.

expense expenses
NOUN
1 Expense is the money that something costs.
EXAMPLE A second car is an expense we cannot afford.
■ Similar word: cost
▶ *PLURAL NOUN*
2 Expenses are the money somebody spends in connection with their work.
EXAMPLE She claimed her travelling expenses every month.

expensive
ADJECTIVE
If something is expensive, it costs a lot of money.
EXAMPLE Wine is so expensive in this country.

experience experiences experiencing experienced
NOUN
1 Experience is knowledge or understanding gained through personal observation or involvement.
EXAMPLE She has personal experience of what it is like to be bullied.
2 An experience is something that you do or something that happens to you.
EXAMPLE The funeral was a painful experience.
3 Experience is knowledge or skill in a particular job or activity.
EXAMPLE He lacked experience for the job.
▶ *VERB*
4 If you experience something, it happens to you or you are affected by it.
EXAMPLE I have never experienced such rudeness.

experiment experiments experimenting experimented   SCIENCE
NOUN
1 An experiment is practical work aimed at finding out the answer to a question.
EXAMPLE The experiment showed which foods contained starch.
▶ *VERB*
2 If you experiment with something or on something, you do a scientific test on it.
EXAMPLE The company experimented on rabbits.

expert experts
NOUN
An expert is a person who is very skilled at something or who knows a lot about something.
EXAMPLE She was an expert on Greek drama.
■ Similar words: authority, specialist

explain explains explaining explained
VERB
If you explain something, you give information about it or reasons for it.
EXAMPLE She tried to explain her decision to me.
■ Similar words: clarify, make clear

explanation explanations
NOUN
An explanation is a detailed description of something or an account of why it happened.
EXAMPLE He could offer no explanation for his behaviour.

explode explodes exploding exploded
VERB
If something explodes, it bursts with great force.
EXAMPLE The bomb exploded, killing both men.

explore explores exploring explored
VERB
If you explore a place, you travel around it to discover what it is like.
EXAMPLE The best way to explore the area is by boat.

explosion explosions
NOUN
An explosion is a sudden violent burst of energy.
EXAMPLE Six soldiers were injured in the explosion.

export exports exporting exported   GEOGRAPHY
VERB
1 To export goods means to sell them to another country.
EXAMPLE The country's main export is coffee.
▶ *NOUN*
2 An export is a product sold to a foreign country.
EXAMPLE The company's exports to China increased.

expose exposes exposing exposed
VERB
1 To expose something means to uncover it.
EXAMPLE For a moment his back was exposed.
2 To expose a person to something means to put them in a situation in which it might harm them.
EXAMPLE He was exposed to dangerous chemicals.

express expresses expressing expressed
VERB
1 When you express an idea or feeling, you show what you think or feel by saying or doing something.
EXAMPLE He expressed his admiration for my work.
▶ *ADJECTIVE*
2 Express means very fast.
EXAMPLE She went to London on an express train.

expression expressions
NOUN
1 The expression of ideas or feelings is the act of showing them through words, actions or art.
EXAMPLE Laughter is an expression of emotion.

A B C D E F G H I J K L M N O P Q R S T U V W X Y Z

2 Your expression is the look on your face which shows what you are thinking or feeling.
EXAMPLE His expression suddenly changed.

ENGLISH

3 An expression is a word or phrase.
EXAMPLE 'Pom' is an Australian expression for an Englishman.

extend extends extending extended

VERB

1 If something extends for a particular distance or time, it continues for that distance or time.
EXAMPLE The caves extend for 18 kilometres.

2 If you extend something, you make it larger or longer.
EXAMPLE We're thinking of extending the house.

extent

NOUN

The extent of a situation is how great or serious it is.
EXAMPLE The full extent of the damage is not yet known.

extraordinary

ADJECTIVE

Extraordinary means very unusual or surprising.
EXAMPLE What an extraordinary thing to say!

▪ **Similar words:** remarkable, unusual

extreme extremes

ADJECTIVE

1 Extreme means very great in degree.
EXAMPLE Many people in Africa live in extreme poverty.

2 Extreme means at the furthest point or edge of something.
EXAMPLE They lived in the extreme north of Norway.

▸ NOUN

3 Extreme is the highest or furthest degree of something.
EXAMPLE They suffered extremes of heat and cold on their travels.

extremely

ADVERB

Extremely means very.
EXAMPLE You did extremely well.

A B C D E **F** G H I J K L M N O P Q R S T U V W X Y Z

fabric fabrics
NOUN
Fabric is cloth.
EXAMPLE The shop sold silk and other delicate fabrics.

face faces facing faced
NOUN
1 The face is the front part of your head from your chin to your forehead.
EXAMPLE His face was covered in sweat.

2 A face is a surface or side of something.
EXAMPLE They climbed the north face of the mountain.

▶ VERB
3 To face something means to be opposite it.
EXAMPLE They stood facing each other.

4 To be faced with something means to have to deal with it.
EXAMPLE We are faced with a serious problem.

facility facilities
NOUN
Facilities are buildings, equipment or services which are provided for a particular purpose.
EXAMPLE The town has excellent shopping facilities.

fact facts
NOUN
1 A fact is a piece of information which is true.
EXAMPLE This doesn't alter the fact that he was wrong.

▶ PHRASES
2 'In fact' and 'as a matter of fact' mean 'actually' or 'really'.
EXAMPLE In fact, this was what happened.

factor factors
NOUN
1 A factor is something that affects an event or situation.
EXAMPLE Hard work is a major factor in our success.

▱ Similar words: cause, element, part

MATHS

2 The factors of a number are the whole numbers that will divide exactly into it.
EXAMPLE 2 and 5 are factors of 10.

factory factories   **TECHNOLOGY**
NOUN
A factory is a building or group of buildings where goods are made in large quantities.
EXAMPLE The tables were made in a large furniture factory.

fade fades fading faded
VERB
When something fades, it slowly becomes less bright or less loud.
EXAMPLE The light was fading.

faeces   **SCIENCE**
🔊 Said: fee-seez
NOUN
Faeces are semi-solid substances that the body cannot digest and which the body gets rid of.
EXAMPLE The faeces showed what the animal had eaten.

fail fails failing failed
VERB
1 If you fail to do something, you do not succeed in doing it.
EXAMPLE He failed to win enough votes to be elected.

▱ Similar words: be unsuccessful, flop
2 If you fail an exam, your marks are too low to pass.
EXAMPLE I failed my driving test twice.

3 If something fails, it stops working properly.
EXAMPLE His grandmother's eyesight began to fail.

▶ PHRASE
4 'Without fail' means definitely.
EXAMPLE Every day her mum would phone her without fail.

failure failures
NOUN
Failure is a lack of success in doing something.
EXAMPLE The attempt ended in failure.

fairly
ADVERB
1 Fairly means to quite a large degree.
EXAMPLE He's fairly bright.

2 If something is done fairly it is done in a fair and reasonable way.
EXAMPLE They divided up their winnings fairly.

faith faiths
NOUN
1 Faith is a feeling of confidence or trust in something.
EXAMPLE People have lost faith in politicians.

RE

2 Faith is religious belief.
EXAMPLE She has a strong Christian faith.

A
B
C
D
E
F
G
H
I
J
K
L
M
N
O
P
Q
R
S
T
U
V
W
X
Y
Z

false
ADJECTIVE
False means untrue, incorrect or not real.
EXAMPLE He gave the police a false name.

familiar
ADJECTIVE
1 Familiar means well-known or easy to recognize.
EXAMPLE The room was full of familiar faces.

■ Similar word: well-known

2 If you are familiar with something, you know it or understand it well.
EXAMPLE He was not very familiar with the area.

family families
NOUN
A family is parents and their children, and sometimes other close relations.
EXAMPLE Our family always argued at Christmas.

fantasy fantasies
NOUN
1 A fantasy is an imagined story or situation.
EXAMPLE His fantasy was to play football at Wembley.

2 Fantasy is the activity of imagining things.
EXAMPLE What is fantasy and what is reality?

fare fares faring fared
NOUN
1 The fare is the money that you pay for a journey.
EXAMPLE He had just enough for the bus fare.

▶ VERB
2 How someone fares in a particular situation is how successful they are.
EXAMPLE The team have not fared well this season.

fascism
HISTORY

◫ Said: *fash*-izm
NOUN
Fascism is a political movement aiming to run a country with the help of a dictator.
EXAMPLE He saw fascism at work in Mussolini's Italy.

fashion fashions
NOUN
1 A fashion is a style of dress or way of behaving which is popular at a particular time.
EXAMPLE The latest Paris fashions are very expensive to buy.

■ Similar words: style, trend

2 The fashion in which something is done is the way in which it is done.
EXAMPLE He greeted us in his usual friendly fashion.

fate fates
NOUN
1 Fate is a power that some people believe controls everything that happens.
EXAMPLE Fate seemed to be working against him.

2 Someone's fate is what happens to them.
EXAMPLE She accepted her fate.

fault faults faulting faulted
NOUN
1 If something is your fault, you are to blame for it.
EXAMPLE It was all his fault.

2 A fault is a weakness.
EXAMPLE His biggest fault was his desire to do too much.

▶ VERB
3 If you cannot fault someone or something, you cannot find any reason to criticize them.
EXAMPLE You can't fault his enthusiasm.

favour favours favouring favoured
NOUN
1 If you do someone a favour, you do something which helps them.
EXAMPLE Can you do me a favour?

▶ PHRASE
2 If you are 'in favour of' something, you agree with it.
EXAMPLE I'm in favour of the new proposals.

▶ VERB
3 If you favour something, you prefer it to something else.
EXAMPLE Some people favour a different approach.

favourite favourites
ADJECTIVE
1 Your favourite person or thing is the one you like best.
EXAMPLE She's my favourite writer.

▶ NOUN
2 A favourite is the animal or person expected to win in a contest.
EXAMPLE The race was won by the favourite.

feature features featuring featured
NOUN
1 A feature of something is an interesting or important part of it.
EXAMPLE Pollution is an unpleasant feature of modern life.

2 Your features are your eyes and other parts of your face.
EXAMPLE His features expressed fear.

▶ VERB
3 When a film or exhibition features someone or something, they are an important part of it.
EXAMPLE The series features top stars from the world of sport.

February
NOUN
February is the month that follows January.
EXAMPLE February was a stormy month.

feel feels feeling felt
VERB
1 If you feel an emotion or sensation, you experience it.
EXAMPLE I felt very angry.

■ Similar words: be aware of, experience

2 If you feel something, you touch it.
EXAMPLE The doctor felt my head.

3 If you feel that something is the case, you believe it to be true.
EXAMPLE She feels that he treated her badly.

▣ **Similar words:** believe, consider, think

▶ *PHRASE*
4 If you 'feel like' doing something, you want to do it.
EXAMPLE I felt like having a party.

feeling feelings
NOUN
1 A feeling is an emotion.
EXAMPLE It gave me a feeling of satisfaction.

2 A feeling is a physical sensation.
EXAMPLE I had a strange feeling in my neck.

3 Your feelings are your general attitudes or thoughts about something.
EXAMPLE I had mixed feelings about meeting him.

fellow fellows
NOUN
1 A fellow is a man.
EXAMPLE I knew a fellow by that name.

▶ *ADJECTIVE*
2 You use fellow to describe people who have something in common with you.
EXAMPLE He liked his fellow teachers.

female females
NOUN
1 A female is a person or animal that belongs to the sex that can have babies or young.
EXAMPLE More females than males are affected.

▶ *ADJECTIVE*
2 Female means to do with females.
EXAMPLE She is his favourite female singer.

fertilization fertilizations   SCIENCE
NOUN
Fertilization is the joining together of a male and a female nucleus to start a new life.
EXAMPLE If an egg is fertilized it may grow into a baby.

festival festivals
NOUN
A festival is a series of events and performances; also a period of religious celebration.
EXAMPLE Diwali is the Hindu festival of light.

fiction   ENGLISH
NOUN
Fiction is stories which have been invented.
EXAMPLE *Treasure Island* is a piece of fiction.

fierce fiercer fiercest
ADJECTIVE
Fierce means very aggressive or intense.
EXAMPLE He was attacked by a fierce dog.

▣ **Similar words:** savage, wild.

fight fights fighting fought
VERB
1 To fight is to take part in a battle or contest.
EXAMPLE They often fought over their toys.

▶ *NOUN*
2 A fight is a battle or contest.
EXAMPLE The fight ended in tragedy.

figure figures
NOUN
1 A figure is a written number or the amount a number stands for.
EXAMPLE He wrote the figure down.

2 A figure is the shape of a person whom you cannot see clearly.
EXAMPLE It seemed to be a figure in a blue dress.

3 Your figure is the shape of your body.
EXAMPLE He has a great figure for his age.

file files filing filed
NOUN
1 A file is a box or folder in which documents are kept; also used of the information kept in the file.
EXAMPLE The police probably have a file on him.

ICT

2 A file is a stored set of information with its own name.
EXAMPLE He stored his work in the file named 'History'.

3 A file is a tool used for smoothing and shaping hard materials.
EXAMPLE She always carried a nail file in her bag.

▶ *VERB*
4 When someone files a document, they put it in its correct place with similar documents.
EXAMPLE They are filed alphabetically under the author's name.

film films filming filmed
NOUN
1 A film is a series of moving pictures shown in a cinema or on television.
EXAMPLE *Star Wars* is one of my favourite films.

2 A film is a strip of thin plastic that you use in a camera to take photographs.
EXAMPLE He loaded the film into his camera.

▶ *VERB*
3 To film is to use a camera to take moving pictures of something.
EXAMPLE A camera crew was filming her for French TV.

finally
ADVERB
1 Finally means after a long delay.
EXAMPLE Finally, he answered the phone himself.

▣ **Similar words:** at last, eventually

2 You use finally to introduce a final point or topic.
EXAMPLE Finally, I would like to thank my wife.

▣ **Similar words:** in conclusion, lastly

finance finances financing financed
VERB
1 To finance a project or purchase is to provide the

A B C D E **F** G H I J K L M N O P Q R S T U V W X Y Z

A B C D E **F** G H I J K L M N O P Q R S T U V W X Y Z

money to pay for it.
EXAMPLE These funds are to finance a major new project.

▸ PLURAL NOUN
2 Your finances are the amount of money that you have.
EXAMPLE An accountant can give advice on how to manage your finances.

financial
ADJECTIVE
Financial means to do with money.
EXAMPLE They have had financial difficulties.

fine finer finest; fines fining fined
ADJECTIVE
1 Fine means very good.
EXAMPLE They went to one of London's finest theatres.

2 Fine describes something that is satisfactory or acceptable.
EXAMPLE Come on in, the water's fine.

3 When the weather is fine, it is sunny and not raining.
EXAMPLE It was a fine summer's day.

4 Fine means very delicate, narrow or small.
EXAMPLE She had fine hairs on her arm.

▸ NOUN
5 A fine is a sum of money paid as a punishment.
EXAMPLE The fine for smoking on buses is still quite small.

▸ VERB
6 To fine means to exact a sum of money as a punishment.
EXAMPLE He was fined £310,000.

finish finishes finishing finished
VERB
1 When you finish something, you do the last part of it and complete it.
EXAMPLE She hopes to finish the book by Christmas.

▣ **Similar words:** complete, conclude, end
2 When something finishes, it ends.
EXAMPLE The film finished around 10 o'clock.

▸ NOUN
3 The finish of something is the last part of it.
EXAMPLE There was a very exciting finish to the match.

▣ **Similar words:** conclusion, end

firm firmer firmest; firms
ADJECTIVE
1 Firm means fairly hard.
EXAMPLE She preferred a firm mattress.

2 Someone who is firm behaves in a fairly strict way and will not change their mind.
EXAMPLE You have to be firm with such children.

▸ NOUN
3 A firm is a business that sells or produces something.
EXAMPLE A firm of engineers built the engine.

flashback flashbacks
NOUN   **ENGLISH**
A flashback in a novel, play or film is a scene that returns to events of the past.
EXAMPLE The flashback showed how the lovers had first met.

flat flats; flatter flattest
NOUN
1 A flat is a set of rooms for living in, which is part of a larger building.
EXAMPLE They lived in a block of flats.

▸ ADJECTIVE
2 Flat means level and smooth.
EXAMPLE The building had a flat roof.

▣ **Similar words:** even, level
3 A flat tyre or ball has not got enough air in it.
EXAMPLE We had a flat tyre and had to stop.

4 A flat battery has lost its electrical charge.
EXAMPLE When he tried to start the car, the battery was flat.

▸ ADVERB
5 If something is done in a particular time flat, it takes exactly that time.
EXAMPLE He reached the house in ten minutes flat.

flavour flavours flavouring flavoured
NOUN
1 The flavour of food is its taste.
EXAMPLE This cheese has a very strong flavour.

▸ VERB
2 If you flavour food, you add something to give it a particular taste.
EXAMPLE She loves strawberry-flavoured sweets.

flee flees fleeing fled
VERB
To flee is to run away.
EXAMPLE He fled from the enemy to avoid being captured.

fleet fleets
NOUN
A fleet is a group of ships or vehicles.
EXAMPLE The fleet sailed into the harbour.

flexible
ADJECTIVE
1 Something that is flexible can be bent easily without breaking.
EXAMPLE She used brushes with long, flexible bristles.

2 Someone or something that is flexible is able to adapt easily to changing circumstances.
EXAMPLE This plan is very flexible.

flight flights
NOUN
1 A flight is a journey made by aeroplane.
EXAMPLE The flight to Paris was delayed.

2 Flight is the action of flying or the ability to fly.
EXAMPLE They watched the flight of the bird.

3 Flight is the act of running away.
EXAMPLE They described their flight from the revolution.

4 A flight of stairs or steps is a row of them.
EXAMPLE The office was up three flights of stairs.

float floats floating floated
VERB

1 If something is floating in a liquid, it is lying at or near the surface of the liquid.
EXAMPLE **A branch was floating down the river.**

2 If something floats in the air, it hangs in the air or moves slowly through it.
EXAMPLE **They watched a leaf floating on the breeze.**

▶ *NOUN*

3 A float is a light object which helps something or someone to float in water.
EXAMPLE **He attached the float to the fishing line.**

flood floods flooding flooded
NOUN

1 A flood is a large amount of water covering an area that is usually dry.
EXAMPLE **More than 70 people were killed in the floods.**

2 A flood of something is a large amount of it occurring suddenly.
EXAMPLE **There was a flood of complaints.**

◻ **Similar words:** stream, torrent

▶ *VERB*

3 To flood is to cover an area with water.
EXAMPLE **He left the tap running and flooded the kitchen.**

▶ *PHRASE*

4 If people or things flood into or out of a place, they arrive or leave in large numbers.
EXAMPLE **The refugees are flooding out of the country.**

floor floors
NOUN

1 The floor is the part of a room that you walk on.
EXAMPLE **Jack is sitting on the floor.**

2 A floor is one of the levels in a building.
EXAMPLE **She was on the fifth floor of the hospital.**

flow flows flowing flowed
VERB

1 If something flows somewhere, it moves there in a steady manner.
EXAMPLE **A stream flowed gently down into the valley.**

▶ *NOUN*

2 A flow of something is a steady movement of it.
EXAMPLE **The doctors noticed an increase in blood flow.**

focus focuses focusing focused
VERB

1 To focus your eyes or a camera means to adjust them so that the image is clear.
EXAMPLE **She focused her eyes on the horizon.**

2 To focus on a particular topic means to concentrate on it.
EXAMPLE **Recently he has focused all his attention on his family.**

▶ *NOUN*

3 The focus of something is the main thing that it is concerned with.
EXAMPLE **The focus of the conversation shifted suddenly.**

▶ *PHRASE*

4 If an image is 'in focus', its edges are clear and sharp. If it is 'out of focus', the edges are blurred.
EXAMPLE **Make sure the picture is in focus.**

Focuses, focusing and focused are also spelt focusses, focussing and focussed.

font fonts   **ICT**
NOUN

A font is a style of letters used on a computer.
EXAMPLE **He changed the font to make the text look nicer.**

football footballs
NOUN

1 Football is any game in which the ball can be kicked, such as soccer and American football.
EXAMPLE **They played football in the park.**

2 A football is a ball used in any of these games.
EXAMPLE **They played with a leather football.**

force forces forcing forced
VERB

1 If you force someone to do something, you make them do it.
EXAMPLE **I can't force you to stay.**

▶ *NOUN*

2 Force is violence or great strength.
EXAMPLE **The rebels seized power by force.**

3 The force of something is its strength or power.
EXAMPLE **The force of the explosion shook the building.**

4 A force is an organized group of people, especially soldiers or police.
EXAMPLE **American forces were sent to the region.**

   SCIENCE

5 A force pushes objects together or pulls them apart.
EXAMPLE **They measured the force of gravity in their experiment.**

forecast forecasts forecasting
NOUN

1 A forecast is a prediction of what will happen.
EXAMPLE **The weather forecast predicted rain.**

▶ *VERB*

2 If you forecast an event, you predict what will happen.
EXAMPLE **He forecast that house prices would start to rise again.**

foreign
ADJECTIVE

1 Foreign means to do with a country that is not your own.
EXAMPLE **He studied a foreign language at school.**

2 Foreign means unfamiliar or strange.
EXAMPLE **Such ideas were completely foreign to him.**

foreigner foreigners
NOUN

A foreigner is someone who belongs to a country that is not your own.
EXAMPLE **They don't like talking to foreigners.**

A
B
C
D
E
F
G
H
I
J
K
L
M
N
O
P
Q
R
S
T
U
V
W
X
Y
Z

A B C D E F G H I J K L M N O P Q R S T U V W X Y Z

forget forgets forgetting forgot forgotten
VERB

1 If you forget something, you cannot remember it.
EXAMPLE I forgot his name.

2 If you forget to do something, you do not remember to do it.
EXAMPLE He forgot to lock the door.

form forms forming formed
NOUN

1 A form of something is a type or kind of it.
EXAMPLE The scientists developed a new form of vaccine.

2 The form of something is its shape.
EXAMPLE She bought a brooch in the form of a lizard.

3 A form is a sheet of paper with questions and spaces for the answers.
EXAMPLE You will be asked to fill in a form.

▶ *VERB*
4 When someone forms something or when it forms, it is created, organized or started.
EXAMPLE The League was formed in 1959.

formal
ADJECTIVE

Formal means official or correct.
EXAMPLE He received a formal letter of apology.

format formats
NOUN

The format of something is the way it is arranged and presented.
EXAMPLE I explained the format of the programme.

formation
NOUN

The formation of something is its start or creation.
EXAMPLE He joined two years after the club's formation.

former
ADJECTIVE

1 Former is used to indicate what someone or something used to be.
EXAMPLE The former tennis champion presented the cup to the winner.

▶ *NOUN*
2 The former refers to the first of two things that you have just mentioned.
EXAMPLE If I had to choose between happiness and money, I would choose the former.

formula formulae formulas
NOUN

1 A formula is a group of letters, numbers or symbols which stand for a mathematical or scientific rule.
EXAMPLE What is the formula for working out the area?

2 A formula is a plan for dealing with a particular problem.
EXAMPLE The politicians came up with a peace formula.

forth
ADVERB

To go forth from a place is a formal way of saying to leave it.
EXAMPLE In 1492 Columbus set forth on his voyage of discovery.

fortunate
ADJECTIVE

Fortunate means lucky.
EXAMPLE He was fortunate to survive.

fortunately
ADVERB

Fortunately means luckily.
EXAMPLE Fortunately, no one was hurt.

fortune fortunes
NOUN

1 Fortune or good fortune is good luck.
EXAMPLE He'd had a bit of good fortune at the racetrack.

2 A fortune is a large amount of money.
EXAMPLE The holiday cost them a fortune.

forward forwards
ADVERB OR ADJECTIVE

1 Forward or forwards means in the front or towards the front.
EXAMPLE We moved forward to get a better view.

2 Forward or forwards means onwards, or in the right direction.
EXAMPLE They just couldn't see any way forward.

◼ **Similar words:** ahead, on

3 Forward or forwards means in or towards a future time.
EXAMPLE It's time to look forward, not back.

▶ *NOUN*
4 In a game such as football or hockey, a forward is a player in an attacking position.
EXAMPLE None of the forwards played well.

fossil fuel fossil fuels   **SCIENCE**
NOUN

Fossil fuels are fuels made from the remains of plant and animal life; once they are used they cannot be replaced.
EXAMPLE Oil and coal are fossil fuels.

foundation foundations
NOUN
The foundations of a building are the layer of concrete or bricks below the ground on which it is built.
EXAMPLE **We wanted to lay the foundations before the winter.**

fraction fractions   **MATHS**
NOUN
A fraction is a part of a whole number.
EXAMPLE **He added the fractions $\frac{1}{4}$ and $\frac{1}{2}$.**

friction   **SCIENCE**
NOUN
Friction is the force created when you try to move one object across the surface of another.
EXAMPLE **Friction helps car tyres to grip the road.**

frame frames framing framed
NOUN
1 A frame is the structure surrounding a door, window or picture.
EXAMPLE **They bought a wooden picture frame.**

2 A frame is an arrangement of connected bars over which something is built.
EXAMPLE **It was a house with a timber frame.**

3 Your frame is your body.
EXAMPLE **The jacket looked big on his bony frame.**

▶ *VERB*   **ART**
4 To frame a picture is to put it into a frame.
EXAMPLE **He framed the photograph of his wife.**

fraud frauds
NOUN
1 Fraud is the crime of getting money dishonestly.
EXAMPLE **He was jailed for two years for fraud.**

2 A fraud is something that deceives people in a dishonest way.
EXAMPLE **Don't believe him – he's a complete fraud.**

free freer freest; frees freeing freed
ADJECTIVE
1 If something is free, you can have it without paying for it.
EXAMPLE **Admission is free.**

2 Something that is free is not controlled or limited.
EXAMPLE **We should be free to dress as we please.**

3 Someone who is free is no longer a prisoner.
EXAMPLE **He walked away from the court a free man.**

4 If something is free, it is not busy or being used.
EXAMPLE **Are you free tonight?**

▶ *VERB*
5 To free someone or something means to release them.
EXAMPLE **Firemen tried to free the trapped man.**

▤ **Similar word:** release

freedom
NOUN
1 If you have the freedom to do something, you are allowed to do it.
EXAMPLE **They were given the freedom to go wherever they liked.**

2 When prisoners gain their freedom, they are released or they escape.
EXAMPLE **He looked forward to the day he would gain his freedom.**

▤ **Similar words:** liberty, release

3 When there is freedom from something unpleasant, people are not affected by it.
EXAMPLE **They are campaigning for freedom from hunger.**

freeze freezes freezing froze frozen   **SCIENCE**
VERB
1 When a liquid freezes it becomes solid because it is very cold.
EXAMPLE **As the temperature fell, the water began to freeze.**

2 If you freeze, you suddenly stop moving.
EXAMPLE **A light came on and she froze.**

French
ADJECTIVE
1 French means to do with France.
EXAMPLE **They spent the holiday in a French chalet.**

▶ *NOUN*
2 French is the main language spoken in France
EXAMPLE **She spoke French as well as German.**

frequent
ADJECTIVE
If something is frequent, it happens often.
EXAMPLE **She gives frequent performances of her work.**

fresh fresher freshest
ADJECTIVE
1 A fresh thing replaces a previous one or is added to it.
EXAMPLE **The footprints had been filled in by fresh snow.**

2 Fresh food has been obtained or prepared recently, and is not tinned or frozen.
EXAMPLE **They preferred locally caught fresh fish.**

3 Fresh water is not salty.
EXAMPLE **Rivers and lakes are fresh water features.**

friend friends
NOUN
A friend is someone you know well and like.
EXAMPLE **She's my best friend.**

▤ **Similar words:** chum, companion, mate, pal

friendly friendlier friendliest
ADJECTIVE
If you are friendly to or with someone, you behave in a kind and pleasant way to them.
EXAMPLE **He was very friendly to us.**

friendship friendships
NOUN
A friendship is a relationship between friends.
EXAMPLE **Sadly, it was the end of a good friendship.**

A
B
C
D
E
F
G
H
I
J
K
L
M
N
O
P
Q
R
S
T
U
V
W
X
Y
Z

front fronts
NOUN

1 The front of something is the part that faces forward.
EXAMPLE He had a jacket with six buttons down the front.

2 In a war, the front is the place where two armies are fighting.
EXAMPLE They marched straight to the front.

▶ ADJECTIVE
3 The front part of something is the part that is nearest to the front.
EXAMPLE She sat in the front seat of the car.

▶ PHRASE
4 Something that is 'in front' is ahead of others.
EXAMPLE Don't drive too close to the car in front.

5 If something is 'in front of' another thing, it is facing it or near the front of it.
EXAMPLE She sat down in front of the mirror.

frustrate frustrates frustrating frustrated
VERB

1 If something frustrates you, it prevents you doing what you want and makes you upset.
EXAMPLE Everyone gets frustrated with their work.

2 To frustrate something is to prevent it.
EXAMPLE They deliberately frustrated my plan.

fry fries frying fried
VERB

When you fry food, you cook it in a pan containing hot fat.
EXAMPLE I love fried fish.

fuel fuels fuelling fuelled
NOUN

1 Fuel is a substance such as gas which provides heat or power.
EXAMPLE They added fuel to the fire.

▶ VERB
2 A machine or vehicle that is fuelled by a substance works by burning that substance.
EXAMPLE Some power stations are fuelled by oil.

fulfil fulfils fulfilling fulfilled
VERB

1 If you fulfil a promise, hope or duty, you carry it out.
EXAMPLE She never fulfilled her dream of becoming an actress.

2 If something fulfils you, it gives you satisfaction.
EXAMPLE Teaching is a fulfilling job.

function functions functioning functioned
NOUN

1 The function of something is the thing it was designed to do.
EXAMPLE The function of this button is to start the engine.

▶ VERB
2 To function means to operate or work.
EXAMPLE Sometimes the lift didn't function at all.

fund funds funding funded
NOUN

1 A fund is an amount of money which is collected for a particular purpose.
EXAMPLE They put money in a fund for their children's education.

▶ VERB
2 To fund something means to provide money for it.
EXAMPLE The research was funded by the government.

⬛ **Similar words:** finance, pay for

fundamental
ADJECTIVE

Fundamental describes something basic and central.
EXAMPLE Fundamental changes are required.

funny funnier funniest
ADJECTIVE

1 Funny means strange or puzzling.
EXAMPLE You get a lot of funny people in the library.

⬛ **Similar words:** odd, strange

2 Funny describes something causing amusement.
EXAMPLE She told a funny story.

⬛ **Similar words:** amusing, humorous

furniture
NOUN

Furniture is movable objects in the home, such as tables, chairs and wardrobes.
EXAMPLE Each piece of furniture has been carefully chosen.

further furthers furthering furthered
ADJECTIVE

1 Further means additional or more.
EXAMPLE Write to us for further information.

▶ VERB
2 If you further something, you help it to progress.
EXAMPLE He wants to further his acting career.

⬛ **Similar words:** advance, promote

future
NOUN

1 The future is the period of time after the present.
EXAMPLE He is already making plans for the future.

▶ ADJECTIVE
2 Future is relating to or occurring at a time after the present.
EXAMPLE His future role in the team is unclear.

▶ PHRASE
3 'In future' means from now on.
EXAMPLE Be more careful in future.

Gg Gg Gg

gather gathers gathering gathered
VERB
1 When people gather, they come together in a group.
EXAMPLE We gathered around the fireplace.
2 To gather things is to bring them together in one place.
EXAMPLE They gathered nuts and berries for food.
◼ Similar word: collect

gear gears
NOUN
1 A gear is a piece of machinery which controls the rate at which energy is converted into movement.
EXAMPLE The car was in fourth gear.
2 Gear means clothes or equipment.
EXAMPLE We took off our riding gear.

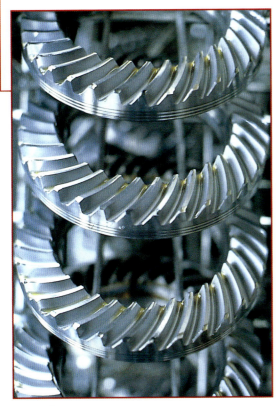

gender genders
NOUN
1 Gender is the sex of a person or animal.
EXAMPLE We discussed gender differences today.
2 Gender is a way of classing nouns as masculine, feminine and neuter in certain languages.
EXAMPLE In French the word 'lemon' is masculine in gender and 'orange' is feminine in gender.

gene genes   SCIENCE
◻ Said: jeen
NOUN
A gene is one of the parts of a cell which controls an organism's characteristics.
EXAMPLE Is there a gene for intelligence?

general generals
ADJECTIVE
1 General means relating to the whole of something or to most things in a group.
EXAMPLE There is a general improvement in his health.
◼ Similar word: overall
▸ NOUN
2 A general is an army officer of very high rank.
EXAMPLE The general inspected his troops.
▸ PHRASE
3 'In general' is used to indicate that a statement is true in most cases.
EXAMPLE In general, people supported us.

general election
general elections   CITIZENSHIP
NOUN
A general election is an election for a new government.
EXAMPLE A general election is held at least every five years in Britain.

generate generates generating generated
VERB
To generate something means to create or produce it.
EXAMPLE Windmills can be used to generate electricity.

generation generations
NOUN
1 A generation is all the people of a similar age.
EXAMPLE The younger generation is full of energy.
2 A generation is the period of time that it takes for children to grow up and have children of their own.
EXAMPLE Within a few generations this knowledge will be lost.

generous
ADJECTIVE
1 A generous person gives more of something than is usual or expected.
EXAMPLE It was generous of him to lend us the money.
2 Something that is generous is larger than usual or expected.
EXAMPLE This is a generous portion of spaghetti.

genre genres   ENGLISH
NOUN
A genre is a particular style in drama, art or literature.
EXAMPLE The soap opera is one of the most popular genres of TV drama.

A B C D E F G H I J K L M N O P Q R S T U V W X Y Z

genuine

🔲 **Said:** *jen-yoo-in*

ADJECTIVE
Genuine means real and exactly what it appears to be.
EXAMPLE It's made of genuine silver.

German Germans

ADJECTIVE
1 German means to do with Germany.
EXAMPLE They spent three weeks in a German village.

▶ *NOUN*
2 A German is someone who comes from Germany.
EXAMPLE The Germans are good at making cars.

3 German is the main language spoken in Germany, Austria and parts of Switzerland.
EXAMPLE She spoke German as well as French.

gesture gestures gesturing gestured

NOUN
1 A gesture is a movement of your hands or head which conveys a message or feeling.
EXAMPLE She made an angry gesture with her fist.

2 A gesture is an action which expresses your attitude or intention.
EXAMPLE The march is meant as a gesture of support.

▶ *VERB*
3 If you gesture, you move your hands or head to emphasize or show what you mean or feel.
EXAMPLE She gestured towards the door.

glance glances glancing glanced

VERB
1 If you glance at something, you look at it quickly.
EXAMPLE He glanced at his watch.

▶ *NOUN*
2 A glance is a quick look.
EXAMPLE The boys exchanged glances.

global

ADJECTIVE
Global means to do with the whole world.
EXAMPLE Global warming is a real problem.

glossary glossaries ENGLISH

NOUN
A glossary is a list of explanations of specialist words.
EXAMPLE She used the glossary to look up 'metaphor'.

goal goals

NOUN
1 In some games the goal is the space into which the players try to get the ball.
EXAMPLE The ball missed the goal by inches.

2 If a player scores a goal they get the ball into the goal.
EXAMPLE They beat us by four goals to three.

3 Your goal is something that you hope to achieve.
EXAMPLE Our goal is to raise as much money as possible.

god gods RE

PROPER NOUN
1 The name God is given to the being who is worshipped by Christians, Jews and Muslims as the creator and ruler of the world.
EXAMPLE Do you believe in God?

▶ *NOUN*
2 A god is any of the beings that are believed in many religions to have power over the world.
EXAMPLE Dionysus is the Greek god of wine.

golf

NOUN
Golf is a game in which players use clubs to hit a ball into holes.
EXAMPLE They played nine holes of golf before lunch.

gone

VERB
Gone is the past participle of go.
EXAMPLE Where has it gone?

good better best; goods

ADJECTIVE
1 Good means pleasant or enjoyable.
EXAMPLE We had a really good time.

2 Good refers to things that are considered to be morally right.
EXAMPLE The forces of good and evil are always with us.

3 Good refers to anything that is desirable or beneficial.
EXAMPLE The break has done me good.

▶ *PLURAL NOUN*
4 Goods are objects that are sold in shops.
EXAMPLE The shop sold a range of electrical goods.

▶ *PHRASE*
5 'For good' means for ever.
EXAMPLE The theatre closed down for good.

6 'As good as' means almost.
EXAMPLE His career is as good as over.

> 'Good' is an adjective, and should not be used as an adverb. You should say that 'a person did well' not 'a person did good'.

govern governs governing governed CITIZENSHIP

VERB
1 To govern a country means to control it.
EXAMPLE She promised to govern the country fairly.

2 Something that governs a situation influences or controls it.
EXAMPLE Much of our behaviour is governed by habit.

government governments CITIZENSHIP

NOUN
1 The government is the people who rule the country and make the laws.
EXAMPLE The government was in power for only two years before an election was called.

2 Government is the control and organization of a country.
EXAMPLE Our system of government is called a democracy.

A B C D E F G H I J K L M N O P Q R S T U V W X Y Z

grade grades grading graded
VERB
1 To grade things means to judge them according to their quality.
EXAMPLE The college does not grade students' work.

▶ NOUN
2 The grade of something is its quality.
EXAMPLE There are different grades of paper.

3 Your grade in an exam is the mark that you get.
EXAMPLE I got a grade B in Maths.

gradual
ADJECTIVE
Gradual means happening slowly over a long period of time.
EXAMPLE Losing weight should be a gradual process.

gradually
ADVERB
Gradually means happening slowly over a long period of time.
EXAMPLE Gradually, her condition improved.

graduate graduates graduating graduated
NOUN
1 A graduate is a person who has completed a first degree at a university.
EXAMPLE She was a history graduate.

▶ VERB
2 To graduate is to complete a first degree at a university.
EXAMPLE She graduated from Manchester University last year.

grain grains
NOUN
1 Grain is a cereal plant, such as wheat, that has been harvested for food.
EXAMPLE The farmer put the grain in bags.

2 A grain of wheat, rice or other cereal plant is a seed from it.
EXAMPLE The peasant planted grains of rice.

3 A grain of sand or salt is a tiny piece of it.
EXAMPLE Each grain of sand is different.

■ Similar word: bit

gram grams gramme SCIENCE
NOUN
A gram is a unit of weight equal to one thousandth of a kilogram.
EXAMPLE It only weighs a few grams.

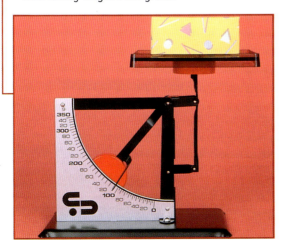

grammar ENGLISH
NOUN
Grammar is the rules of a language relating to the ways you can combine words to form sentences.
EXAMPLE The teacher asked us to get our grammar books out.

grant grants granting granted
NOUN
1 A grant is an amount of money that an official body gives to someone for a particular purpose.
EXAMPLE He was given a grant to carry out repairs.

▶ VERB
2 If you grant something to someone, you allow them to have it.
EXAMPLE Permission was granted a few weeks ago.

graphics DESIGN
NOUN
Graphics are a drawing or drawings which show the shape or design of an object.
EXAMPLE Tarik used stunning graphics for his design project.

grate grates grating grated
NOUN
1 A grate is a framework of metal bars in a fireplace; also, the whole fireplace.
EXAMPLE A wood fire burned in the grate.

▶ VERB
2 If you grate food, you shred it into small pieces.
EXAMPLE He grated some cheese for his omelette.

grave graves; graver gravest
NOUN
1 A grave is a place where a dead person is buried.
EXAMPLE He visits his grandmother's grave every Sunday.

▶ ADJECTIVE
2 Grave means very serious.
EXAMPLE The threat of war was grave.

gravity SCIENCE
NOUN
Gravity is the force that makes things fall when you drop them.
EXAMPLE Gravity caused the apple to fall.

green greener greenest; greens
ADJECTIVE OR NOUN
1 Green is a colour between yellow and blue on the spectrum.
EXAMPLE She wanted a shiny green apple.

▶ NOUN
2 A green is a smooth flat area of grass.
EXAMPLE The children played on the village green.

▶ ADJECTIVE CITIZENSHIP
3 Green is used to describe political movements which are concerned with environmental issues.
EXAMPLE The Green Party campaigns against pollution.

gross grosser grossest
ADJECTIVE
1 Gross means very bad.
EXAMPLE He was dismissed for gross misconduct.

2 Gross means very ugly or disgusting.
EXAMPLE Don't be so gross!

3 A gross amount is the total before any deductions are made.
EXAMPLE His gross income was £33,000 a year.

A B C D E F **G** H I J K L M N O P Q R S T U V W X Y Z

ground grounds
NOUN

1 The ground is the surface of the earth or the floor of a room.
EXAMPLE They sat on the ground.

2 Ground is land.
EXAMPLE They played on a patch of waste ground.

▸ PLURAL NOUN

3 The grounds of a large building is the land that surrounds it.
EXAMPLE They walked through the grounds of the university.

4 The grounds for something are the reasons for it.
EXAMPLE You have no grounds for complaint.

▸ VERB

5 Ground is the past tense and past participle of grind.
EXAMPLE The miller ground the flour.

group groups grouping grouped
NOUN

1 A group of things is a number of them that are linked in some way.
EXAMPLE They met a small group of friends.

■ Similar words: band, bunch, crowd, set

MUSIC

2 A group is a number of musicians who perform music together.
EXAMPLE He's a drummer in a group.

▸ VERB

3 To group things together is to link them in some way.
EXAMPLE Don't group all young people together.

guarantee guarantees guaranteeing guaranteed
NOUN

1 A guarantee is a written promise by a company that if a product develops a fault it will be replaced or repaired free of charge.
EXAMPLE The stereo had a five-year guarantee.

2 If something is a guarantee of something else, it makes it certain that it will happen.
EXAMPLE There is no guarantee that this will work.

▸ VERB

3 If someone guarantees something, they make certain that it will happen.
EXAMPLE I guarantee that he'll come.

■ Similar words: ensure, promise

guard guards guarding guarded
VERB

1 If you guard a person or object, you watch them carefully.
EXAMPLE She was guarded night and day.

■ Similar words: defend, protect, watch over

NOUN

2 A guard is a person whose job is to guard a person, object or place.
EXAMPLE His father was a prison guard.

■ Similar words: protector, sentry, watchman

3 A guard is an official in charge of a train.
EXAMPLE The guard blew his whistle.

guess guesses guessing guessed
VERB

1 If you guess something, you form an opinion about it without knowing all the facts.

EXAMPLE She guessed that he was in his late forties.

■ Similar word: suppose

▸ NOUN

2 A guess is an attempt to give an answer or opinion about something without knowing all the facts.
EXAMPLE If you don't know the answer, have a guess.

guest guests
NOUN

1 A guest is someone who has been invited to stay at your home or attend an event.
EXAMPLE She was a guest at the wedding.

2 The guests in a hotel are the people staying there.
EXAMPLE I was the only guest in the hotel.

guide guides guiding guided
NOUN

1 A guide is someone who shows you round places, or leads the way through difficult country.
EXAMPLE I would have been lost without a good tour guide.

2 A guide is a book which gives information about a particular place or subject.
EXAMPLE They took the *Rough Guide to Paris* on holiday.

▸ VERB

3 To guide is to lead in a particular direction.
EXAMPLE He guided her through the door.

guilt
NOUN

1 Guilt is a feeling of having done something wrong.
EXAMPLE Her emotions ranged from anger to guilt.

2 Someone's guilt is the fact that they have done something wrong.
EXAMPLE I'm not convinced of his guilt.

guilty guiltier guiltiest
ADJECTIVE

1 If someone is guilty of doing something illegal or wrong, they did it.
EXAMPLE Both men were found guilty of murder.

2 If you feel guilty, you are unhappy because you have done something wrong.
EXAMPLE Alex had every reason to feel guilty.

guitar guitars
NOUN

MUSIC

A guitar is a musical instrument with six strings.
EXAMPLE She played an electric guitar in the band.

Hh Hh Hh

habit habits
NOUN
A habit is something that you do often or regularly.
EXAMPLE He had a habit of smiling at everyone he saw.

habitat habitats [SCIENCE]
NOUN
A habitat is an area where a plant or animal lives.
EXAMPLE The North Pole is the natural habitat of the polar bear.

halt halts halting halted
VERB
1 When someone or something halts, they stop moving.
EXAMPLE They halted at a short distance from the house.

▶ PHRASE
2 When something comes 'to a halt', it stops moving or developing.
EXAMPLE The lift came to a halt.

happen happens happening happened
VERB
1 When something happens, it occurs or takes place.
EXAMPLE Tell me what happened.

▣ Similar words: come about, occur, take place
2 If you happen to do something, you do it by chance.
EXAMPLE I happened to notice his name in the paper.

harbour harbours
NOUN
A harbour is a protected area of water where boats can be tied up.
EXAMPLE He watched the boat approaching the harbour.

hardly
ADVERB
1 Hardly means almost not or not quite.
EXAMPLE I could hardly believe it.

2 Hardly means certainly not.
EXAMPLE It's hardly a secret.

You should not use 'hardly' with a negative word such as 'not' or 'no': 'he could hardly hear her' not 'he could not hardly hear her'.

hardware [ICT]
NOUN
Hardware is the name for computer machinery rather than programs.
EXAMPLE A keyboard is part of the computer hardware.

harmony harmonies [MUSIC]
NOUN
Harmony is the pleasant combination of notes.
EXAMPLE The group sang in harmony.

headline headlines
NOUN
1 A headline is the title of a newspaper story.
EXAMPLE The headline said simply, 'New Planet Discovered'.

2 The headlines are the main points of the radio or television news.
EXAMPLE Here are tonight's headlines.

headquarters
NOUN
The headquarters of an organization are its main offices.
EXAMPLE The firm's headquarters are in Buenos Aires.

health
NOUN
1 Your health is the condition that your body is in.
EXAMPLE Smoking is bad for your health.

2 Health is a state in which you are fit and well.
EXAMPLE They nursed me back to health.

healthy healthier healthiest
ADJECTIVE
1 Someone who is healthy is fit and well.
EXAMPLE She was a very healthy child.

▣ Similar words: fit, well
2 Something that is healthy is good for you.
EXAMPLE Fruit and vegetables form part of a healthy diet.

hearing
NOUN
Hearing is the sense that lets you be aware of sounds.
EXAMPLE My hearing is poor.

heart hearts [SCIENCE]
NOUN
1 Your heart is the organ in your chest that pumps the blood around your body.
EXAMPLE He was aware of his heart beating.

2 Your heart is thought of as the centre of your emotions, especially of love.
EXAMPLE His heart filled with pride.

3 The heart of something is its most central or important part.
EXAMPLE This is the heart of the problem.

heaven

NOUN

In some religions, heaven is the place where God lives, and where good people go when they die.
EXAMPLE She told them their mother was now in heaven.

height heights

NOUN

1 The height of something is its measurement from bottom to top.
EXAMPLE The witness said the man was of average height.

2 The height of something is the distance that it is above the ground.
EXAMPLE The plane began to lose height.

3 A height is a high position or place.
EXAMPLE He's afraid of heights.

heir heirs

☐ Said: air

NOUN

Someone's heir is the person who is able to inherit their property or title.
EXAMPLE Prince Charles is the heir to the throne.

helicopter helicopters

NOUN

A helicopter is an aircraft with rotating blades above it instead of wings.
EXAMPLE They watched the helicopter circling overhead.

hell

NOUN

RE

1 In some religions, hell is the place where the Devil lives, and where wicked people go to be punished when they die.
EXAMPLE He told them they would go to hell for their crimes.

2 If you say that something is hell, you mean it is very unpleasant.
EXAMPLE Bullies can make your life hell.

hero heroes

NOUN

ENGLISH

1 The hero is the main character in a book, film or play.
EXAMPLE The hero of the story is a photographer.

2 A hero is a person who has done something brave or good.
EXAMPLE My dad was a war hero.

herself

PRONOUN

1 Herself refers to the same woman, girl or female animal that has already been mentioned.

EXAMPLE She pulled herself out of the water.

2 Herself is used to emphasize the female subject or object of a clause.
EXAMPLE Louise herself then spoke.

high higher highest

ADJECTIVE OR ADVERB

1 High means tall or a long way above the ground.
EXAMPLE He jumped high into the air.

▦ Similar word: tall

▶ ADJECTIVE

2 High refers to how much something measures from the bottom to the top.
EXAMPLE It was a statue nine inches high.

3 Something that is high is near the top of a scale of importance or quality.
EXAMPLE This is one of our highest priorities.

highlight highlights highlighting highlighted

VERB

1 If you highlight something, you draw attention to it.
EXAMPLE The report highlights the problem areas.

▶ NOUN

2 The highlights of an event are the best parts of it.
EXAMPLE The highlights of the match were shown on TV.

ART

3 A highlight is a lighter area of a painting or photograph.
EXAMPLE The highlights drew attention to the subject's face.

highly

ADVERB

Highly means extremely.
EXAMPLE It is highly unlikely I'll be able to attend.

himself

PRONOUN

1 Himself refers to the same man, boy or male animal that has already been mentioned.
EXAMPLE He poured himself a drink.

2 Himself is used to emphasize the male subject or object of a clause.
EXAMPLE The judge himself said so.

Hindu Hindus

RE

☐ Said: hin-doo

NOUN

A Hindu is a person who believes in Hinduism, an Indian religion which has many gods and which teaches that people have another life on Earth after death.
EXAMPLE Many Hindus believe it is wrong to kill animals for food.

hint hints hinting hinted

NOUN

1 A hint is a clue.
EXAMPLE He gave no hint of what his plans might be.

▦ Similar word: clue

2 A hint is a helpful piece of advice.
EXAMPLE The book offers hints on looking after plants.

▶ VERB

3 To hint means to suggest something indirectly.
EXAMPLE The President hinted that he might make some changes.

▦ Similar words: imply, suggest

hire hires hiring hired
VERB

1 If you hire something, you pay money to use it for a period of time.
EXAMPLE Shall we hire a car for the weekend?

2 If you hire someone, you pay them to do a job for you.
EXAMPLE He hired a top lawyer to defend him.

historical
ADJECTIVE   **HISTORY**

1 Historical means happening in the past, or to do with the study of the past.
EXAMPLE They discovered some historical manuscripts.

2 Historical means describing or representing the past.
EXAMPLE I am reading a historical novel.

holiday holidays
NOUN

1 A holiday is a period of time spent away from home for pleasure.
EXAMPLE I went on holiday to Greece.

2 A holiday is a day when people do not go to work or school.
EXAMPLE New Year's Day is a public holiday.

Holocaust   **HISTORY**
▣ **Said:** hol-lo-kawst

NOUN

The Holocaust was the mass murder of the Jews by the Nazis during the Second World War.
EXAMPLE Millions died in the Holocaust.

holy holier holiest   **RE**
ADJECTIVE

1 Something that is holy is to do with God or a particular religion.
EXAMPLE This is a holy place.

▣ **Similar word:** sacred

2 Someone who is holy leads a pure and good life.
EXAMPLE The monk was known to be a holy man.

homeless
ADJECTIVE

Someone who is homeless has nowhere to live.
EXAMPLE She worked in a hostel for homeless people.

homophone homophones   **ENGLISH**
NOUN

A homophone is a word with the same sound as another, but with a different meaning.
EXAMPLE 'Pair' and 'pear' are homophones.

homosexual
ADJECTIVE

Homosexual means sexually attracted to people of the same sex.
EXAMPLE The book describes a homosexual relationship.

honest
ADJECTIVE

Honest means truthful and trustworthy.
EXAMPLE I'll be honest with you.

▣ **Similar word:** truthful

honour honours honouring honoured
NOUN

1 Your honour is your good reputation.
EXAMPLE He felt that his honour was at stake.

2 An honour is an award.
EXAMPLE She was given many honours, including an Oscar.

▶ VERB

3 If you honour someone, you give them special praise, or an award.
EXAMPLE He was honoured by the Pope.

4 If you honour an agreement or promise, you do what was agreed or promised.
EXAMPLE He made promises that he was not able to honour.

horizontal
ADJECTIVE

Horizontal means flat and level with the ground.
EXAMPLE She drew a horizontal line across the page.

horror horrors
NOUN

Horror is a strong feeling of alarm.
EXAMPLE He gazed in horror at the knife.

hospital hospitals
NOUN

A hospital is a place where sick people are looked after.
EXAMPLE The nurse worked at the local hospital.

host hosts hosting hosted
NOUN

1 The host at a party is the person who is holding it.
EXAMPLE He was always the perfect host.

▶ VERB

2 To host an event means to organize it or act as host at it.
EXAMPLE Atlanta hosted the Olympic Games in 1996.

hostage hostages
NOUN

A hostage is a person who is held prisoner until certain demands are met.
EXAMPLE The hostages were released once the money had been handed over.

however
ADVERB

1 However adds a comment which contrasts with what has just been said.
EXAMPLE However, that is not the case.

2 You use 'however' to say that something makes no difference to a situation.
EXAMPLE However hard she tried, nothing seemed to work.

A B C D E F G **H** I J K L M N O P Q R S T U V W X Y Z

human humans

ADJECTIVE

1 Human means to do with people.
EXAMPLE We belong to the human race.

▶ NOUN

2 A human is a person.
EXAMPLE Pollution affects animals as well as humans.

humour humours humouring humoured

NOUN

1 Humour is the quality of being funny.
EXAMPLE He failed to see the humour of the situation.

▪ **Similar words:** comedy, wit

2 Humour is the ability to be amused by certain things.
EXAMPLE Helen has a great sense of humour.

▶ VERB

3 If you humour someone, you try to please them.
EXAMPLE He nodded, partly to humour her.

hymn hymns

RE

▪ **Said:** him

NOUN

A hymn is a song of praise.
EXAMPLE We sang a hymn in assembly this morning.

ideal
ADJECTIVE
The ideal thing or person is the best possible one.
EXAMPLE He's the ideal person for the job.

identify identifies identifying identified
VERB
1 If you identify someone or something, you are able to recognize them or name them.
EXAMPLE The boy's father had to identify the body.

2 If you identify with someone, you understand their feelings and ideas.
EXAMPLE I couldn't identify with the central character of the film.

identity identities
NOUN
Your identity is who you are.
EXAMPLE The police soon discovered his true identity.

ignore ignores ignoring ignored
VERB
To ignore someone or something means to take no notice of them.
EXAMPLE I ignored his unkind remarks.

illegal
ADJECTIVE
Illegal means forbidden by the law.
EXAMPLE It is illegal to marry until you are sixteen.

■ Similar word: unlawful

illustrate illustrates illustrating illustrated
VERB
1 If something illustrates a fact, it shows that the fact is true.
EXAMPLE This incident illustrates what I mean.

2 To illustrate a book means to put pictures in it.
EXAMPLE She was given an illustrated Bible.

EXAM TERM

3 To illustrate means to explain and give examples.
EXAMPLE Illustrate how you might gather information about the rainfall.

image images
NOUN
1 An image is a picture or photograph.
EXAMPLE Her image filled the TV screen.

2 Image is the appearance that a person or organization presents to the public.
EXAMPLE The government tried to improve its image.

imagination
NOUN
Your imagination is your ability to form pictures and ideas in your mind.
EXAMPLE She has a lively imagination.

imagine imagines imagining imagined
VERB
1 If you imagine something, you form a picture or idea of it in your mind.
EXAMPLE Can you imagine how I felt?

2 If you imagine something, you think you have experienced it but actually you have not.
EXAMPLE I must have imagined the whole thing.

3 If you imagine that something is true, you think it is true.
EXAMPLE I imagine he's dead now.

■ Similar words: believe, suppose, think

immediate
ADJECTIVE
1 Immediate means without delay.
EXAMPLE The announcement had an immediate effect.

2 Immediate means very close in time, space or relationship.
EXAMPLE He never got on with his immediate superior.

immediately
ADVERB
Immediately means without any delay.
EXAMPLE She answered his letter immediately.

immigrant immigrants   **CITIZENSHIP**
NOUN
An immigrant is someone who has come to live in a country from another country.
EXAMPLE He is descended from Chinese immigrants.

immigration   **CITIZENSHIP**
NOUN
Immigration is people coming into a country in order to live and work there.
EXAMPLE There was a queue at the immigration desk.

immune
🔊 Said: im-yoon
ADJECTIVE
If you are immune to something, you cannot be affected by it.
EXAMPLE This test will show if you are immune to the disease.

A B C D E F G H I J K L M N O P Q R S T U V W X Y Z

impact impacts
NOUN
1 An impact is a strong effect on something or someone.
EXAMPLE Her speech had a powerful impact on them.
2 The impact of one object on another is the force with which it hits it.
EXAMPLE The car crumpled under the impact of the crash.

implication implications
NOUN
The implications of something are the things that are likely to happen as a result of it.
EXAMPLE He fully understood the implications of his decision.

imply implies implying implied
VERB
To imply means to suggest something in an indirect way.
EXAMPLE Are you implying that it was my fault?

import imports importing imported
GEOGRAPHY
VERB
1 To import means to buy goods from another country.
EXAMPLE The cost of importing goods from Europe decreased.
▶ NOUN
2 An import is a product bought from a foreign country.
EXAMPLE Bananas are an import from the West Indies.

importance
NOUN
The importance of something is its quality of being important.
EXAMPLE This is a matter of some importance.

important
ADJECTIVE
Something that is important is very valuable, necessary or significant.
EXAMPLE Her sons are the most important thing in her life.
◼ Similar word: significant

impose imposes imposing imposed
VERB
If you impose something on people, you force it on them.
EXAMPLE Don't impose your view on me.

impossible
ADJECTIVE
Something that is impossible cannot happen or be done.
EXAMPLE This question is impossible to answer.

impress impresses impressing impressed
VERB
If something impresses you, it causes you to admire them.
EXAMPLE The boys tried to impress their girlfriends.

impression impressions
NOUN
An impression of something is the way it seems to you.
EXAMPLE What were your first impressions of college?

impressive
ADJECTIVE
If something is impressive, you admire it.
EXAMPLE The film has impressive special effects.

improve improves improving improved
VERB
If something improves or if you improve it, it gets better.
EXAMPLE He wants to improve his French.

improvement improvements
NOUN
If there is an improvement in something, it becomes better.
EXAMPLE There's still room for improvement.

incident incidents
NOUN
An incident is an event.
EXAMPLE It was a really unpleasant incident.

include includes including included
VERB
If one thing includes another, the second thing is part of the first thing.
EXAMPLE Meals are included in the price.
◼ Similar word: contain

including
PREPOSITION
You use 'including' to give examples of things that you are talking about.
EXAMPLE Six people, including two children, were injured.

income incomes
NOUN
Income is the money a person earns.
EXAMPLE The government promised to help those on low incomes.

increase increases increasing increased
VERB
1 If something increases, or if you increase it, it becomes larger.
EXAMPLE The population continued to increase.
▶ NOUN
2 An increase is a rise in the number, level or amount of something.
EXAMPLE There was an increase in the number of road accidents in August.

A
B
C
D
E
F
G
H
I
J
K
L
M
N
O
P
Q
R
S
T
U
V
W
X
Y
Z

incredible
ADJECTIVE
1 Incredible means wonderful.
EXAMPLE I had an incredible holiday.
Similar words: amazing, unbelievable
2 Incredible means difficult to believe.
EXAMPLE It's incredible that he survived.

indeed
ADVERB
You use indeed to emphasize a point that you are making.
EXAMPLE The meal was very good indeed.

independence
NOUN
Independence means not having to rely on others.
EXAMPLE Jane is beginning to show her independence.

independent
ADJECTIVE
1 Independent means not controlled by other people or things.
EXAMPLE They demanded an independent inquiry.
2 Someone who is independent does not need other people's help.
EXAMPLE She was always a fiercely independent woman.

index indexes
NOUN
An index is an alphabetical list of items at the back of a book.
EXAMPLE He looked up 'France' in the index.

Indian Indians
ADJECTIVE
1 Indian means to do with India.
EXAMPLE The Indian parliament met today.

▸ NOUN
2 An Indian is someone who comes from India.
EXAMPLE The Indians are delightful people.
3 An Indian is someone descended from the native peoples of North, South or Central America.
EXAMPLE The settlers drove the Indians westwards.

indicate indicates indicating indicated
VERB
1 If something indicates something, it shows that it is true.
EXAMPLE The test pilot's smile clearly indicated his relief.
Similar word: show

2 If you indicate something to someone, you point to it.
EXAMPLE He indicated the chair beside him.

individual
ADJECTIVE
Individual means to do with one particular person or thing.
EXAMPLE Each person needs individual attention.

industrial
ADJECTIVE
Industrial means to do with industry.
EXAMPLE The company made industrial equipment.

industry industries
NOUN
GEOGRAPHY
1 Industry is the work and processes involved in making things in factories.
EXAMPLE The use of robots in industry is very common.
TECHNOLOGY
2 An industry is all the people and processes involved in manufacturing a particular thing.
EXAMPLE The film industry creates a lot of jobs.

infect infects infecting infected
VERB
To infect someone or something is to cause them to have a disease.
EXAMPLE People infected with HIV may become very ill.

infection infections
NOUN
An infection is a disease caused by germs.
EXAMPLE He developed a chest infection.

inflation
NOUN
Inflation is an increase in the price of goods and services in a country.
EXAMPLE The rate of inflation increased last month.

influence influences influencing influenced
NOUN
1 Influence is the power to make other people do what you want.
EXAMPLE She has no influence on him at all.
Similar word: power
▸ VERB
2 To influence someone or something means to have an effect on them.
EXAMPLE I didn't want him to influence my choice.

inform informs informing informed
VERB
If you inform someone of something, you tell them about it.
EXAMPLE My daughter informed me that she was pregnant.
Similar word: tell

information
NOUN
Information about something is knowledge about it.
EXAMPLE For further information, contact the number below.
Similar words: data, facts

A B C D E F G H I J K L M N O P Q R S T U V W X Y Z

ingredient ingredients
NOUN
Ingredients are the things that something is made from, especially in cookery.
EXAMPLE Mix the ingredients in a bowl.

initial initials
▪ Said: in-*nish*-ul
ADJECTIVE
1 Initial describes something that happens at the beginning of a process.
EXAMPLE My initial reaction was shock.

▸ *NOUN*
2 Your initials are the capital letters that begin each word of your name.
EXAMPLE Please give your surname and initials.

injure injures injuring injured
VERB
If you injure someone, you damage part of their body.
EXAMPLE Several policemen were injured in the riots.

injury injuries
NOUN
An injury is damage done to someone's body.
EXAMPLE He escaped without injury.

innocent
ADJECTIVE
1 Innocent means not guilty of a crime.
EXAMPLE She was sure he was innocent of the crime.

2 Innocent means without experience of evil or unpleasant things.
EXAMPLE He seemed so young and innocent.

inquiry inquiries
NOUN
1 An inquiry is a question that you ask in order to get information.
EXAMPLE He made some inquiries at the post office.

2 An inquiry is an official investigation.
EXAMPLE They demanded an inquiry into the incident.

Inquiry is also spelt enquiry.

insist insists insisting insisted
VERB
If you insist on something, you demand it.
EXAMPLE She insisted on joining us.

inspect inspects inspecting inspected
VERB
If you inspect something, you examine it carefully.
EXAMPLE The nurse inspected the wound.

install installs installing installed
VERB
If you install a piece of equipment in a place, you put it there so that it is ready to use.
EXAMPLE They installed a new computer.

institute institutes
NOUN
An institute is an organization for teaching or research.
EXAMPLE My sister works at a research institute.

institution institutions
NOUN
1 An institution is a large, important organization.
EXAMPLE It is Hong Kong's largest financial institution.

2 An institution is a place where people are looked after.
EXAMPLE He spent several years in a mental institution.

instruct instructs instructing instructed
VERB
1 To instruct means to order.
EXAMPLE I've been instructed to take you to London.

2 To instruct means to teach.
EXAMPLE He instructed them in basic survival techniques.

instruction instructions
NOUN
1 Instructions are information on how to do something.
EXAMPLE Simply follow the instructions below.

2 Instructions are something that someone tells you to do.
EXAMPLE He claimed he was just following instructions.

instrument instruments
NOUN
1 An instrument is a tool or device.
EXAMPLE The instrument cut straight through the metal.

MUSIC

2 An instrument is anything used to play music.
EXAMPLE Which instrument do you play?

insulator insulators
SCIENCE
NOUN
An insulator is any substance that does not allow energy to pass through it easily.
EXAMPLE Wood is a good insulator.

insurance
NOUN
Insurance is an arrangement in which you pay money to a company to protect yourself if something unpleasant happens to you.
EXAMPLE Remember to take out travel insurance.

integrate integrates integrating integrated
VERB
1 If a person integrates into a group, they become a part of it.
EXAMPLE The new boy tried to integrate with the rest of the class.

2 If you integrate things, you link them closely.
EXAMPLE The government planned to integrate the road and rail networks.

intelligence
NOUN
Your intelligence is your ability to understand and learn things.
EXAMPLE She was a woman of exceptional intelligence.

■ **Similar words:** brains, understanding

intelligent
ADJECTIVE
Intelligent means able to think and learn things quickly.
EXAMPLE The student was very intelligent.

intend intends intending intended
VERB
If you intend to do something, you have decided or planned to do it.
EXAMPLE She intended to move back to France.

intense
ADJECTIVE
Intense means very great in strength or amount.
EXAMPLE The fire gave off an intense heat.

intention intentions
NOUN
An intention is an idea or plan of what you are going to do.
EXAMPLE I have no intention of resigning.

interactive `ICT`
ADJECTIVE
Computer programs that can be influenced by their users are described as interactive.
EXAMPLE This interactive story on CD-ROM has several possible endings.

interest interests interesting interested
NOUN
1 If you have an interest in something, you want to know more about it.
EXAMPLE He showed no interest in the idea.

2 Your interests are the things you enjoy doing.
EXAMPLE His interests include cooking and photography.

3 If something is in the interests of a person or group, it will benefit them.
EXAMPLE Did he act in the best interests of the company?

4 Interest is an extra payment that you receive if you have invested money, or an extra payment that you make if you have borrowed money.
EXAMPLE Does your bank account pay interest?

▶ VERB
5 If something interests you, you want to know more about it.
EXAMPLE This is the area that most interests me.

interested
ADJECTIVE
If you are interested in something, you want to know more about it.
EXAMPLE I'm not very interested in sport.

interesting
ADJECTIVE
If you find something interesting, it holds your attention.
EXAMPLE It's a very interesting book.

interior interiors
NOUN
The interior is the inside part of something.
EXAMPLE The interior of the building was brightly lit.

internal
ADJECTIVE
Internal means happening inside.
EXAMPLE The fall had caused internal bleeding.

international
ADJECTIVE
International means involving different countries.
EXAMPLE The three countries signed an international trade agreement.

Internet `ICT`
NOUN
The Internet is a worldwide communication system which people use through computers.
EXAMPLE He researched the topic on the Internet.

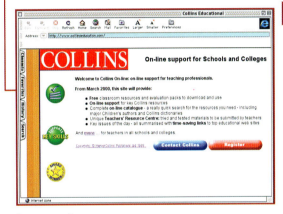

interview interviews interviewing interviewed
NOUN
1 An interview is a meeting at which an employer finds out if you are suitable for a job.
EXAMPLE I had an interview at Boots.

2 An interview is a conversation in which a journalist asks someone questions.
EXAMPLE They listened to the interview with the prime minister.

▶ VERB
3 When an employer interviews you, they ask you questions to find out if you are suitable for a job.
EXAMPLE He was interviewed for a management job.

4 When a journalist interviews someone, they ask them questions.
EXAMPLE She was interviewed live on TV.

introduce introduces introducing introduced
VERB
1 If you introduce something, you cause it to exist in a place or system for the first time.
EXAMPLE The government introduced two new laws.

2 If you introduce one person to another, you tell them each other's name.
EXAMPLE Let me introduce my wife, Jane.

invasion invasions `HISTORY`
NOUN
If there is an invasion of a country, a foreign army enters it by force.
EXAMPLE They studied the Roman invasion of Britain.

A
B
C
D
E
F
G
H
I
J
K
L
M
N
O
P
Q
R
S
T
U
V
W
X
Y
Z

investigate investigates investigating investigated
VERB
To investigate means to try to find out all the facts about something.
EXAMPLE Police are still investigating the incident.

▪ **Similar words:** examine, look into, study

invitation invitations
NOUN
An invitation is a request to come to an event.
EXAMPLE He received an invitation to his cousin's wedding.

invite invites inviting invited
VERB
1 If you invite someone to an event, you ask them to come to it.
EXAMPLE I wasn't invited to the party.

2 If you invite someone to do something, you ask them to do it.
EXAMPLE Andrew has been invited to speak at the conference.

involve involves involving involved
VERB
1 If a situation involves something, that thing is a necessary part of it.
EXAMPLE His work involves a lot of travelling.

2 If a situation involves someone, they are taking part in it.
EXAMPLE There was a demonstration involving a group of students.

Irish
ADJECTIVE
1 Irish means to do with the Irish Republic, or to the whole of Ireland.
EXAMPLE They studied Irish history at college.

▸ *NOUN*
2 Irish is a language spoken in some parts of Ireland.
EXAMPLE The Celts of Ireland spoke Irish.

irony ironies　　　　　ENGLISH
NOUN
Irony is a device used in a play or story to make an unusual connection between things.
EXAMPLE Shakespeare used irony to great effect in *Macbeth*.

Islam　　　　　RE
▪ **Said:** *iz*-lahm
NOUN
Islam is the Muslim religion, which teaches that there is only one God, Allah, and that Muhammad is his Prophet.
EXAMPLE Islam is one of the world's great religions.

island islands　　　　　GEOGRAPHY
▪ **Said:** *eye*-lund
NOUN
An island is a piece of land surrounded by water.
EXAMPLE Crete, Majorca and Sri Lanka are islands.

issue issues issuing issued
▪ **Said:** *ish*-yoo
NOUN
1 An issue is an important subject.
EXAMPLE Gay rights was becoming a major political issue.

2 An issue is a particular edition of a newspaper or magazine.
EXAMPLE He bought the latest issue of *Q Magazine*.

▸ *VERB*
3 If you are issued with something, it is officially given to you.
EXAMPLE Staff will be issued with new uniforms.

Italian Italians
ADJECTIVE
1 Italian means to do with Italy.
EXAMPLE They looked forward to their Italian holiday.

▸ *NOUN*
2 Italian is the main language spoken in Italy.
EXAMPLE She taught Italian at university.

3 An Italian is someone who comes from Italy.
EXAMPLE He's an Italian, not a Frenchman.

item items
NOUN
An item is one of a collection or list of objects.
EXAMPLE The necklace was the most valuable item on the list.

its
ADJECTIVE OR PRONOUN
Its refers to something belonging to or relating to a thing that has already been mentioned.
EXAMPLE The dog is fighting for its life.

Don't confuse 'its' with 'it's'. 'Its', without an apostrophe, means 'belonging to it'. 'It's', with an apostrophe, is a short form of 'it is' or 'it has'.

itself
PRONOUN
1 Itself refers to the same thing that has already been mentioned.
EXAMPLE Paris prides itself on its luxurious hotels.

2 Itself is used to emphasize the thing you are referring to.
EXAMPLE This task itself took three hours.

Jj

jacket jackets
NOUN

1 A jacket is a short coat.
EXAMPLE He wore a leather jacket.

2 A jacket is an outer covering for something.
EXAMPLE The book jacket was very colourful.

January
NOUN

January is the first month of the year.
EXAMPLE Snow fell throughout January.

Jew Jews
NOUN **RE**

A Jew is someone who believes in Judaism; also someone of Hebrew descent.
EXAMPLE Both Jews and Muslims live in Jerusalem.

join joins joining joined
VERB

1 When two things join they come together.
EXAMPLE This road eventually joins the motorway.

Similar words: connect, link, unite

2 If you join a club or organization, you become a member of it.
EXAMPLE He joined the Army five years ago.

joint joints
ADJECTIVE

1 Joint means shared by or belonging to two or more people.
EXAMPLE They had a joint bank account.

▶ *NOUN* **SCIENCE**

2 A joint is a part of your body where two bones meet.
EXAMPLE She massaged her elbow and knee joints.

journal journals
NOUN

1 A journal is a magazine which deals with a specialized subject.
EXAMPLE She enjoyed reading scientific journals.

2 A journal is a diary.
EXAMPLE Each morning he wrote in his journal.

journalist journalists
NOUN

A journalist is a person whose job is to write or talk about news.
EXAMPLE She is a journalist on *The Times*.

journey journeys
NOUN

A journey is the act of travelling from one place to another.
EXAMPLE It was a long journey to the hotel.

Judaism
RE

▢ Said: *joo-day-i-zm*

NOUN

Judaism is the religion of the Jewish people, which is based on a belief in one God.
EXAMPLE The Hebrew Scriptures tell how Judaism began.

judge judges judging judged
NOUN **CITIZENSHIP**

1 A judge is someone who presides over a law court.
EXAMPLE The judge delayed the case until Tuesday.

2 A judge is someone who chooses the winner of a competition.
EXAMPLE The panel of judges announced the winner.

▶ *VERB*

3 If you judge someone or something, you form an opinion about them.
EXAMPLE It's hard to judge her age.

judgement judgements
NOUN

A judgement is an opinion that you have after thinking carefully about something.
EXAMPLE What has changed, in your judgement?

A B C D E F G H I J K L M N O P Q R S T U V W X Y Z

juice juices
NOUN
Juice is the liquid that can be obtained from fruit or other food.
EXAMPLE He has orange juice with his breakfast.

junior
ADJECTIVE
A junior official or employee holds a lower position in an organization.
EXAMPLE He was a junior minister for sport.

jury juries
CITIZENSHIP
NOUN
A jury is a group of people in a court of law who decide whether the accused person is guilty or not.
EXAMPLE The jury found him guilty of murder.

just
ADVERB
1 If something has just happened, it happened a short time ago.
EXAMPLE I've just bought a new car.

2 If you just do something, you do it by a very small amount.
EXAMPLE They only just won.

3 Just means simply or only.
EXAMPLE It was just an excuse not to cut the grass.

4 Just means exactly.
EXAMPLE It's just what she wanted.

▸ ADJECTIVE
5 Just means right or fair.
EXAMPLE She arrived at a just decision.

justice
NOUN
Justice is fairness in the way that people are treated.
EXAMPLE The families of his victims are demanding justice.

justify justifies justifying justified
VERB
If you justify an action or idea, you prove or explain why it is a good one.
EXAMPLE How can you justify what you've done?

keyboard keyboards

NOUN

ICT

1 A keyboard is a set of keys on a computer.
EXAMPLE Her fingers flew over the keyboard.

MUSIC

2 A keyboard is a musical instrument played by hitting a row of buttons or keys.
EXAMPLE Jenny plays keyboards with the local rock group.

kilo kilos

NOUN

SCIENCE

A kilo is a kilogram.
EXAMPLE It weighs around 5 kilos.

kilogram kilograms

NOUN

SCIENCE

A kilogram is a unit of weight equal to 1000 grams.
EXAMPLE It weighs 3 kilograms.

kilometre kilometres

NOUN

A kilometre is a unit of distance equal to 1000 metres.
EXAMPLE They were 20 kilometres from the border.

kitchen kitchens

NOUN

A kitchen is a room used for cooking and preparing food.
EXAMPLE Come and help me in the kitchen.

knife knives

NOUN

A knife is a sharp metal tool used for cutting things.
EXAMPLE He used a knife to cut himself free.

know knows knowing knew known

VERB

1 If you know something, you have it in your mind and you do not need to learn it.
EXAMPLE She knows how to swim.

2 If you know a person, place or thing, you are familiar with them.
EXAMPLE I've known him for five years.

knowledge

NOUN

Knowledge is information about a subject.
EXAMPLE My knowledge of French is poor.

A
B
C
D
E
F
G
H
I
J
K
L
M
N
O
P
Q
R
S
T
U
V
W
X
Y
Z

label labels labelling labelled
NOUN

1 A label is a piece of paper or plastic attached to something and giving information about it.
EXAMPLE Read the label on the bottle.

▸ *VERB*

2 If you label something, you put a label on it.
EXAMPLE Some of the boxes weren't labelled.

labour labour
NOUN

1 Labour is hard work.
EXAMPLE The book was the result of two years' labour.

■ **Similar word:** work

2 Labour refers to the people who work in a country or industry.
EXAMPLE There was a shortage of skilled labour in the area.

3 Labour is the last stage of pregnancy when a woman gives birth to a baby.
EXAMPLE She went into labour late last night.

lack lacks lacking lacked
NOUN

1 If there is a lack of something, there is not enough of it.
EXAMPLE Despite his lack of experience, he got the job.

■ **Similar words:** absence, shortage

▸ *VERB*

2 If someone lacks something, they do not have enough of that thing.
EXAMPLE Francis lacked stamina.

landscape landscapes
NOUN

1 The landscape is everything you can see when you look across an area of land.
EXAMPLE The desert landscape of Arizona is spectacular.

ART

2 A landscape is a painting of the countryside.
EXAMPLE The painter Constable was famous for his landscapes.

language languages
NOUN

1 A language is a system of words used by people to communicate with each other.
EXAMPLE It is good to know a foreign language.

2 The language in which something is written or performed is the style in which it is expressed.
EXAMPLE The show was full of bad language.

largely
ADVERB

You use largely to say that a statement is mostly but not completely true.
EXAMPLE The public are largely unaware of this.

last lasts lasting lasted
ADJECTIVE

1 The last thing or event is the most recent one.
EXAMPLE I went to America last year.

2 The last one of a group of things is the only one that remains.
EXAMPLE Jenny ate the last piece of pizza.

▸ *ADVERB*

3 If something happens last, it happens after everything else.
EXAMPLE He added the milk last.

▸ *VERB*

4 If something lasts, it continues to exist or happen.
EXAMPLE Her speech lasted fifty minutes.

▸ *PHRASE*

5 'At last' means after a long time.
EXAMPLE The coffee arrived at last.

late later latest
ADVERB OR ADJECTIVE

1 Late means near the end of a period of time.
EXAMPLE It's getting late, we'd better go.

2 Late means after the time that was arranged or expected.
EXAMPLE Steve arrived late.

▸ *ADJECTIVE*

3 Late means dead.
EXAMPLE His late father founded the company.

latitude latitudes   **GEOGRAPHY**
NOUN

Latitude is the position north or south of the equator, measured in degrees.
EXAMPLE York is at latitude 54 degrees north.

launch launches launching launched
VERB

1 To launch a ship means to put it into water for the first time.
EXAMPLE The ship was launched in 1926.

2 To launch a rocket means to send it into space.
EXAMPLE They launched two more satellites that year.

3 When a company launches a new product, it makes it available to the public.
EXAMPLE Fiat launched a new estate in April.

law laws
CITIZENSHIP
NOUN
A law is a rule which sets down what we are free and not free to do.
EXAMPLE He broke the law when he stole from the music shop.

lawyer lawyers
NOUN
A lawyer is someone who advises people about the law and represents them in court.
EXAMPLE Their lawyer then spoke to the jury.

layer layers
NOUN
A layer is a single thickness of something.
EXAMPLE A fresh layer of snow covered the street.

lead leads leading led
Said: rhymes with *feed*
VERB
1 To lead someone means to go in front of them in order to show them the way.
EXAMPLE A nurse led me to a large room.

2 If you lead in a race or competition, you are winning.
EXAMPLE Henman leads by two games to one.

3 To lead to something means to cause it to happen.
EXAMPLE What led to the outbreak of violence?

4 To lead a group of people is to be in charge of them.
EXAMPLE He led the country well.

▸ *NOUN*
5 If you take the lead in a race or competition, or if you are in the lead, you are winning.
EXAMPLE England took the lead with a goal from Beckham.

6 A lead is a length of leather or chain used for controlling a dog.
EXAMPLE She put her dog on a lead.

lead
Said: rhymes with *fed*
NOUN
Lead is a soft, grey, heavy metal.
EXAMPLE The pipes were made of lead.

leader leaders
NOUN
1 A leader is someone in charge of a group of people.
EXAMPLE The Conservative leader made a speech.

2 A leader is a person who is winning in a race or competition.
EXAMPLE Lynne was the leader after the first lap.

leaf leaves
NOUN
A leaf is a flat, thin and usually green part of a tree or plant.
EXAMPLE Each leaf on the plant was the same shape.

league leagues
Said: leeg
NOUN
A league is a group of people, clubs or countries that have joined together for a particular purpose.
EXAMPLE They were promoted to the Premier League.

learn learns learning learnt learned
VERB
1 When you learn something, you gain knowledge or a skill through study or training.
EXAMPLE He's learning to play the piano.

2 If you learn of something, you find out about it.
EXAMPLE She first learnt of the fire that morning.

Similar words: discover, find out, hear

lease leases leasing leased
NOUN
1 A lease is a legal agreement which allows someone to use a house or flat in return for rent.
EXAMPLE The lease still has five years left to run.

▸ *VERB*
2 To lease property to someone means to allow them to use it in return for rent.
EXAMPLE She hopes to lease the building to students.

least
ADJECTIVE OR ADVERB
1 Least means the smallest.
EXAMPLE He has the least money of all of them.

▸ *PHRASE*
2 You use 'at least' to suggest that the true amount may be greater.
EXAMPLE At least 200 people were injured.

3 You use 'at least' to refer to something good that still exists in a bad situation.
EXAMPLE At least he's still alive.

leave leaves leaving left
VERB
1 When you leave a place or person, you go away from them.
EXAMPLE They left the hotel early.

Similar words: depart, go

2 If you leave something somewhere, you put it there before you go away.
EXAMPLE I left my bags in the car.

3 If you leave a job or organization, you stop being a part of it.
EXAMPLE He left school with no qualifications.

4 If something leaves an amount of something, that amount remains.
EXAMPLE That won't leave us much time.

A B C D E F G H I J K L M N O P Q R S T U V W X Y Z

lecture lectures
NOUN
A lecture is a formal talk intended to teach people about a subject.
EXAMPLE He is giving a lecture on modern art.

legal
CITIZENSHIP
ADJECTIVE
1 Legal means to do with the law.
EXAMPLE The British legal system is complicated.
2 Legal means allowed by the law.
EXAMPLE The strike was perfectly legal.

legislation
CITIZENSHIP
NOUN
Legislation is a law or set of laws.
EXAMPLE The new legislation on the health service was praised.

lend lends lending lent
VERB
If you lend something to someone, you let them have it for a time.
EXAMPLE Will you lend me your jacket?

length lengths
NOUN
The length of something is the distance from one end to the other.
EXAMPLE They measured the length of the fish.

lens lenses
NOUN
A lens is a thin, curved piece of glass or plastic which makes things appear larger or clearer.
EXAMPLE I'm changing the lens on this camera.

lesbian lesbians
NOUN
A lesbian is a homosexual woman.
EXAMPLE The council set up a youth group for lesbians and gays.

less
ADJECTIVE OR ADVERB
1 Less means a smaller amount of something, or to a smaller extent.
EXAMPLE A shower uses less water than a bath.

You use 'less' to talk about things that can't be counted: 'less time'. When you are talking about amounts that can be counted you should use 'fewer': 'fewer than six people'.

level levels
NOUN
1 A level is a point on a scale.
EXAMPLE We have the lowest level of inflation for years.
■ Similar words: grade, position, stage
2 The level of something is its height.
EXAMPLE He held the gun at waist level.
▶ *ADJECTIVE*
3 Level means completely flat.
EXAMPLE They built the park on an area of level ground.
4 If one thing is level with another, it is at the same height.
EXAMPLE Her face was level with the boy's.

liable
ADJECTIVE
1 Liable means probable or likely.
EXAMPLE Grant was liable to get angry.
2 Liable means legally responsible.
EXAMPLE When the firm collapsed, he was liable for the debt.

liberal
ADJECTIVE
Liberal means tolerant and easy-going.
EXAMPLE My father had liberal views on drugs.

liberty
NOUN
Liberty is freedom.
EXAMPLE Prisoners suffer from their loss of liberty.

library libraries
NOUN
A library is a building in which books are kept.
EXAMPLE Sally borrowed books from the library.

licence licences
NOUN
A licence is a document which gives you permission to do, use or own something.
EXAMPLE He sent off for a driving licence.

likely likelier likeliest
ADJECTIVE
Likely means probable.
EXAMPLE It's more likely that she forgot.

limb limbs
NOUN
Your limbs are your arms and legs.
EXAMPLE He was tall with long limbs.

limit limits limiting limited
NOUN
1 A limit is the largest or smallest amount of something that is possible or allowed.
EXAMPLE Make sure you stick to the speed limit.
▶ *VERB*
2 If you limit something, you prevent it from developing or becoming bigger.
EXAMPLE He did all he could to limit the damage.

limited
ADJECTIVE
Limited means not very great in amount or extent.
EXAMPLE We have a limited amount of time.

listen listens listening listened
VERB
To listen means to pay attention to a sound or what someone is saying.
EXAMPLE He listened to the radio.

literature
ENGLISH
NOUN
Novels, plays and poetry are referred to as literature.
EXAMPLE He was a lecturer in English Literature.

litmus
SCIENCE
NOUN
Litmus is a substance that turns red in acids and blue in alkalis.
EXAMPLE The litmus turned blue, which showed that the solution was an alkali.

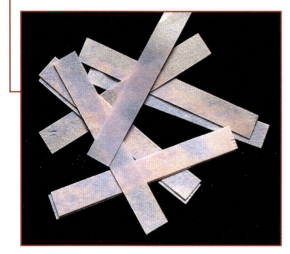

little less lesser least
ADJECTIVE
1 Little means small in size or amount.
EXAMPLE I have a little boy of eight.

▶ *ADVERB OR PRONOUN*
2 A little is a small amount or degree of something.
EXAMPLE He seemed a little anxious.

live lives living lived
☐ **Said:** rhymes with *give*
VERB
1 To live means to be alive.
EXAMPLE She lived in the sixteenth century.

2 If you live in a place, that is where your home is.
EXAMPLE He still lives with his parents.

live
☐ **Said:** rhymes with *dive*
ADJECTIVE OR ADVERB
1 Live television or radio is broadcast while the event is taking place.
EXAMPLE The match will be shown live tonight.

▶ *ADJECTIVE*
2 Live means alive.
EXAMPLE The fisherman had a basket of live crabs.

liver livers
SCIENCE
NOUN
The liver is the organ in your body that cleans your blood.
EXAMPLE Having a healthy liver is important.

loan loans loaning loaned
NOUN
1 A loan is a sum of money which you borrow.
EXAMPLE I arranged a bank loan to buy some furniture.

▶ *VERB*
2 To loan means to lend.
EXAMPLE He never loaned his car to anyone.

local locals
ADJECTIVE
1 Local means to do with the area where you live.
EXAMPLE She always read the local newspaper.

▶ *NOUN*
2 A local is someone who lives in a particular area.
EXAMPLE That's where the locals go to drink.

location locations
NOUN
A location is a place.
EXAMPLE What is the exact location of the church?

☐ **Similar words:** place, position

logic
NOUN
Logic is a way of thinking or reasoning.
EXAMPLE I don't follow the logic of your argument.

logical
ADJECTIVE
Logical means reasonable.
EXAMPLE This is the logical answer to the problem.

log on logs on logging on logged on
ICT
VERB
To log on means to gain access to a computer system.
EXAMPLE He logged on by typing in the password.

longitude longitudes
GEOGRAPHY
NOUN
Longitude is the position east or west on the globe, measured in degrees.
EXAMPLE Swansea is at longitude 4 degrees west.

loose looser loosest
ADJECTIVE
1 Loose means not firmly held or fixed in place.
EXAMPLE He wobbled his loose tooth.

▶ *ADVERB*
2 Loose means free.
EXAMPLE She broke loose from his embrace.

The adjective and adverb 'loose' is spelt with two 'o's. Do not confuse it with the verb 'lose'.

lose loses losing lost
VERB
1 If you lose something, you cannot find it, or you no longer have it because it has been taken from you.
EXAMPLE He lost his place in the team.

2 If you lose a fight or a game of something, you are beaten.
EXAMPLE She hates losing arguments.

loss losses
NOUN
A loss is no longer having something.
EXAMPLE Big job losses are expected.

A B C D E F G H I J K **L** M N O P Q R S T U V W X Y Z

loud louder loudest
ADJECTIVE OR ADVERB
Loud means having a high volume of sound.
EXAMPLE **He turned the television up loud.**

lovely lovelier loveliest
ADJECTIVE
Lovely means very beautiful or pleasant.
EXAMPLE **You look lovely tonight.**

lover lovers
NOUN
1 A person's lover is someone that they have a sexual relationship with but are not married to.
EXAMPLE **They became lovers three months later.**

2 Someone who is a lover of something is very fond of it.
EXAMPLE **The gallery was full of art lovers.**

lower lowers lowering lowered
VERB
1 If you lower something, you move it downwards.
EXAMPLE **She lowered herself into a chair.**

2 To lower an amount, value or quality means to make it less.
EXAMPLE **They decided to lower interest rates.**

▸ *ADJECTIVE*
3 The lower one of a pair of things is the bottom one.
EXAMPLE **She sat on the lower deck of the bus.**

lucky luckier luckiest
ADJECTIVE
1 Someone who is lucky has a lot of good luck.
EXAMPLE **He had always been lucky at cards.**

2 Something that is lucky has good effects or consequences.
EXAMPLE **It's lucky that no one was injured.**

luxury luxuries
NOUN
1 Luxury is great comfort.
EXAMPLE **He led a life of luxury.**

▤ **Similar word:** treat

2 A luxury is something that you enjoy very much but do not often have.
EXAMPLE **Foreign holidays are a luxury we can no longer afford.**

A B C D E F G H I J K **L** M N O P Q R S T U V W X Y Z

Mm Mm Mm

machine machines — TECHNOLOGY
NOUN
A machine is a piece of equipment which uses power to make it work.
EXAMPLE The machine pumped the oil out of the ground.

magazine magazines
NOUN
A magazine is a weekly or monthly publication with articles and photographs.
EXAMPLE She bought a women's magazine at the newsagent's.

magic
NOUN
1 In fairy stories, magic is a special power which can make impossible things happen.
EXAMPLE They believe in magic.
2 Magic is the art of performing tricks to entertain people.
EXAMPLE The boy bought a book on tricks and magic.

mail mails mailing mailed
NOUN
1 Mail is the letters and parcels delivered to you by the post office.
EXAMPLE Was there any mail today?
2 Mail is the system used for collecting and delivering letters and parcels.
EXAMPLE You will be contacted by mail.
▸ VERB
3 If you mail a letter, you send it by post.
EXAMPLE I mailed a letter to you yesterday.

main mains
ADJECTIVE
1 Main means most important.
EXAMPLE This is the main entrance to the building.
▪ Similar words: chief, major, principal
▸ PLURAL NOUN
2 The mains are the large pipes or wires that carry gas, water or electricity to a building.
EXAMPLE Switch off the electricity at the mains!

mainly
ADVERB
You use mainly to show that a statement is true in most cases.
EXAMPLE The staff were mainly women.

maintain maintains maintaining maintained
VERB
1 If you maintain something, you make it continue or keep it at a particular rate or level.
EXAMPLE I've maintained contact with the children.
2 If you maintain a machine or a building, you keep it in good condition.
EXAMPLE The house costs a fortune to maintain.

major majors
ADJECTIVE
1 Major means very important or serious.
EXAMPLE Drug abuse is a major problem here.
▸ NOUN
2 A major is an army officer of the rank immediately above captain.
EXAMPLE Major Chapman was in charge of the parade.

majority majorities
NOUN
The majority of people or things in a group is more than half of them.
EXAMPLE The majority of people in our survey agreed.

You should use 'majority' only to talk about things that can be counted: 'the majority of car owners'. To talk about an amount that cannot be counted you should use 'most': 'most of the harvest was saved'.

make-up
NOUN
Make-up is coloured creams and powders which women and actors put on their faces.
EXAMPLE She puts on too much make-up.

male males
NOUN
1 A male is a person or animal belonging to the sex that cannot have babies or lay eggs.
EXAMPLE There were two males and four females in the nest.
▸ ADJECTIVE
2 Male means to do with men rather than women.
EXAMPLE He had a deep male voice.

manage manages managing managed
VERB
1 If you manage to do something, you succeed in doing it.
EXAMPLE We managed to find somewhere to sit.
▪ Similar word: succeed
2 If you manage an organization or business, you are responsible for controlling it.
EXAMPLE Within two years he was managing the company.

A B C D E F G H I J K L M N O P Q R S T U V W X Y Z

A B C D E F G H I J K L **M** N O P Q R S T U V W X Y Z

management

NOUN

1 Management is the control and organizing of something.
EXAMPLE **The zoo needed better management.**

■ **Similar words:** administration, control

2 The management is the people who control an organization.
EXAMPLE **Hanna asked the management about the new salary scale.**

manager managers

NOUN

A manager is a person responsible for running a business or organization.
EXAMPLE **The bank manager came in late.**

In business, the word manager can apply to either a man or a woman.

manner manners

NOUN

1 The manner in which you do something is the way you do it.
EXAMPLE **The workers behaved in a most professional manner.**

▶ PLURAL NOUN

2 If you have good manners, you behave very politely.
EXAMPLE **She dressed well and had beautiful manners.**

manufacture manufactures manufacturing manufactured `TECHNOLOGY`

VERB

To manufacture goods is to make them on a large scale using machinery.
EXAMPLE **This table has been manufactured abroad.**

march marches marching marched

NOUN

1 A march is an organized protest in which a large group of people walk somewhere together.
EXAMPLE **She went on the march against racism.**

▶ VERB

2 When soldiers march, they walk with regular steps as a group.
EXAMPLE **They saw some soldiers marching down the street.**

margin margins

NOUN

The margin is the blank space at each side of a written or printed page.
EXAMPLE **The teacher wrote a comment in the margin.**

marine marines

NOUN

1 A marine is a soldier who is trained for duties at sea.
EXAMPLE **He joined the Royal Marines when he was twenty-one.**

▶ ADJECTIVE

2 Marine means to do with the sea.
EXAMPLE **She loved to study marine life.**

marked

ADJECTIVE

Marked describes something which is very obvious.
EXAMPLE **There was a marked improvement in his health.**

market markets marketing marketed

NOUN

1 A market is a place where goods are bought and sold.
EXAMPLE **She found a bargain at the antiques market.**

2 The market for a product is the people who want to buy it.
EXAMPLE **The market for soft drinks is mainly made up of children.**

▶ VERB

3 To market a product is to sell it in an organized way.
EXAMPLE **They decided to market their product abroad.**

marriage marriages

NOUN

Marriage is the relationship between a husband and wife.
EXAMPLE **Their marriage lasted for twenty years.**

mass masses

NOUN

1 Mass is a large amount of something.
EXAMPLE **She had a mass of red hair.**

`RE`

2 Mass is a Christian religious service in which people eat bread and drink wine.
EXAMPLE **She went to Mass each day.**

`SCIENCE`

3 Mass is the amount of matter that an object has, measured in grams.
EXAMPLE **The mass of the iron block was 780 grams.**

▶ ADJECTIVE

4 Mass describes something which involves or affects a large number of people.
EXAMPLE **Nuclear bombs are weapons of mass destruction.**

master masters mastering mastered

NOUN

1 A master is a man who is in charge of others.
EXAMPLE **We saw a dog walking next to its master.**

▶ VERB

2 If you master something, you succeed in learning how to do it or understand it.
EXAMPLE **I never mastered French.**

mate mates mating mated

NOUN

1 Your mates are your friends.
EXAMPLE **He's in the pub with his mates.**

2 An animal's mate is its sexual partner.
EXAMPLE **The males guard their mates closely.**

▶ VERB

3 When animals mate, they have sex in order to produce young.
EXAMPLE **The pandas were now ready to mate.**

material materials

NOUN **TECHNOLOGY**

1 Material is cloth.
EXAMPLE The thick material of her skirt made her hot.

2 Material is a solid substance.
EXAMPLE The recycling of materials is a good way of preventing waste.

TECHNOLOGY

3 The equipment used for a particular activity can be referred to as materials.
EXAMPLE The materials she used to make her kite were wood and plastic.

matter matters mattering mattered

NOUN

1 A matter is a task or situation.
EXAMPLE This is a matter for the police.

▣ Similar words: situation, subject

SCIENCE

2 Matter is any substance.
EXAMPLE We carried out an experiment to see how matter behaves at extreme temperatures.

▶ *VERB*
3 If something matters, it is important.
EXAMPLE It doesn't matter to me how old she is.

maximum

ADJECTIVE

The maximum amount is the most that is possible or allowed.
EXAMPLE The car's maximum speed is 90 miles per hour.

maybe

ADVERB

You use maybe to express uncertainty.
EXAMPLE I met him once, maybe twice.

mayor mayors

NOUN **CITIZENSHIP**

A mayor is a person who has been elected to represent the people of a town or city.
EXAMPLE The Mayor of New York made a speech on television.

meaning meanings

NOUN

The meaning of a word or action is the thing that it refers to or expresses.
EXAMPLE 'Big' and 'huge' have similar meanings.

▣ Similar word: sense

meanwhile

ADVERB

Meanwhile means while something else is happening.
EXAMPLE She ate her dinner. Meanwhile, he prepared the pudding.

measure measures measuring measured

VERB

1 If you measure something, you find out how big or good it is by using a particular method or instrument.
EXAMPLE We measured how tall he was.

2 If something measures a particular distance, that is how long or wide it is.
EXAMPLE The door measured 65 by 16 inches.

▶ *NOUN*
3 A measure of something is a certain amount of it.
EXAMPLE We've had a measure of success.

4 A measure is an action carried out to achieve a particular result.
EXAMPLE The council introduced new measures to fight crime.

medal medals

NOUN

A medal is a small metal disc given as an award for bravery or as a prize in sport.
EXAMPLE He won three Olympic gold medals.

media

PLURAL NOUN

The television, radio and newspapers are the media.
EXAMPLE The media have a fascination with the royal family.

Although media is a plural noun, it is becoming more common for it to be used as a singular: 'the media is obsessed with violence'.

medical

ADJECTIVE

1 Medical means to do with the prevention and treatment of illness and injuries.
EXAMPLE She studied at medical school in London.

▶ *NOUN*
2 A medical is an examination of your body by a doctor.
EXAMPLE He failed his army medical because of poor eyesight.

medicine medicines

NOUN

1 Medicine is the treatment of illness and injuries by doctors and nurses.
EXAMPLE He hoped to have a long career in medicine.

2 A medicine is a substance that you drink to help cure an illness.
EXAMPLE The chemist gave him a bottle of cough medicine.

medieval

HISTORY

▣ Said: med-ee-*ee*-vul

ADJECTIVE

Medieval refers to the Middle Ages in Europe.
EXAMPLE Castles were a feature of the medieval period.

A B C D E F G H I J K L **M** N O P Q R S T U V W X Y Z

A B C D E F G H I J K L **M** N O P Q R S T U V W X Y Z

medium
ADJECTIVE
Medium means neither large nor small.
EXAMPLE **He was of medium height.**

meeting meetings
NOUN
1 A meeting is an event at which people discuss things or make decisions.
EXAMPLE **The teachers held a staff meeting after school.**

2 A meeting is an occasion when you meet someone.
EXAMPLE **He remembers his first meeting with Alice.**

megabyte megabytes   ICT
NOUN
A megabyte is a unit of storage in a computer.
EXAMPLE **There are 1000 bytes in a megabyte.**

melodrama melodramas   DRAMA
NOUN
A melodrama is a story or play in which people's emotions are exaggerated.
EXAMPLE **The melodrama was set in a ruined castle.**

melody melodies   MUSIC
NOUN
A melody is a tune.
EXAMPLE **The song has a lovely melody.**

member members
NOUN
A member of a group is one of the people or things belonging to it.
EXAMPLE **She disliked the other members of the family.**

membership
NOUN
1 Membership of an organization is the state of being a member of it.
EXAMPLE **David applied for membership of the youth club.**

2 The membership of an organization is the people who belong to it.
EXAMPLE **Membership of the party doubled in two years.**

memory memories
NOUN
1 Your memory is your ability to remember things.
EXAMPLE **The details are still fresh in my memory.**

■ Similar word: recall

2 A memory is something you remember about the past.
EXAMPLE **He had happy memories of his schooldays.**

ICT

3 A computer's memory is its capacity to store information.
EXAMPLE **My computer has 128 megabytes of memory.**

mental
ADJECTIVE
Mental means to do with the mind and the process of thinking.
EXAMPLE **Schools work hard to develop the mental abilities of children.**

mention mentions mentioning mentioned
VERB
If you mention something, you say something about it, usually briefly.
EXAMPLE **I thought I mentioned it to you.**

■ Similar words: bring up, refer to, touch upon

menu menus   ICT
NOUN
1 A menu is a list of different options shown on a computer screen.
EXAMPLE **He selected 'Save' from the menu.**

2 A menu is a list of the food or meals that you can buy in a café or restaurant.
EXAMPLE **Can I look at the menu?**

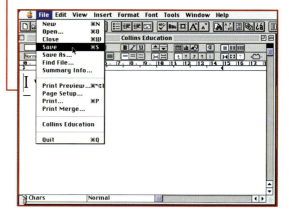

mere
ADJECTIVE
You use mere to emphasize how unimportant or small something is.
EXAMPLE **Tickets are a mere £37.50.**

merely
ADVERB
You use merely to emphasize that something is only what you say and not better or more important.
EXAMPLE **Michael is merely a good friend.**

message messages
NOUN
A message is a piece of information or a request which you send someone or leave for them.
EXAMPLE **I got a message that you were trying to reach me.**

metaphor metaphors   ENGLISH
NOUN
A metaphor is a way of using the qualities of one thing to describe another.
EXAMPLE **'He was a bull of a man' is a metaphor.**

method methods
NOUN
1 A method is a particular way of doing something.
EXAMPLE **He has found a new method of making wine.**

SCIENCE

2 A method is a description of an experiment.
EXAMPLE **Under the heading 'Method', Jenny wrote what she did in the experiment.**

metre metres
NOUN
A metre is a unit of length equal to 100 centimetres.
EXAMPLE **The scarves are 2.3 metres long.**

middle class middle classes
NOUN
The middle class or the middle classes are the people in a society who are not working class or upper class, for example managers and lawyers.
EXAMPLE **Teachers are members of the middle classes.**

migration migrations GEOGRAPHY

NOUN

Migration is the movement of people to settle in a different place.

EXAMPLE **Migration has been an important factor in the make-up of the American population.**

mild milder mildest

ADJECTIVE

Mild means not very strong or severe.

EXAMPLE **The weather was mild for December.**

mile miles

NOUN

A mile is a unit of distance equal to 1760 yards or about 1.6 kilometres.

EXAMPLE **The nearest doctor is five miles away.**

military

ADJECTIVE

Military means to do with the armed forces.

EXAMPLE **The soldiers returned to the military base.**

mill mills

NOUN

1 A mill is a building where grain is crushed to make flour.

EXAMPLE **The old mill still produced flour for the bakery.**

2 A mill is a factory for making materials such as steel, wool or cotton.

EXAMPLE **The woman worked in a cotton mill.**

million millions MATHS

NOUN

A million is the number 1,000,000.

EXAMPLE **Millions of people attended the rally.**

mime mimes miming mimed DRAMA

VERB

To mime is to use only movements and gestures to express something.

EXAMPLE **They had to mime their feeling of anger.**

mind minds minding minded

NOUN

1 Your mind is your ability to think, together with all the thoughts you have and your memory.

EXAMPLE **You must be strong in mind and body.**

▶ PHRASE

2 If you 'change your mind', you change a decision that you have made or an opinion that you have.

EXAMPLE **I was going to vote for him, but I changed my mind.**

▶ VERB

3 If you mind something, you are annoyed by it.

EXAMPLE **I hope you don't mind me phoning you at home.**

4 If you do not mind what happens or what something is like, you do not have a strong preference about it.

EXAMPLE **I don't mind where we go.**

5 If you tell someone to mind something, you are warning them to be careful.

EXAMPLE **Mind how you go!**

mine mines

PRONOUN

1 Mine refers to something belonging or relating to the person who is speaking or writing.

EXAMPLE **Her hand was inches from mine.**

▶ NOUN

2 A mine is a place where deep holes or tunnels are dug under the ground in order to take out minerals.

EXAMPLE **He hated working in a coal mine.**

3 A mine is a bomb hidden in the ground or underwater, which explodes when something touches it.

EXAMPLE **The army found a mine under the man's car.**

minimum

ADJECTIVE

1 A minimum amount is the smallest amount that is possible or allowed.

EXAMPLE **The minimum age for leaving school is 16.**

▶ NOUN

2 A minimum is the smallest amount that is possible or allowed.

EXAMPLE **This will take a minimum of one hour.**

minister ministers CITIZENSHIP

NOUN

1 A minister is a person who is in charge of a particular government department.

EXAMPLE **The Minister of Defence spoke next.**

RE

2 A minister is a priest, especially in a Protestant church.

EXAMPLE **They were married by a Methodist minister.**

ministry ministries CITIZENSHIP

NOUN

A ministry is a government department.

EXAMPLE **The Ministry of Defence is in charge of the army.**

minor

ADJECTIVE

Minor means less important or serious than other things.

EXAMPLE **The player suffered a minor injury in the tackle.**

minority minorities

NOUN

A minority of people or things in a group is a number of them forming less than half of the group.

EXAMPLE **Only a small minority of people agree with you.**

minute minutes

Said: *min-*it

NOUN

A minute is a unit of time equal to 60 seconds.

EXAMPLE **The pizza takes about 20 minutes to cook.**

A
B
C
D
E
F
G
H
I
J
K
L
M
N
O
P
Q
R
S
T
U
V
W
X
Y
Z

minute

☐ **Said:** *my-nyoot*

ADJECTIVE
Minute means extremely small.
EXAMPLE Only a minute amount of salt is needed.

missile missiles

NOUN
A missile is a weapon which is launched into the air, or thrown.
EXAMPLE They aimed nuclear missiles at the major cities.

mission missions

NOUN
A mission is an important task that someone has to do.
EXAMPLE He flew to Rome on a secret mission.

mist mists   GEOGRAPHY

NOUN
Mist is a thin fog consisting of many tiny drops of water in the air.
EXAMPLE A sea mist made it difficult for them to see the land.

mistake mistakes mistaking mistook mistaken

NOUN
1 A mistake is something you do wrong without intending to.
EXAMPLE You've made two spelling mistakes.

■ **Similar words:** error, slip

▶ *VERB*
2 If you mistake something for something else, you wrongly think that it is that other thing.
EXAMPLE I mistook him for someone I knew.

mixture mixtures

NOUN
A mixture is two or more things mixed together.
EXAMPLE He watched the match with a mixture of nervousness and excitement.

■ **Similar words:** blend, mix

mob mobs

NOUN
A mob is a large, disorganized crowd of people.
EXAMPLE A violent mob attacked the bus.

mobile

ADJECTIVE
Mobile describes the ability to move or be moved easily.
EXAMPLE He's much more mobile since getting his new wheelchair.

mode modes

NOUN
A mode of something is one of the different forms it can take.
EXAMPLE Road and rail are two modes of transport.

model models

NOUN
1 A model is a smaller copy of something which shows what it looks like or how it works.
EXAMPLE His hobby was making tiny models of famous ships.

2 A model is a system which people might want to copy.

EXAMPLE The school followed the French model.

■ **Similar words:** example, pattern

3 A model is a type or version of a machine.
EXAMPLE Which model of washing machine did you choose?

4 A model is a person who poses for a painter or photographer.
EXAMPLE She became a fashion model when she left school.

moderate

ADJECTIVE
Moderate means neither large nor small.
EXAMPLE She had a moderate amount of success in her exams.

modest

ADJECTIVE
1 Modest describes a quite small size or amount.
EXAMPLE There was a modest improvement in his behaviour.

2 Someone who is modest does not boast about their abilities or possessions.
EXAMPLE He is modest about his achievements.

molecule molecules   SCIENCE

NOUN
A molecule is two or more atoms chemically joined together.
EXAMPLE There are two atoms in a molecule of oxygen.

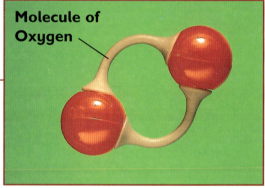

Molecule of Oxygen

moment moments

NOUN
1 A moment is a very short period of time.
EXAMPLE He paused for a moment.

■ **Similar word:** second

▶ *PHRASE*
3 If something is happening 'at the moment', it is happening now.
EXAMPLE He's abroad at the moment.

monitor monitors monitoring monitored

VERB
1 If you monitor something, you regularly check how it is doing.
EXAMPLE Her health will be monitored daily.

▶ *NOUN*
2 A monitor is a machine used to check or record things.
EXAMPLE The patient was put on a heart monitor.

ICT

3 The monitor is the visual display unit of a computer.
EXAMPLE He switched on the monitor.

monarch monarchs   HISTORY

⌨ **Said:** mon-nark

NOUN
A monarch is a ruler, especially a king or queen.
EXAMPLE Elizabeth I was the last Tudor monarch.

monologue monologues   DRAMA

⌨ **Said:** mon-o-log

NOUN
A monologue is a long speech made by one person.
EXAMPLE He gave a monologue on the cruelty of life.

moral morals

PLURAL NOUN
1 Morals are principles and beliefs about right and wrong behaviour.
EXAMPLE Such people have no morals.

▶ ADJECTIVE
2 Moral means to do with beliefs about what is right and wrong.
EXAMPLE She had clear moral values and tried to live a good life.

mortgage mortgages

⌨ **Said:** mor-gij

NOUN
A mortgage is a loan which you get from a bank or building society in order to buy a house.
EXAMPLE He had problems getting a mortgage from the bank.

mosque mosques   RE

⌨ **Said:** mosk

NOUN
A mosque is a building where Muslims worship.
EXAMPLE They entered the mosque to pray.

mostly

ADVERB
Mostly is used to show that a statement is generally true.
EXAMPLE Her friends are mostly men.

moth moths

NOUN
A moth is an insect like a butterfly which usually flies at night.
EXAMPLE He watched a moth fly around the candle.

motion motions motioning motioned

NOUN
1 Motion is the process of continually moving or changing position.
EXAMPLE He felt sick because of the motion of the ship.

2 Motion describes an action or gesture.
EXAMPLE Apply with a brush, using circular motions.

3 A motion is a proposal which people discuss and vote on at a meeting or in a debate.
EXAMPLE The motion was heavily defeated.

▶ VERB
4 If you motion to someone, you move your hand or head in order to show them what they should do.
EXAMPLE I motioned to him across the room.

motivate motivates motivating motivated

VERB
If you motivate someone, you make them feel determined to do something.
EXAMPLE A manager should know how to motivate his players.

motor motors

NOUN
1 A motor is a part of a vehicle or a machine which produces movement so that the machine can work.
EXAMPLE She got into her car and started the motor.

▶ ADJECTIVE
2 Motor describes anything relating to vehicles with an engine.
EXAMPLE He worked in the motor industry.

mount mounts mounting mounted

VERB
1 To mount a campaign or event is to organize it and carry it out.
EXAMPLE They mounted a campaign against drinking and driving.

2 If something is mounting, it is increasing.
EXAMPLE The team's injury problems are mounting.

3 If you mount a horse or bicycle, you climb on to it.
EXAMPLE They mounted their bikes and rode off.

▶ NOUN   GEOGRAPHY
4 Mount is used as part of the name of a mountain.
EXAMPLE Mount Everest is in the Himalayas.

mountain mountains   GEOGRAPHY

NOUN
A mountain is a very high piece of land with steep sides.
EXAMPLE Ben Nevis is Britain's highest mountain.

mouse mice

NOUN   ICT
1 A mouse is a hand-held control which moves the position of the cursor on a computer screen.
EXAMPLE She used the mouse to move the cursor up and down.

2 A mouse is a small creature with a long tail.
EXAMPLE He saw a mouse running across the floor.

movement movements

NOUN
Movement is the process of changing position or going from one place to another.
EXAMPLE He heard a movement behind him.

A B C D E F G H I J K L **M** N O P Q R S T U V W X Y Z

A B C D E F G H I J K L **M** N O P Q R S T U V W X Y Z

multimedia
ADJECTIVE
A computer program that uses text, sound, graphics and sometimes video is described as multimedia.
EXAMPLE He enjoyed using his new multimedia program.

multiple multiples
MATHS
NOUN
The multiples of a number are the numbers you get when you multiply it by any whole number over 1.
EXAMPLE 20 and 50 are multiples of 10.

mural murals
ART
NOUN
A mural is a picture painted on a wall.
EXAMPLE The murals on the west wall of the church are especially good.

murder murders murdering murdered
NOUN
1 Murder is the deliberate killing of a person.
EXAMPLE He was found guilty of murder.

Similar word: killing

▶ *VERB*
2 To murder someone means to kill them deliberately.
EXAMPLE He murdered three people in a single year.

muscle muscles
SCIENCE
NOUN
Your muscles are the internal parts of your body which allow you to make a movement.
EXAMPLE This exercise develops your stomach muscles.

museum museums
NOUN
A museum is a public building where interesting or valuable objects are kept and displayed.
EXAMPLE They saw the dinosaurs in the Natural History Museum.

music
MUSIC
NOUN
Music is the sounds produced by people singing or playing instruments.
EXAMPLE I love listening to music.

Muslim Muslims
RE
NOUN
A Muslim is a person who believes in Islam.
EXAMPLE He was a devout Muslim who prayed every day.

mutual
ADJECTIVE
You use mutual to describe something that is experienced or shared by both of two people.
EXAMPLE They had a mutual interest in rugby.

Similar word: shared

mystery mysteries
NOUN
A mystery is something that is not understood or known about.
EXAMPLE Who committed the murder is still a mystery.

myth myths
ENGLISH
NOUN
1 A myth is a story which was made up long ago to explain events or to justify religious beliefs.
EXAMPLE We are learning about the Greek myth of Troy.

2 A myth is an untrue belief or explanation.
EXAMPLE It's a myth that men are better drivers than women.

Nn Nn Nn

narrator narrators ENGLISH
NOUN
The narrator in a play or story is the person who tells or explains parts of the story to the reader or audience.
EXAMPLE The narrator described what had led to the war.

narrow narrower narrowest
ADJECTIVE
Something that is narrow measures a small distance from one side to the other.
EXAMPLE The town's narrow streets caused traffic problems.

nation nations
NOUN
Nation is another name for a country.
EXAMPLE The whole nation was interested in the match.

national
ADJECTIVE
National means to do with the whole of a country.
EXAMPLE The Times is a national newspaper.

native natives
ADJECTIVE
1 Your native country is the country where you were born.
EXAMPLE Scotland was his native country.

▶ NOUN
2 A native of a place is someone who was born there.
EXAMPLE He is a native of Barbados.

natural
ADJECTIVE
1 Anything natural is normal and to be expected.
EXAMPLE It is only natural for youngsters to enjoy theme parks.

2 Natural also describes anything existing or happening in nature.
EXAMPLE An earthquake is a natural disaster.

nature natures
NOUN
1 Nature is animals, plants and all the other things in the world not made by people.
EXAMPLE The night sky is one of the most beautiful sights in nature.

2 The nature of a person or thing is their basic quality or character.
EXAMPLE She liked his warm, generous nature.

navy navies
NOUN
A navy is the part of a country's armed forces that fights at sea.
EXAMPLE He had once been in the navy.

nearby
ADJECTIVE OR ADVERB
Nearby means a short distance away.
EXAMPLE They ate at a nearby restaurant.

necessary
ADJECTIVE
Something that is necessary is needed or must be done.
EXAMPLE We will do whatever is necessary.

■ Similar words: essential, needed

need needs needing needed
VERB
1 If you need something, you cannot achieve what you want without it.
EXAMPLE I need help.

▶ NOUN
2 Need is a strong feeling that you must have or do something.
EXAMPLE I felt the need to write about it.

negative
ADJECTIVE
1 A negative answer means 'no'.
EXAMPLE He asked for more pocket money but got a negative response.

2 Something that is negative is unpleasant or harmful.
EXAMPLE The news is not all negative.

negotiate negotiates negotiating negotiated
VERB
When people negotiate, they talk about a situation in order to reach agreement about it.
EXAMPLE The Prime Minister refused to negotiate with terrorists.

negotiation negotiations
NOUN
A negotiation is a discussion between people with different interests.
EXAMPLE Negotiations between the two sides broke down quickly.

A B C D E F G H I J K L M N O P Q R S T U V W X Y Z

neighbour neighbours CITIZENSHIP
NOUN
Your neighbour is someone who lives next door to you or near you.
EXAMPLE We had several visits from the neighbours.

neither
CONJUNCTION, ADJECTIVE OR PRONOUN
You use neither to show that a negative statement refers to each of two things.
EXAMPLE He spoke neither English nor German.

When the word neither is followed by a plural noun, the verb can be plural too: 'Neither of these books are useful.' When you have two singular subjects the verb should be singular too: 'Neither Jack nor John has done the work.'

nerve nerves SCIENCE
NOUN
1 Nerves are long thin fibres that send messages between your brain and other parts of your body.
EXAMPLE His spinal nerves were damaged in the car crash.

2 Someone has nerves if they can remain calm in a difficult situation.
EXAMPLE This needs confidence and strong nerves.

nervous
ADJECTIVE
To be nervous is to be worried and frightened.
EXAMPLE I was nervous about meeting him.
▤ Similar words: anxious, worried

net nets
NOUN
1 A net is a piece of material made of threads woven together with small spaces in between.
EXAMPLE She used a fishing net to land the trout.

2 The Net is the same as the Internet.

network networks
NOUN
1 A network is a large number of lines or roads which cross each other at many points.
EXAMPLE A network of paths made their journey through the woods easy.

2 A large number of people or things that work together as a system is called a network.
EXAMPLE Their network of offices covered the south of England.

ICT
3 A network is a group of computers connected to each other.
EXAMPLE The computers in the network shared the same printer.

neutral SCIENCE
ADJECTIVE
Neutral means neither acid nor alkali, or that an object does not carry an electrical charge.
EXAMPLE Pure water is a neutral substance.

never
ADVERB
When you say 'never' you mean at no time in the past, present or future.
EXAMPLE You'll never see her again.

nevertheless
ADVERB
You use nevertheless when you say something that contrasts with what has just been said.
EXAMPLE I know it is true; it's crazy nevertheless.

news
NOUN
News is information about things that have happened recently.
EXAMPLE Chris had some good news about his sister.

newspaper newspapers
NOUN
A newspaper is a regular publication which contains news and articles.
EXAMPLE The man behind them was reading a newspaper.

night nights
NOUN
Night is the time between sunset and sunrise when it is dark.
EXAMPLE So where were you on Friday night?

nightmare nightmares
NOUN
A nightmare is a very frightening dream.
EXAMPLE She had a nightmare about a vicious dog.

noise noises
NOUN
A noise is a sound, especially one that is loud or unpleasant.
EXAMPLE There were complaints about the noise.
▤ Similar words: din, racket, sound

noon
NOUN
Noon is midday.
EXAMPLE An inspection will be held at noon today.

nor
CONJUNCTION
You use 'nor' after 'neither' or after a negative statement to add something else that the negative statement applies to.
EXAMPLE They had neither the time nor the money for the sport.

normal
ADJECTIVE
Normal means usual and ordinary.
EXAMPLE That's the normal response.
▤ Similar words: conventional, ordinary, usual

normally
ADVERB
You use the word normally to refer to what usually

A B C D E F G H I J K L M N O P Q R S T U V W X Y Z

happens or what you usually do.
EXAMPLE I don't normally like dancing.

note notes noting noted
NOUN
1 A note is a short letter to someone.
EXAMPLE I'll leave a note for Karen.

2 A note is something that you write down that helps you to remember something.
EXAMPLE You should take notes during the meeting.

MUSIC

3 A note is a musical sound of a particular pitch, or a written symbol that represents it.
EXAMPLE She played a few notes on the piano.

▸ *VERB*
4 If you note a fact, you become aware of it or write it down.
EXAMPLE Please note that there are a limited number of tickets.

nothing
PRONOUN
Nothing means not a single thing.
EXAMPLE There is nothing wrong with the car.

▪ **Similar words:** none, zero

notice notices noticing noticed
VERB
1 If you notice something, you become aware of it.
EXAMPLE I noticed he was acting strangely.

▪ **Similar words:** detect, observe

▸ *NOUN*
2 A notice is a written announcement.
EXAMPLE She saw a 'No Vacancies' notice in the window of the hotel.

3 Notice is advance warning about something.
EXAMPLE Thank you all for coming along at such short notice.

notion notions
NOUN
A notion is an idea or belief.
EXAMPLE She had old-fashioned notions about love.

noun nouns
ENGLISH
NOUN
A noun is a word for a person, place, thing or idea.
EXAMPLE Ruth underlined all the nouns in the passage.

1 Common nouns indicate every example of a certain type of thing. They begin with a small letter: 'girl', 'city', 'shop'.
2 Proper nouns give the name of a particular person, place or object. They begin with a capital letter: 'Sally', 'Belfast', 'Sainsburys'.

novel novels
NOUN
ENGLISH
1 A novel is a book which tells an invented story.
EXAMPLE *Oliver Twist* is a classic novel.

▸ *ADJECTIVE*
2 Novel describes something that is new and interesting.
EXAMPLE Riding a camel was a novel experience.

nuclear
SCIENCE
ADJECTIVE
Nuclear refers to anything relating to the energy produced when atoms are split.
EXAMPLE Sellafield is a nuclear power station in Cumbria.

nucleus nuclei
SCIENCE
▫ **Said:** *nyoo-klee-uss*
NOUN
1 In biology, the nucleus is the control centre of a cell.
EXAMPLE James used his microscope to see the nucleus in the cell.

2 In chemistry or physics, the nucleus is the centre of an atom.
EXAMPLE Every atom has a nucleus.

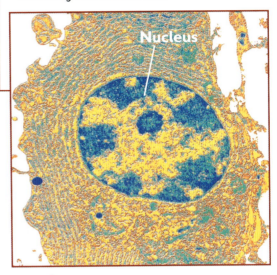
Nucleus

numb
ADJECTIVE
Numb describes when you are unable to feel anything.
EXAMPLE She was numb with grief.

number numbers numbering numbered
NOUN
MATHS
1 A number is a word or symbol which is used for counting or calculating something.
EXAMPLE Fred said that thirteen was his lucky number.

▪ **Similar words:** digit, figure

2 A number of things or people is several of them.
EXAMPLE Sam made a surprising number of errors.

▸ *VERB*
3 If you number something, you give it a number in a series or write the number on it.
EXAMPLE I haven't numbered the pages.

numeral numerals
MATHS
NOUN
A numeral is a symbol which represents a number.
EXAMPLE IV is the Roman numeral for four.

numerous
ADJECTIVE
Numerous means a large number of.
EXAMPLE I have numerous aunts and cousins.

nurse nurses nursing nursed
NOUN
1 A nurse is a person whose job is to look after those who are ill.
EXAMPLE The nurse lifted the patient carefully.

▸ *VERB*
2 If you nurse someone, you look after them when they are ill.
EXAMPLE They nursed me back to health.

A B C D E F G H I J K L M **N** O P Q R S T U V W X Y Z

object objects objecting objected

📖 **Said:** *ob*-ject

NOUN

1 An object is anything solid that you can touch or see.
EXAMPLE The sky was filled with flying objects.

2 The object of something is the reason for doing it.
EXAMPLE The object of the exercise is to raise money.

ENGLISH

3 The object of a sentence is the thing being acted on, which is usually the word after the verb.
EXAMPLE In the sentence 'Lisa threw the ball', the object is 'ball'.

▶ *VERB*

📖 **Said:** ob-*ject*

4 If you object to something, you dislike it or disapprove of it.
EXAMPLE I strongly object to that statement.

📖 **Similar words:** oppose, protest

objective objectives

NOUN

1 Your objective is the thing that you are trying to achieve.
EXAMPLE His main objective was to win the race.

▶ *ADJECTIVE*

2 If you are objective, you are not influenced by personal feelings.
EXAMPLE A journalist should be completely objective.

observe observes observing observed

VERB

1 To observe something is to watch it carefully.
EXAMPLE The social worker observed the behaviour of the child.

2 To observe something is to notice it.
EXAMPLE She observed a tall man entering the building.

3 To observe a law or custom is to obey or follow it.
EXAMPLE You must observe the speed limit.

obtain obtains obtaining obtained

VERB

If you obtain something, you get it.
EXAMPLE Peter was trying to obtain a new passport.

obtuse angle obtuse angles **MATHS**

NOUN

An obtuse angle is an angle which measures between 90 and 180 degrees.
EXAMPLE The obtuse angle measured 135 degrees.

obvious

ADJECTIVE

If something is obvious, it is easy to see or understand.
EXAMPLE It was obvious that she wasn't going to call him.

📖 **Similar words:** clear, plain

occasion occasions

NOUN

1 An occasion is a time when something happens.
EXAMPLE I met her on only one occasion.

2 An important event is often called an occasion.
EXAMPLE The first night was quite an occasion.

occasional

ADJECTIVE

Occasional means happening sometimes but not often.
EXAMPLE I've had occasional headaches.

occupation occupations

NOUN

An occupation is a job or profession.
EXAMPLE My main occupation is designing gardens.

occupy occupies occupying occupied

VERB

1 To occupy means to live in a place or to take control of it.
EXAMPLE Demonstrators occupied the square.

2 If something occupies you, you spend your time doing it.
EXAMPLE Lawrence's work occupies him completely.

occur occurs occurring occurred

VERB

1 If something occurs, it happens or exists.
EXAMPLE The attack occurred at a swimming pool.

2 If something occurs to you, you suddenly think of it.
EXAMPLE That possibility hadn't occurred to them.

If an event has been planned, you should not say that it occurred or happened: 'The wedding took place on Saturday.' Only something unexpected occurs or happens: 'An accident has occurred.'

ocean oceans **GEOGRAPHY**

NOUN

The five oceans are the five large areas of sea in the world.
EXAMPLE He crossed the Atlantic Ocean to visit America.

odd odder oddest; odds
ADJECTIVE
1 Odd means strange or unusual.
EXAMPLE It was odd that they should both choose to stay in the same hotel.

2 Odd things do not match each other.
EXAMPLE He only had odd socks in his drawer.

MATHS

3 Odd numbers are numbers that cannot be divided exactly by two.
EXAMPLE Three and seven are odd numbers.

▶ PLURAL NOUN
4 In gambling, the probability of something happening is called the odds.
EXAMPLE The odds on him winning look pretty good.

offence offences
NOUN
An offence means a crime.
EXAMPLE Blackmail is a serious offence.

offensive
ADJECTIVE
Something offensive is rude and upsetting.
EXAMPLE She was known for her offensive behaviour.

offer offers offering offered
VERB
1 If you offer something to someone, you ask them if they would like it.
EXAMPLE She offered him a cup of tea.

▶ NOUN
2 An offer is something that someone says they will give you or do for you.
EXAMPLE He refused the offer of a drink.

office offices
NOUN
1 An office is a room where people work at desks.
EXAMPLE They worked in a large, air-conditioned office.

2 A government department is also known as an office.
EXAMPLE He worked in the Foreign Office.

officer officers
NOUN
An officer is a person with a position of authority in the armed forces, the police or a government organization.
EXAMPLE He was a high-ranking army officer.

official officials
ADJECTIVE
1 Anything which is official is approved by the government or by someone in authority.
EXAMPLE She received her third official warning.

▶ NOUN
2 An official is a person who holds a position of authority in an organization.
EXAMPLE They were met by a senior official at the American embassy.

oil oils oiling oiled
NOUN
1 Oil is a thick, sticky liquid which is used as a fuel and for lubricating machines.
EXAMPLE The Middle East has vast resources of oil.

2 Oil is a thick, greasy liquid made from plants or animals.
EXAMPLE He fried the vegetables in olive oil.

▶ VERB
3 If you oil something, you put oil in it or on it.
EXAMPLE The machine needs to be oiled regularly.

once
ADVERB
1 If something happens once, it happens one time only.
EXAMPLE Mary only went to Manchester once.

2 If something was once true, it was true in the past, but is no longer true.
EXAMPLE The island was once covered by trees.

▶ CONJUNCTION
3 If something happens once another thing has happened, it happens immediately afterwards.
EXAMPLE I'll go back to the hotel once the game is over.

▶ PHRASE
4 If you do something 'at once', you do it immediately.
EXAMPLE We must go home at once.

only
ADJECTIVE OR ADVERB
1 You use only to indicate the one thing or person involved.
EXAMPLE Only Tony was able to continue.

▶ ADVERB
2 You use only to introduce a condition which must happen before something else can happen.
EXAMPLE You will be paid only if you win.

3 You use only to emphasize that something is unimportant.
EXAMPLE He's only a little boy.

▶ CONJUNCTION
4 Only means but or except.
EXAMPLE He was like you, only with blond hair.

open opens opening opened
VERB
1 When you open something, it is moved so that it is no longer closed.
EXAMPLE She opened the door.

2 When a shop or office opens, people are able to go in.
EXAMPLE The bank opens at nine o'clock.

3 To open something also means to start it.
EXAMPLE Ramesh opened the batting with Michael.

▶ ADJECTIVE
4 Something that is open is not closed.
EXAMPLE They sat by an open window.

5 Someone who is open is honest and frank.
EXAMPLE He was quite open about his debts.

A
B
C
D
E
F
G
H
I
J
K
L
M
N
O
P
Q
R
S
T
U
V
W
X
Y
Z

opening openings

ADJECTIVE

1 Opening means coming first.
EXAMPLE They had a good win on the opening day of the season.

▸ *NOUN*

2 The opening of a book or film is the first part of it.
EXAMPLE That would be a great opening for a novel.

3 An opening is a hole or gap.
EXAMPLE There was a small opening in the mound.

▉ **Similar words:** gap, hole

opera operas

MUSIC

NOUN

An opera is a play in which the words are sung to music rather than spoken.
EXAMPLE He is writing an opera about Joan of Arc.

operate operates operating operated

VERB

1 To operate is to work.
EXAMPLE A healthy diet makes your body operate efficiently.

2 When you operate a machine, you make it work.
EXAMPLE Beth knew how to operate the controls.

3 When surgeons operate, they cut open a person's body to remove or repair a damaged part.
EXAMPLE We shall have to operate to remove the bullet.

operation operations

NOUN

1 An operation is an organized, planned event.
EXAMPLE The enemy carried out a secret operation against the American forces.

2 An operation is a form of medical treatment in which a surgeon cuts open a person's body to remove or repair a damaged part.
EXAMPLE Elizabeth had just had an operation on her back.

▸ *PHRASE*

3 If something is 'in operation', it is working or being used.
EXAMPLE There are still three machines in operation.

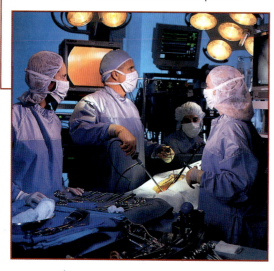

operator operators

NOUN

1 An operator is someone who works at a telephone exchange or on a switchboard.
EXAMPLE He asked the operator to connect him to the bank.

2 An operator is someone who operates a machine.
EXAMPLE The computer operator will be with you soon.

3 An operator is someone who runs a business.
EXAMPLE They are one of Britain's largest tour operators.

opinion opinions

NOUN

An opinion is a belief or view.
EXAMPLE I am not interested in your opinion.

▉ **Similar words:** belief, judgement, view

opponent opponents

NOUN

An opponent is someone who is against you in an argument or a contest.
EXAMPLE He was aware of his opponents' weaknesses.

opportunity opportunities

NOUN

An opportunity is a chance to do something that you want to do.
EXAMPLE I had an opportunity to go to Lisbon.

opposed

ADJECTIVE

1 If you are opposed to something, you disagree with it.
EXAMPLE He was totally opposed to fox hunting.

▸ *PHRASE*

2 If you refer to one thing 'as opposed to' another, you are emphasizing the first thing in contrast to the second.
EXAMPLE Let us now look at pop music as opposed to jazz.

opposite

PREPOSITION OR ADVERB

1 If one thing is opposite another, it is facing it.
EXAMPLE She lives in the house opposite.

▸ *ADJECTIVE*

2 The opposite part of something is the part farthest away from you.
EXAMPLE The cinema is on the opposite side of town.

3 If things are opposite, they are completely different.
EXAMPLE I take the opposite view to you.

▉ **Similar word:** reverse

opposition

NOUN

If there is opposition to something, people disagree with it.
EXAMPLE There was strong opposition to the new road.

opt opts opting opted

VERB

If you opt for something, you choose it.
EXAMPLE I opted to study History at GCSE.

optimistic

ADJECTIVE

If you are optimistic you are hopeful about the future.
EXAMPLE She is optimistic that she will get a good job when she leaves school.

option options

NOUN

If you have an option you have a choice between two or more things.
EXAMPLE I was offered the option of leaving or staying on.

oral orals
ADJECTIVE

1 Oral means that something is spoken rather than written.
EXAMPLE I gave an oral account of what had happened.

▶ *NOUN*

2 An oral is an examination that is spoken rather than written.
EXAMPLE My French oral is on Friday.

orchestra orchestras   MUSIC

◻ **Said:** or-kess-tra

NOUN

An orchestra is a large group of musicians who play together.
EXAMPLE Viv played second violin in the school orchestra.

order orders ordering ordered
NOUN

1 An order is a command given by someone in authority.
EXAMPLE The lieutenant gave the order to arrest them.

2 An order means a particular arrangement or sequence.
EXAMPLE The names were listed in alphabetical order.

3 Order is a situation in which everything is in the correct place.
EXAMPLE The police arrived to restore order.

▶ *VERB*

4 To order means to command.
EXAMPLE He ordered his men to stop firing.

5 When you order something, you ask for it to be brought or sent to you.
EXAMPLE Jim ordered another plate of cakes.

▶ *PHRASE*

6 If you do something 'in order to' achieve a particular thing, you do it because you want to achieve that thing.
EXAMPLE Naseem came to Britain in order to study.

ordinary
ADJECTIVE

Ordinary means not special or different.
EXAMPLE It was just an ordinary day.

◻ **Similar words:** conventional, normal, usual

ore ores   SCIENCE
NOUN

An ore is a rock which contains large amounts of a mineral.
EXAMPLE A lot of iron ore comes from Russia.

organ organs
NOUN   SCIENCE

1 Your organs are parts of your body that have a particular purpose.
EXAMPLE The heart and lungs are vital organs.

MUSIC

2 An organ is a large musical keyboard instrument.
EXAMPLE He plays the organ on Sundays.

organism organisms   SCIENCE
NOUN

An organism is any living animal or plant.
EXAMPLE They studied the organisms under the microscope.

organization organizations
NOUN

1 An organization is a group or business.
EXAMPLE The Labour Party is a powerful political organization.

◻ **Similar words:** body, company, group

2 The organization of something is the way that the different parts are arranged.
EXAMPLE The key to Chelsea's victory was the organization of their defence.

Organization is also spelt organisation.

organize organizes organizing organized
VERB

1 If you organize an event, you plan and arrange it.
EXAMPLE We decided to organize a concert for Easter.

2 If you organize things, you arrange them in a sensible order.
EXAMPLE Filing cabinets allow people to organize their work better.

Organize is also spelt organise.

origin origins
NOUN

1 The origin is the beginning or cause of something.
EXAMPLE The origin of the word is not known.

◻ **Similar words:** root, source

2 You can refer to someone's family background as their origin or origins.
EXAMPLE She was of Swedish origin.

original originals
ADJECTIVE

1 Original describes things that existed at the beginning.
EXAMPLE The new kitchen is twice its original size.

2 Original means imaginative and clever.
EXAMPLE He is a highly original thinker.

▶ *NOUN*

3 An original is a work of art or a document which is the one that was first produced, and not a copy.
EXAMPLE The pictures on the walls were all originals.

otherwise
ADVERB

1 You use otherwise to say a different situation would exist if a particular fact was not the case.
EXAMPLE You had to learn to swim pretty quickly, otherwise you sank.

2 Otherwise means apart from the thing mentioned.
EXAMPLE She wrote to her daughter; otherwise she did nothing.

A B C D E F G H I J K L M N O P Q R S T U V W X Y Z

ought

🔲 **Said:** awt

VERB

1 If you say that someone ought to do something, you mean that they should do it.
EXAMPLE **He ought to see a doctor.**

2 If you say that something ought to be the case, you mean that you expect it to be the case.
EXAMPLE **It ought to be quite easy.**

Do not use the words 'did' and 'had' with ought: 'He ought not to come' is correct. 'He didn't ought to come' is not correct.

ounce ounces

NOUN

An ounce is a unit of weight equal to one sixteenth of a pound or about 28.35 grams.
EXAMPLE **She bought three ounces of cheese.**

outline outlines outlining outlined

VERB

1 If you outline a plan or idea, you explain it in a general way.
EXAMPLE **The mayor outlined his plan.**

▸ *NOUN*

2 The outline of something is its shape.
EXAMPLE **The hill had an unmistakable outline.**

outside outsides

NOUN

1 The outside of something is the part that surrounds the rest of it.
EXAMPLE **We wandered around the outside of the house.**

▸ *ADVERB, ADJECTIVE OR PREPOSITION*

2 Outside means not inside.
EXAMPLE **The house had an outside toilet.**

Do not use 'of' after the word outside. You should write 'She was waiting outside the school', not 'outside of the school'.

outstanding

ADJECTIVE

1 Outstanding means extremely good.
EXAMPLE **The collection contains many outstanding paintings.**

2 Money that is outstanding is still owed.
EXAMPLE **I promise to pay back the outstanding debt.**

oval ovals

NOUN

An oval is an egg shape.
EXAMPLE **The teacher drew a large oval on the blackboard.**

overall overalls

ADJECTIVE OR ADVERB

1 Overall means taking into account all the parts or aspects of something.
EXAMPLE **Overall, things are not too bad.**

▸ *PLURAL NOUN*

2 Overalls are what you wear to protect your other clothes when you are working.
EXAMPLE **The men on the building site wore overalls.**

overcome overcomes overcoming overcame overcome

VERB

If you overcome a problem or a feeling, you successfully deal with it or control it.
EXAMPLE **She eventually overcame her fear of flying.**

overnight

ADJECTIVE OR ADVERB

1 Overnight means during the night.
EXAMPLE **Further rain was forecast overnight.**

2 Overnight is used to describe something that happens suddenly.
EXAMPLE **The pop singer became an overnight success.**

overseas

ADJECTIVE OR ADVERB

Overseas describes something that happens or exists abroad.
EXAMPLE **I enjoy travelling overseas.**

owe owes owing owed

VERB

1 If you owe someone money, they have lent it to you and you have not yet paid it back.
EXAMPLE **You still owe me five pounds.**

2 If you owe a quality or skill to someone, you only have it because of them.
EXAMPLE **He owes his success to his mother.**

▸ *PHRASE*

3 'Owing to' something means because of that thing.
EXAMPLE **I was late owing to a traffic jam.**

owner owners

NOUN

The owner of something is the person it belongs to.
EXAMPLE **The owner of the car was furious.**

pace paces pacing paced
NOUN

1 The pace of something is the speed at which it moves or happens.
EXAMPLE He quickened his pace to win the race.

▶ *VERB*

2 To pace means to step.
EXAMPLE I paced up and down the room.

pack packs packing packed
VERB

1 If you pack, you put your belongings into a bag before leaving a place.
EXAMPLE We barely had time to pack.

2 To pack or pack into a place means to fill it.
EXAMPLE Thousands of people packed into the stadium.

▶ *NOUN*

3 A pack is a packet or collection of something.
EXAMPLE He sent for an information pack from the museum.

package packages
NOUN

A package is a small parcel.
EXAMPLE The package was addressed to his wife.

page pages
NOUN

A page is one side of one of the pieces of paper in a book or magazine.
EXAMPLE Turn to page 4.

pain pains
NOUN

1 Pain is a feeling of discomfort in your body caused by an illness or injury.
EXAMPLE I felt a sharp pain in my lower back.

◼ **Similar words:** ache, hurt

2 Pain is unhappiness.
EXAMPLE He felt the pain of losing his girlfriend.

painful
ADJECTIVE

If something is painful it causes physical or emotional pain.
EXAMPLE He suffered a painful injury in the accident.

paint paints painting painted
NOUN

1 Paint is a coloured liquid used to decorate buildings and make pictures.
EXAMPLE The paint was still wet on the walls.

▶ *VERB*

2 If you paint something, you add paint to a surface.
EXAMPLE He painted several pictures of her.

painting paintings　　ART
NOUN

A painting is a picture which someone has painted.
EXAMPLE He was painting a picture of the countryside.

pair pairs
NOUN

1 A pair of things are two things of the same type that are meant to be used together.
EXAMPLE He took out a pair of socks.

2 Objects which have two main parts of the same size and shape come in pairs.
EXAMPLE He cut his toenails with a pair of scissors.

palace palaces
NOUN

A palace is a large, grand house, especially the home of a king or queen.
EXAMPLE There were huge crowds outside Buckingham Palace.

pale paler palest
ADJECTIVE

If something is pale it is not strong or bright in colour.
EXAMPLE They painted the bedroom pale blue.

panel panels
NOUN

1 A panel is a small group of people who are chosen to do something.
EXAMPLE The panel of judges decided that Wesley gave the best speech.

2 A panel is a flat piece of wood or other material that is part of a larger object.
EXAMPLE One of the door panels was damaged by the burglar.

panic panics panicking panicked
NOUN

1 Panic is a sudden strong feeling of fear or anxiety.
EXAMPLE The earthquake caused panic among the villagers.

▸ *VERB*

2 If you panic, you become so afraid or anxious that you cannot act sensibly.
EXAMPLE The crowd panicked when the lights went out.

paper papers
NOUN

1 Paper is a material that you write on or wrap things with.
EXAMPLE She typed her work on to A4 paper.

2 A paper is a newspaper.
EXAMPLE He went to the newsagent's to buy the Sunday paper.

parade parades
NOUN

A parade is a line of people or vehicles moving together as part of a show.
EXAMPLE The crowd cheered the parade as it passed through the town.

paragraph paragraphs   ENGLISH
NOUN

A paragraph is a section of a piece of writing which deals with the same topic.
EXAMPLE Barney's essay had a good opening paragraph.

parallel   MATHS
ADJECTIVE

A parallel line is the same distance from another line at all points.
EXAMPLE She drew three parallel lines with a ruler.

parent parents
NOUN

Your parents are your father and mother.
EXAMPLE This is where a lot of parents go wrong.

parliament parliaments   CITIZENSHIP
NOUN

Parliament is the group of elected representatives who run the country.
EXAMPLE Parliament met to discuss a new reform bill.

participate participates participating participated
VERB

If you participate in an activity, you do it together with other people.
EXAMPLE Both sides agreed to participate in talks.

▣ **Similar words:** be involved in, join in, take part

particular
ADJECTIVE

1 The word particular emphasizes that you are talking about one thing rather than other similar ones.
EXAMPLE One particular memory still bothers me.

2 Particular means greater or more intense than usual.
EXAMPLE Pay particular attention to the following advice.

particularly
ADVERB

You use particularly to show that what you are saying applies especially to one thing or situation.
EXAMPLE This is hard for young children, particularly when they are ill.

partly
ADVERB

Partly means to some extent but not completely.
EXAMPLE It's partly my fault.

partner partners
NOUN

1 Someone's partner is the person they are married to or living with.
EXAMPLE Discuss the problem with your partner.

2 Your partner is the person you are doing something with, for example in a dance or a game.
EXAMPLE He was asked to dance with a partner he had not met before.

party parties
NOUN

1 A party is a social event, often in order to celebrate something.
EXAMPLE We threw a huge birthday party for my sister.

CITIZENSHIP

2 A party is an organization whose members share the same political beliefs.
EXAMPLE He was a member of the Labour Party.

pass passes passing passed
VERB

1 To pass something means to move past it.
EXAMPLE We passed the street where I used to live.

▣ **Similar words:** go past, overtake

2 If you pass something to someone, you hand it to them.
EXAMPLE Pass the salt, please.

3 When a period of time passes, it happens and ends.
EXAMPLE Several minutes passed before anyone spoke.

4 If you pass a test, you are considered to be of an acceptable standard.
EXAMPLE Kevin has just passed his driving test.

▸ *PHRASE*

5 If someone 'passes out', they faint or collapse.
EXAMPLE He was so drunk that he passed out.

▸ *NOUN*

6 A pass is a document that allows you to go somewhere.
EXAMPLE Don't let anyone in unless they have a pass.

passage passages
NOUN
1 A passage is a corridor or space which connects two places.
EXAMPLE A narrow passage led to a door.
2 A passage is a section of a book or piece of music.
EXAMPLE He read a passage from Shakespeare.

passenger passengers
NOUN
A passenger is a person travelling in a vehicle, aircraft or ship.
EXAMPLE Fewer than a hundred passengers survived.

passion passions
NOUN
Passion is a very strong feeling, especially of sexual attraction.
EXAMPLE I felt such extraordinary passion for her.
▪ Similar word: emotion

past
NOUN
1 The past is the period of time before the present.
EXAMPLE In the past this was never a problem.
PREPOSITION OR ADVERB
2 If you go past something, you move beyond it.
EXAMPLE An ambulance drove past.

patient patients
ADJECTIVE
1 If you are patient, you stay calm in a difficult or irritating situation.
EXAMPLE I've got to be patient and wait.
▶ NOUN
2 A patient is a person receiving treatment from a doctor.
EXAMPLE All of the cancer patients were kept in one ward.

pattern patterns
NOUN
1 A pattern is a design of shapes repeated at regular intervals.
EXAMPLE She drew a pattern of red and gold stripes.
DESIGN
2 A pattern is a diagram or shape used as a guide for making something.
EXAMPLE She laid the pattern on the material and then cut around it.

pause pauses pausing paused
VERB
If you pause, you stop speaking or doing something for a short time.
EXAMPLE She paused at the door to listen.

payment payments
NOUN
Payment is the act of paying money.
EXAMPLE Players now expect payment for interviews.

peace
NOUN
Peace is a state of undisturbed calm and quiet.
EXAMPLE One more question and I'll leave you in peace.

peaceful
ADJECTIVE
Peaceful means quiet and calm.
EXAMPLE It's so peaceful without the children here.

peak peaks
NOUN
1 The peak of an activity or process is the point at which it is strongest or most successful.
EXAMPLE Eight o'clock is the peak of the morning rush hour.
2 The peak is the pointed top of a mountain.
EXAMPLE The snow-covered peaks of the Alps could be seen in the distance.

peer pressure
NOUN
Peer pressure is the influence of a group of people to which we belong.
EXAMPLE Adam started smoking only because of peer pressure.

penalty penalties
NOUN
1 A penalty is a punishment for breaking a rule or law.
EXAMPLE Some countries have the death penalty for murder.
2 In soccer, a penalty is a free kick at goal that is given to the attacking team.
EXAMPLE They were awarded a penalty in the last minute.

pension pensions
NOUN
A pension is a regular sum of money paid to a retired or disabled person.
EXAMPLE He receives a company pension.

people peoples
PLURAL NOUN
1 People are men, women and children.
EXAMPLE Thousands of people have lost their homes in the disaster.
▶ NOUN
2 A people is all the men, women and children of a particular country or race.
EXAMPLE It's a triumph for the American people.
▪ Similar words: nation, population, race

pepper peppers
NOUN
1 Pepper is a hot-tasting powdered spice used for flavouring in cooking.
EXAMPLE He liked to use salt and pepper on his soup to add taste.
2 A pepper is a green, red or yellow vegetable, with sweet-flavoured flesh.
EXAMPLE The supermarket had run out of peppers.

A B C D E F G H I J K L M N O P Q R S T U V W X Y Z

per
PREPOSITION
Per means each when expressing rates and ratios.
EXAMPLE We are travelling at 70 miles per hour.

per cent
MATHS
NOUN
Per cent is a fraction expressed as a number of hundredths.
EXAMPLE Half marks in the test is equal to 50 per cent.

percentage percentages
MATHS
NOUN
Percentage is the name given to a fraction of an amount expressed as a number of hundredths.
EXAMPLE How do you work out percentages on your calculator?

percussion
MUSIC
NOUN
Percussion is the name for instruments that make sound by being hit.
EXAMPLE Tubular bells are percussion instruments.

perfect
ADJECTIVE
Something that is perfect is as good as it can possibly be.
EXAMPLE His English was perfect.

perfectly
ADVERB
1 Perfectly emphasizes the word it goes with.
EXAMPLE They are perfectly safe to eat.
2 If something is done perfectly, it could not be done better.
EXAMPLE The system worked perfectly.

perform performs performing performed
VERB
1 If you perform a task or action, you do it.
EXAMPLE Lifeboatmen have performed outstanding acts of bravery.

2 The way that something performs is how well it works.
EXAMPLE SATs are a measure of how different schools are performing.
DRAMA

3 To perform is to act, dance or play music in front of an audience.
EXAMPLE She loves to perform on stage.

performance performances
DRAMA
NOUN
1 A performance is an entertainment provided for an audience.
EXAMPLE They watched a performance of Beauty and the Beast.

2 Someone's or something's performance is how successful they are.
EXAMPLE The team gave a poor performance in the final.

perhaps
ADVERB
You use the word perhaps when you are not sure whether something is true or possible.
EXAMPLE It will cost hundreds, perhaps thousands, to repair.

perimeter perimeters
MATHS
NOUN
The perimeter of an area or figure is the whole of its outer edge; also the length of that edge.
EXAMPLE They measured the perimeter of the field.

period periods
NOUN
1 A period is a particular length of time.
EXAMPLE The film was made over a period of a few months.

2 When a woman has a period, she bleeds from her womb, usually once a month.
EXAMPLE She thought she was pregnant because she had missed her period.

permanent
ADJECTIVE
If something is permanent it lasts forever.
EXAMPLE The car crash left him with permanent brain damage.

permission
NOUN
If you have permission to do something, you are allowed to do it.
EXAMPLE He asked permission to leave the room.

permit permits permitting permitted
VERB
1 If someone permits you to do something, they allow it or make it possible.
EXAMPLE You are permitted to use the golf course.
▪ Similar words: allow, give permission, let
▶ NOUN
2 A permit is a document which says that you are allowed to do something.
EXAMPLE He wasn't allowed to work until he received a work permit.

personal
ADJECTIVE
If something is personal it is to do with a particular person.
EXAMPLE That's my personal opinion.
▪ Similar words: individual, own, private

personality personalities
NOUN

1 Your personality is your character and nature.
EXAMPLE She's got a very lively personality.

2 A personality is a famous person.
EXAMPLE There were many television personalities at the party.

personally
ADVERB

1 The word personally emphasizes that you are giving your own opinion.
EXAMPLE Personally, I think it's a waste of time.

2 If you do something personally, you do it yourself rather than letting someone else do it for you.
EXAMPLE I'll deal with it personally.

perspective perspectives
NOUN

1 A particular perspective is one way of thinking about something.
EXAMPLE The death of his father gave him a new perspective on life.

ART

2 Perspective is the process of drawing objects on a flat surface so that they look realistic.
EXAMPLE He used perspective to show the street disappearing in the distance.

persuade persuades persuading persuaded
VERB

If someone persuades you to do something, they cause you to do it by giving you good reasons for it.
EXAMPLE My husband persuaded me to come.

■ **Similar words:** convince, talk into

phase phases
NOUN

A phase is a particular stage in the development of something.
EXAMPLE The laying of the foundations was the first phase of the building.

philosophy philosophies
NOUN

Philosophy is the study of ideas about basic things such as the nature of existence or how we should live.
EXAMPLE Gregor went on to study philosophy at university.

phone phones
NOUN

A phone is a telephone.
EXAMPLE Jamie answered the phone.

photograph photographs
NOUN

A photograph is a picture which is made using a camera.
EXAMPLE Her photograph was on the front page of the paper.

photosynthesis **SCIENCE**
NOUN

Photosynthesis is the process by which a plant makes its food.
EXAMPLE Plants need water, sunlight and carbon dioxide for photosynthesis.

phrase phrases **ENGLISH**
NOUN

A phrase is a group of words which is not a sentence.
EXAMPLE A phrase only makes full sense as part of a sentence.

physical
ADJECTIVE

Physical means to do with the body rather than the mind.
EXAMPLE The army first gave him a physical examination.

picture pictures **ART**
NOUN

1 A picture is a drawing, painting or other image of someone or something.
EXAMPLE There was a picture of him in the paper.

▸ *PLURAL NOUN*
2 The pictures means the cinema.
EXAMPLE We're going to the pictures tonight.

piece pieces
NOUN

A piece is a portion or part of something.
EXAMPLE She wrote her answers on a piece of paper.

pilgrimage pilgrimages **RE**
NOUN

A pilgrimage is a journey to a holy place.
EXAMPLE The pilgrimage to Makkah is important to Muslims.

pill pills
NOUN

1 A pill is a medicine tablet which you swallow.
EXAMPLE She took a sleeping pill before she went to bed.

2 The pill is a type of drug that women can take regularly to prevent pregnancy.
EXAMPLE She had been on the pill for three years.

pilot pilots
NOUN

A pilot is a person who is trained to fly an aircraft.
EXAMPLE He wanted to be an airline pilot when he was old enough.

pitch pitches
NOUN

1 A pitch is an area of ground marked out for playing a game such as football or cricket.
EXAMPLE The football pitch was very muddy.

MUSIC

2 The pitch of a sound is how high or low it is.
EXAMPLE He raised his voice to an even higher pitch.

place places
NOUN
1 A place is any point, building or area.
EXAMPLE This is a good place to camp.

Similar words: location, site, spot

▶ PHRASE
2 When something 'takes place', it happens.
EXAMPLE The elections will take place in November.

plain plainer plainest; plains
ADJECTIVE
1 If something is plain it is very simple in style with no pattern or decoration.
EXAMPLE She wore a plain white skirt.

Similar words: bare, simple

2 If something is plain it is obvious or easy to understand.
EXAMPLE He made his feelings quite plain.

▶ NOUN
3 A plain is a large, flat area of land with very few trees.
EXAMPLE There were no signs of the buffalo that once roamed the plains.

plan plans planning planned
NOUN
1 A plan is a method of achieving something that has been worked out beforehand.
EXAMPLE I told them of my plan.

▶ VERB
2 If you plan to do something, you intend to do it.
EXAMPLE They plan to marry in the summer.

Similar words: intend, mean, propose

plane planes
NOUN
A plane is a vehicle with wings and engines which can fly.
EXAMPLE He had plenty of time to catch his plane.

planet planets   SCIENCE
NOUN
A planet is a large round object in space which moves around the sun or a star.
EXAMPLE There are nine planets in the solar system.

plant plants planting planted
NOUN
1 A plant is a living thing which grows in the earth and has a stem, leaves and roots.
EXAMPLE Water each plant as often as required.

2 A plant is the name given to a factory or power station.
EXAMPLE He worked in a car assembly plant.

▶ VERB
3 If you plant a seed or plant, you put it into the ground.
EXAMPLE He wants to plant fruit trees and vegetables.

plastic plastics   TECHNOLOGY
NOUN
Plastic is a light but strong material made by a chemical process.
EXAMPLE They covered the furniture with sheets of plastic to protect it.

plate plates
NOUN
1 A plate is a flat dish used to hold food.
EXAMPLE She pushed her plate away.

2 A plate is a flat piece of metal, for example on a machine.
EXAMPLE The ship's hull is made from heavy steel plates.

platform platforms
NOUN
A platform is a raised structure on which someone or something can stand.
EXAMPLE The speaker mounted the platform to talk to the crowds.

player players
NOUN
A player is a person who takes part in a sport or game.
EXAMPLE Some of Liverpool's top players were in the England team.

plea pleas
NOUN
A plea is an emotional request.
EXAMPLE The refugees made a plea for help.

pleasant
ADJECTIVE
Pleasant means nice, enjoyable or attractive.
EXAMPLE They had a pleasant evening with friends.

Similar words: nice, pleasing

pleased
ADJECTIVE
If you are pleased, you are happy about something.
EXAMPLE I was very pleased with the results.

pleasure pleasures
NOUN
Pleasure is a feeling of happiness, satisfaction or enjoyment.
EXAMPLE Seeing her win gave him great pleasure.

plot plots
NOUN
1 A plot is a secret plan made by a group of people.
EXAMPLE The police discovered a plot to kidnap the president.

ENGLISH

2 The plot of a film, novel or play is the story.
EXAMPLE The novel has a complicated plot.

plunge plunges plunging plunged
VERB
1 If you plunge somewhere, you fall or rush there.
EXAMPLE The bus plunged into the river.

Similar words: dive, drop, fall

2 If you plunge an object into something, you push it in quickly.
EXAMPLE She plunged the knife into his chest.

poem poems ENGLISH
NOUN
A poem is a piece of writing in which words are arranged in rhythmic lines, often with a rhyme.
EXAMPLE 'Daffodils' is a famous poem by Wordsworth.

poet poets
NOUN
A poet is a person who writes poems.
EXAMPLE He was a painter and a poet.

poetry ENGLISH
NOUN
Poetry means verse or poems.
EXAMPLE Shakespeare wrote a great deal of poetry.

point points pointing pointed
NOUN
1 A point is an opinion or fact expressed by someone.
EXAMPLE That's a very good point.

2 The point of something is its purpose.
EXAMPLE What's the point in even trying?

3 A point is a single mark in a competition.
EXAMPLE New Zealand have beaten Scotland by 21 points to 18.

4 The point is the thin, sharp end of something.
EXAMPLE Only the point of the blade was visible.

▶ VERB
5 If you point at something, you hold out your finger to show where it is.
EXAMPLE She pointed to a picture on the wall.

6 If you point something at someone, you aim the end of it towards them.
EXAMPLE A man pointed a gun at them.

▶ PHRASE
7 If you point something out to someone, you draw their attention to it by pointing to it or explaining it.
EXAMPLE She pointed her boss out to us.

pointed
ADJECTIVE
A pointed object has a thin, sharp end.
EXAMPLE She wore pointed shoes.

point of view points of view
NOUN
Your point of view is your opinion about something or your attitude towards it.
EXAMPLE Try to see things from my point of view.

pole poles
NOUN
1 A pole is a long rounded piece of wood or metal.
EXAMPLE There was a large telegraph pole outside the house.

 GEOGRAPHY
2 The earth's poles are the two opposite ends of its axis.
EXAMPLE It is very cold at the North Pole.

police CITIZENSHIP
PLURAL NOUN
The police are the organization that is responsible for making sure that people obey the law.
EXAMPLE The police are looking for him.

policy policies
NOUN
A policy is a set of plans and ideas, especially in politics or business.
EXAMPLE What is their policy on drugs?

politician politicians CITIZENSHIP
NOUN
A politician is a person whose job is in politics, especially a member of parliament.
EXAMPLE She was a Labour politician.

politics CITIZENSHIP
NOUN
Politics is the activity concerned with achieving power in a country or organization.
EXAMPLE Foreign Minister is one of the key jobs in British politics.

poll polls CITIZENSHIP
NOUN
A poll is a survey in which people are asked their opinions about something.
EXAMPLE An opinion poll revealed how popular the government was.

pollination SCIENCE
NOUN
Pollination is the transfer of pollen from one flower to another.
EXAMPLE Bees and other insects pollinate flowers as they collect nectar.

pollution GEOGRAPHY
NOUN
Pollution is poisonous substances in water, air or land.
EXAMPLE The pollution on the beach put visitors off.

popular
ADJECTIVE
Popular describes something which is liked or approved of by a lot of people.
EXAMPLE She was the most popular singer in France.

▤ Similar words: fashionable, well-liked

A B C D E F G H I J K L M N O **P** Q R S T U V W X Y Z

population populations GEOGRAPHY
NOUN

The population of a place is the people who live there, or the number of people living there.
EXAMPLE The country is unable to feed its population.

port ports
NOUN

1 A port is a town or area which has a harbour or docks.
EXAMPLE They landed at the Mediterranean port of Marseille.

2 Port is a kind of strong, sweet red wine.
EXAMPLE She enjoyed a glass of port.

porter porters
NOUN

A porter is a person whose job is to carry things.
EXAMPLE The porter carried his bag to the train.

portion portions
NOUN

1 A portion is a part of something.
EXAMPLE I spent a large portion of my life there.

Similar words: bit, part, piece

2 A portion is an amount of food sufficient for one person.
EXAMPLE The portions were very generous.

portrait portraits ART
NOUN

A portrait is a picture or photograph of someone.
EXAMPLE The students drew portraits of their friends.

pose poses posing posed
VERB

1 If you pose a question, you ask it.
EXAMPLE She posed several questions to the politician.

2 If you pose as someone else, you pretend to be that person.
EXAMPLE The robber was posing as a workman.

3 Pose also means to stay in a particular position so that someone can photograph or paint you.
EXAMPLE The musicians agreed to pose for photographs.

▸ NOUN

4 A pose is a way of standing, sitting or lying.
EXAMPLE The boys were photographed in a variety of poses.

position positions
NOUN

The position of someone or something is the place where they are.
EXAMPLE The ship's position was reported to the coastguard.

positive
ADJECTIVE

1 If you are feeling positive you are completely sure about something.
EXAMPLE I was positive he'd be there.

2 If you feel positive you feel confident and hopeful.
EXAMPLE I feel very positive about everything.

3 If a medical test is positive, it shows that something is present.
EXAMPLE The pregnancy test was positive.

possibility possibilities
NOUN

A possibility is something that might be true or might happen.
EXAMPLE We must accept the possibility that we are wrong.

Similar word: chance

possible
ADJECTIVE

1 If it is possible to do something, it can be done.
EXAMPLE I hope it is possible to find him.

2 If you do something as soon as possible or as quickly as possible, you do it as soon or as quickly as you can.
EXAMPLE I'll be there as soon as possible.

possibly
ADVERB

You use the word possibly to show that you are not sure whether something is true.
EXAMPLE Television is possibly to blame for this.

potential
NOUN

Your potential is your ability to achieve success in the future.
EXAMPLE He's got great potential.

pound pounds pounding pounded
NOUN

1 The pound is the main unit of currency in Britain.
EXAMPLE Beer cost three pounds a bottle.

2 A pound is a unit of weight equal to 16 ounces or 0.454 kilograms.
EXAMPLE He bought a pound of cheese.

▸ VERB

3 If you pound something, you hit it repeatedly with your fist.
EXAMPLE Someone was pounding on the door.

pour pours pouring poured
VERB

1 If you pour a liquid, you tip it out of a container.
EXAMPLE She poured the tea down the sink.

2 To pour with rain means to rain heavily.

EXAMPLE It's been pouring all day.

poverty
NOUN
Poverty is the state of being very poor.
EXAMPLE They lived in great poverty.

power powers
NOUN
1 Power means control over people and events.
   EXAMPLE She held a position of great power and influence.
2 Your power to do something is your ability or right to do it.
   EXAMPLE I will do everything in my power to help.
3 The power of something is its physical strength.
   EXAMPLE He pressed the accelerator and felt the power of the engine.
▪ **Similar words:** force, strength

SCIENCE

4 Power is energy obtained, for example, by burning fuel or using the wind or waves.
   EXAMPLE Nuclear power is one way of making electricity.

powerful
ADJECTIVE
1 Powerful means being able to control or influence people and events.
   EXAMPLE America is the most powerful country in the world.
2 Powerful means very strong.
   EXAMPLE The weight lifter had powerful muscles.

practical
ADJECTIVE
1 If something is practical it involves real situations rather than ideas or theories.
   EXAMPLE She gave practical suggestions for healthy eating.
2 Someone who is practical is able to deal effectively and sensibly with problems.
   EXAMPLE You were always so practical, Maria.

practice practices
NOUN
1 A practice is something that people do regularly.
   EXAMPLE The practice of kissing hands has more or less died out.
2 Practice is regular training in a skill or activity.
   EXAMPLE I need more practice at tackling.

The noun 'practice' ends in 'ice'; the verb 'practise' ends in 'ise'.

practise practises practising practised
VERB
To practise is to train regularly in a skill or activity.
EXAMPLE She practised her goal kicks all afternoon.

praise praises praising praised
VERB
If you praise someone or something, you express your strong approval of them.
EXAMPLE He praised the fans for their continued support.

pray prays praying prayed
VERB
When someone prays, they speak to God to give thanks or to ask for help.
EXAMPLE They were praying for peace.

prayer prayers
RE
NOUN
1 Prayer is the activity of praying.
   EXAMPLE Let us now kneel in prayer.
2 A prayer is the words said when someone prays.
   EXAMPLE We each said our own prayer.

precipitation
GEOGRAPHY
NOUN
Precipitation is the term that describes rain, snow, hail, sleet, drizzle and dew.
EXAMPLE Precipitation is measured with a rain gauge.

precise
ADJECTIVE
Precise means exact.
EXAMPLE We will never know the precise details of his death.

precisely
ADVERB
Precisely means accurately and exactly.
EXAMPLE The baby was born at 4 p.m. precisely.

predict predicts predicting predicted
VERB
If you predict an event, you say that it will happen.
EXAMPLE He predicted that my hair would grow back.
▪ **Similar word:** forecast

prefer prefers preferring preferred
VERB
If you prefer one thing to another, you like it better than the other thing.
EXAMPLE I preferred books to people.

prefix prefixes
ENGLISH
NOUN
A prefix is a letter or a group of letters added to the beginning of a word to make a new word.
EXAMPLE 'Semi-', 'pre-' and 'un-' are all prefixes.

pregnant
ADJECTIVE
A woman who is pregnant has a baby growing in her body.
EXAMPLE I hear Hannah is pregnant again.

A B C D E F G H I J K L M N O P Q R S T U V W X Y Z

preparation preparations
NOUN
Preparation is the process of getting something ready.
EXAMPLE Months of preparation lay ahead.

prepare prepares preparing prepared
VERB
If you prepare for something, you get ready for it.
EXAMPLE She told them to prepare for their exams.

prepared
ADJECTIVE
1 If you are prepared to do something, you are willing to do it.
EXAMPLE He's not prepared to compromise.
2 If you are prepared for something, you are ready for it.
EXAMPLE Be prepared for a surprise.

preposition prepositions   ENGLISH
NOUN
A preposition is a word used before a noun to link it to other words.
EXAMPLE 'In', 'over' and 'around' are all prepositions.

presence
NOUN
1 Someone's presence in a place is the fact that they are there.
EXAMPLE His presence only made things worse.
2 If you are in someone's presence, you are in the same place as they are.
EXAMPLE I always feel nervous in her presence.

present presents presenting presented
ADJECTIVE
☐ Said: *prez*-ent
1 If someone is present somewhere, they are there.
EXAMPLE He had been present at the birth of his son.
2 A present situation is one that exists now rather than in the past or future.
EXAMPLE His present job is just what he wants.
☐ **Similar words:** contemporary, current, existing
▶ *NOUN*
☐ Said: *prez*-ent
3 The present is the period of time that is taking place now.
EXAMPLE The search is continuing right up to the present.
4 A present is something that you give to someone for them to keep.
EXAMPLE She was pleased with her Christmas presents.
▶ *VERB*
☐ Said: pri-*zent*
5 If you present something, you formally give it to them.
EXAMPLE She presented an award to the girl.

preserve preserves preserving preserved
VERB
If you preserve something, you make sure that it stays as it is.
EXAMPLE We will do everything to preserve peace.

president presidents   CITIZENSHIP
NOUN
The president of a country that has no king or queen is the leader of the country.
EXAMPLE The President of the United States lives in the White House.

press presses pressing pressed
VERB
1 If you press something, you push it or hold it firmly against something else.
EXAMPLE He pressed the button and a door opened.
▶ *NOUN*
2 Newspapers and the journalists who work for them are called the press.
EXAMPLE The British press is full of articles on the subject.

pressure pressures
NOUN
1 Pressure is the force that is produced by pushing on something.
EXAMPLE It bends when you put any pressure on it.
2 If there is pressure on you to do something, someone is trying to make you do it.
EXAMPLE He may have put pressure on her to agree.

presumably
ADVERB
If you say that something is presumably the case, you mean that you assume it is the case.
EXAMPLE Presumably the front door was locked?

pretty prettier prettiest
ADJECTIVE
Pretty means attractive and pleasant.
EXAMPLE She is a pretty girl.

prevent prevents preventing prevented
VERB
If you prevent something, you stop it from happening.
EXAMPLE Further treatment will prevent the cancer from developing.
☐ **Similar words:** avert, forestall, stop

previous
ADJECTIVE
A previous time or thing is one that occurred before the present one.
EXAMPLE They went to Italy the previous year.
☐ **Similar words:** earlier, former

previously
ADVERB
Previously means at a time before the present.
EXAMPLE Previously she had very little time to work.

pride
NOUN
Pride is a feeling of satisfaction that you have when you or people close to you have done something well.
EXAMPLE His mother looked at him with pride.

priest priests RE

NOUN
A priest is a minister in some Christian churches.
EXAMPLE **She was visited in hospital by a Catholic priest.**

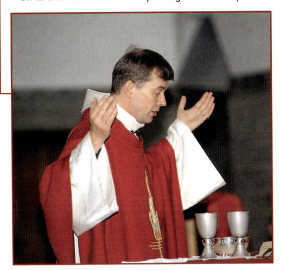

primary

ADJECTIVE
Primary means the first or most important.
EXAMPLE **The primary aim of his research was to find a cure for cancer.**

prime

ADJECTIVE
1 Prime means the main or most important.
EXAMPLE **He was the prime suspect for the crime.**

2 Prime means of the best quality.
EXAMPLE **The house was in prime condition.**

prime number

prime numbers MATHS
NOUN
A prime number can only be divided without remainder by itself or one.
EXAMPLE **Three, five and seven are prime numbers.**

prince princes

NOUN
A prince is the son of a king or queen.
EXAMPLE **The Prince of Wales visited the new factory.**

princess princesses

NOUN
A princess is the daughter of a king or queen, or the wife of a prince.
EXAMPLE **Princess Anne works for several charities.**

principal

ADJECTIVE
Principal means main or most important.
EXAMPLE **The principal source of food is farming.**

Do not confuse the adjective 'principal' with the noun 'principle'.

principle principles

NOUN
A principle is a belief that you have about the way you should behave.
EXAMPLE **I try to live according to my principles.**

print prints printing printed

VERB
1 To print a newspaper or book means to reproduce it mechanically in large quantities.
EXAMPLE **10,000 copies of the pamphlet were printed.**

2 If numbers or letters are printed on something, they appear on it.
EXAMPLE **He looked for the number printed on the receipt.**

▶ NOUN
3 The words on the pages of a book or newspaper are referred to as the print.
EXAMPLE **The newspaper was made up of columns of tiny print.**

prior

ADJECTIVE
1 Prior means planned or done at an earlier time.
EXAMPLE **No prior knowledge is required.**

▶ PHRASE
2 Something that happens 'prior to' a particular time or event happens before it.
EXAMPLE **The police wanted to know his movements prior to the shooting.**

priority priorities

NOUN
A priority means that needs to be dealt with before everything else.
EXAMPLE **Her first priority is to get fit again.**

private

ADJECTIVE
Private means for the use of one person or group rather than for the general public.
EXAMPLE **He travelled to London in his father's private plane.**

pro pros

NOUN
1 A pro is a professional, especially a professional sports person.
EXAMPLE **Some of Europe's top pros play football in the Premier League.**

▶ PHRASE
2 The 'pros and cons' of a situation are its advantages and disadvantages.
EXAMPLE **He considered the pros and cons of getting married.**

probably

ADVERB
Something that is probably the case is likely to be the case.
EXAMPLE **You probably won't agree with this.**

problem problems

NOUN
1 A problem is an unsatisfactory situation that causes difficulties.
EXAMPLE **The main problem was my age.**

Similar words: difficulty

2 A problem is a puzzle or question which you solve using logical thought or mathematics.
EXAMPLE **The maths problem was difficult without a calculator.**

procedure procedures

NOUN
A procedure is a way of doing something.
EXAMPLE **The entire procedure takes about 15 minutes.**

A B C D E F G H I J K L M N O P Q R S T U V W X Y Z

A B C D E F G H I J K L M N O **P** Q R S T U V W X Y Z

proceed proceeds proceeding proceeded
VERB

1 If you proceed to do something, you do it after doing something else.
EXAMPLE He then proceeded to tell us everything.

2 To proceed means to continue doing something.
EXAMPLE Before we proceed any further, please listen.

▶ *PLURAL NOUN*

3 The proceeds of an event are the money that is obtained from it.
EXAMPLE The proceeds from the concert will go towards famine relief.

process processes processing processed
NOUN

1 A process is a series of actions or events which have a particular result.
EXAMPLE We can't stop the ageing process.

▶ *PHRASE*

2 If you are 'in the process' of doing something, you have not yet finished it.
EXAMPLE They are in the process of making new rules.

▶ *VERB* `TECHNOLOGY`

3 When something is processed, it is treated or dealt with in a particular way.
EXAMPLE Processed foods can be found in any supermarket.

produce produces producing produced
VERB

⬛ Said: pro-*duce*

1 To produce something means to make it or cause it to happen.
EXAMPLE You produce wine from grapes.

2 If you produce something, you show it so that it can be seen.
EXAMPLE To hire a car you must produce a passport.

▶ *NOUN*

⬛ Said: *pro*-duce

3 Produce is food that is grown to be sold.
EXAMPLE The shop sells local farm produce.

producer producers
NOUN

The producer of a record, film, play or programme is the person in charge of making it.
EXAMPLE The actor fell out with the producer.

product products
NOUN `TECHNOLOGY`

1 A product is something that is made to be sold.
EXAMPLE The advert told the viewers about the new product.

2 The product is the result of something.
EXAMPLE Her good exam results are the product of hard work.

production productions
NOUN `TECHNOLOGY`

1 Production is the process of manufacturing or growing something in large quantities.
EXAMPLE Germany is famous for the production of cars.

`DRAMA`

2 A production of a play or other show is a series of performances of it.
EXAMPLE Their production of *The Tempest* was a great success.

profession professions
NOUN

A profession is a type of job that requires advanced education or training.
EXAMPLE Teaching is a demanding profession.

professional
ADJECTIVE

1 Professional means to do with the work of someone who is qualified in a particular profession.
EXAMPLE I think you need professional advice.

2 Professional describes activities which are done to earn money rather than as a hobby.
EXAMPLE When he left school he became a professional footballer.

3 Professional also means of a very high standard.
EXAMPLE The team gave a very professional performance.

professor professors
NOUN

A professor is a senior teacher in a British university, or a teacher at an American college or university.
EXAMPLE The students showed their work to the professor.

profile profiles
NOUN

Your profile is the outline of your face seen from the side.
EXAMPLE The photo was of her profile.

profit profits profiting profited
NOUN

1 A profit is an amount of money that you gain when you are paid more for something than it cost you.
EXAMPLE They made a large profit on the deal.

⬛ Similar words: gain, proceeds

▶ *VERB*

2 If you profit from something, you gain or benefit from it.
EXAMPLE He profits from other people's misfortunes.

program programs
NOUN `ICT`

A program is a set of instructions which allows a computer to perform specific tasks.
EXAMPLE What word processing program do you use?

programme programmes
NOUN

1 A programme is a planned series of events.
EXAMPLE The programme for the trip includes a visit to a museum.

⬛ Similar words: plan, schedule

2 A programme is something that is broadcast on television or radio.

EXAMPLE They heard about the car crash on a local news programme.

3 A programme is a booklet giving information about a play, concert or show.
EXAMPLE They bought a programme to find out the names of the actors.

progress
NOUN

1 Progress is the process of improving or getting near to achieving something.
EXAMPLE Gerry is now making real progress at school.

Similar word: advance

▸ *PHRASE*

2 Something that is 'in progress' has started and is still continuing.
EXAMPLE A cricket match was in progress.

project projects projecting projected
NOUN

Said: *pro*-ject

1 A project is a carefully planned task that requires a lot of time or effort.
EXAMPLE His next project was to design the theatre.

▸ *VERB*

Said: pro-*ject*

2 If you project an image on to a screen, you make it appear there.
EXAMPLE The teacher projected pictures on to the wall.

prominent
ADJECTIVE

If something or someone is prominent they are important, well known or noticeable.
EXAMPLE John had a prominent nose.

promise promises promising promised
VERB

1 If you promise to do something, you say that you will definitely do it.
EXAMPLE Promise me that you'll come.

Similar word: guarantee

▸ *NOUN*

2 Something that shows promise is likely to be successful.
EXAMPLE She gave a performance full of promise.

promote promotes promoting promoted
VERB

1 If someone promotes something, they try to sell it or make it popular.
EXAMPLE The band went on tour to promote their latest album.

2 To promote someone is to give them a more important job at work.
EXAMPLE I was promoted to manager.

prompt prompts prompting prompted
VERB

1 If something prompts someone to do something, it makes them decide to do it.
EXAMPLE His mother prompted him to say thank you.

▸ *ADJECTIVE*

2 A prompt action is done without any delay.
EXAMPLE She gave a prompt reply to the question.

pronoun pronouns
NOUN

A pronoun is a word used to replace a noun.
EXAMPLE 'He', 'she' and 'it' are all pronouns.

pronunciation pronunciations

Said: pron-nun-see-*ay*-shn

NOUN

Pronunciation is the way a word is said.
EXAMPLE We practised the pronunciation of some German words today.

proof
NOUN

Proof of something is evidence that it is true or exists.
EXAMPLE There is no proof that he actually said that.

Similar word: evidence

prop props
NOUN

The props in a play are the objects and furniture used by the actors.
EXAMPLE A chair was the only prop in this scene.

propaganda
NOUN

Propaganda is information used to make people think something is good or bad.
EXAMPLE The propaganda made them think that the war was good and just.

proper
ADJECTIVE

If something is proper it is suitable or satisfactory.
EXAMPLE He was no nearer having a proper job.

property properties
NOUN

1 A person's property is the things that belong to them.
EXAMPLE He tries hard to look after his own property.

2 A property is the special quality a material has.
EXAMPLE Mint has powerful healing properties.

prophet prophets
NOUN

1 A prophet is someone who claims to speak for God.
EXAMPLE Isaiah is an important prophet in the Hebrew Scriptures.

2 The Prophet is a title Muslims give to Muhammad.
EXAMPLE The Prophet Muhammad was born in Makkah.

proportion proportions
NOUN
1 A proportion of an amount or group is a part of it.
EXAMPLE A large proportion of students were sick.

▶ PLURAL NOUN
2 You can refer to the size of something as its proportions.
EXAMPLE She carried a red umbrella of vast proportions.

proposal proposals
NOUN
A proposal is a suggestion or plan.
EXAMPLE His new business proposal pleased his partner.

propose proposes proposing proposed
VERB
1 If you propose a plan or idea, you suggest it.
EXAMPLE The head teacher proposed changes in the school rules.

2 If you propose to do something, you intend to do it.
EXAMPLE And how do you propose to do that?

3 If you propose to someone, you ask them to marry you.
EXAMPLE She said yes after he had proposed to her.

prose   ENGLISH
NOUN
Prose is ordinary written language which is not poetry.
EXAMPLE George studied twentieth-century American prose.

prospect prospects
NOUN
1 If there is a prospect of something, it is likely to happen.
EXAMPLE There was little prospect of winning.

▶ PLURAL NOUN
2 Someone's prospects are their chances of being successful.
EXAMPLE Your career prospects are excellent.

protect protects protecting protected
VERB
To protect someone or something means to prevent them from being harmed.
EXAMPLE What can women do to protect themselves from heart disease?

protection
NOUN
If something provides protection, it prevents people or things from being harmed.
EXAMPLE This diet offers protection against a number of diseases.

protein proteins   SCIENCE
NOUN
A protein is a substance needed by bodies for growth.
EXAMPLE Milk is a good source of protein.

protest protests protesting protested
VERB
If you protest, you say or show that you disapprove of something.
EXAMPLE He opened the letter before she could protest.

Protestant Protestants   RE
NOUN
A Protestant is a member of one of the Christian churches that are not Catholic.
EXAMPLE Many Protestants read from the Bible every day.

proud prouder proudest
ADJECTIVE
1 If you are proud of something, you feel satisfaction at something you own or have achieved.
EXAMPLE I was proud of our players today.

2 Someone who is proud has a lot of dignity and self-respect.
EXAMPLE He was too proud to ask his family for help.

prove proves proving proved
VERB
To prove something is to show by means of argument or evidence that it is true.
EXAMPLE A letter from Kathleen proved that he lived there.

▪ Similar words: confirm, show

provide provides providing provided
VERB
If you provide something for someone, you give it to them or make it available for them.
EXAMPLE They would not provide us with any details.

provoke provokes provoking provoked
VERB
To provoke something bad is to make it happen.
EXAMPLE Don't try to provoke a fight with me.

psychological
▫ Said: sigh-kol-oj-ikl
ADJECTIVE
Psychological means to do with a person's mind and thoughts.
EXAMPLE He was in hospital with psychological problems.

public
NOUN
1 You can refer to people in general as the public.
EXAMPLE The gardens are open to the public.

▶ ADJECTIVE
2 Something that is public relates to people in general, or is provided for everyone to use.
EXAMPLE He always used public transport when he could.

publication publications
NOUN
1 The publication of a book is the act of printing it and making it available.
EXAMPLE The dictionary is due for publication in October.

2 A publication is a book or magazine.
EXAMPLE This magazine is the latest publication for teenagers.

publicity
NOUN
Publicity is information or advertisements about an item or event.
EXAMPLE There was some advance publicity for the book.

publish publishes publishing published
VERB
To publish a book, newspaper or magazine means to print copies of it and distribute it.
EXAMPLE The writer was famous even before the book was published.

pump pumps pumping pumped
NOUN
1 A pump is a machine which is used to force a liquid or gas to move in a particular direction.
EXAMPLE He filled his car with petrol at the petrol pump.

▶ *VERB*
2 To pump something means to force it to flow in one direction, using a pump.
EXAMPLE The factory pumped its waste into the river.

punch punches punching punched
VERB
If you punch someone, you hit them hard with your fist.
EXAMPLE He was punching and kicking me.

purchase purchases purchasing purchased
VERB
When you purchase something, you buy it.
EXAMPLE She purchased three tickets at the office.

punctuation
ENGLISH
NOUN
Punctuation is the use of marks in written sentences to make their meaning clear.
EXAMPLE Commas and full stops are important aspects of punctuation.

pure purer purest
ADJECTIVE
1 Something that is pure is not mixed with anything else.
EXAMPLE He bought a pure wool sweater from the clothes shop.

2 Pure means clean and free from harmful substances.
EXAMPLE The water is pure enough to drink.

■ **Similar word:** clean

purpose purposes
NOUN
1 The purpose of something is the reason for it.
EXAMPLE What is the purpose of your visit?

2 Your purpose is the thing that you want to achieve.
EXAMPLE Her only purpose in life was to get rich.

▶ *PHRASE*
3 If you do something 'on purpose', you do it deliberately.
EXAMPLE Was it an accident or did he do it on purpose?

pursue pursues pursuing pursued
VERB
If you pursue someone or an activity, you follow them or it.
EXAMPLE Peter was pursuing a career in photography.

A B C D E F G H I J K L M N O **P** Q R S T U V W X Y Z

A B C D E F G H I J K L M N O P Q R S T U V W X Y Z

qualify qualifies qualifying qualified
VERB
1 When someone qualifies, they pass the examinations that they need in order to do a particular job.
EXAMPLE She qualified as an accountant.

2 If you qualify for something, you have the right to do it or have it.
EXAMPLE She failed to qualify for the finals.

quality qualities
NOUN
1 The quality of something is how good it is.
EXAMPLE The quality of the food here is very poor.

2 A quality is a characteristic.
EXAMPLE Not all people have leadership qualities.

quantity quantities
NOUN
A quantity is an amount.
EXAMPLE There was a small quantity of water.

quarter quarters
NOUN   **MATHS**
1 A quarter is one of four equal parts.
EXAMPLE Cut the pies into quarters.

2 When you are telling the time, quarter refers to the fifteen minutes before or after the hour.
EXAMPLE It was a quarter to six.

queen queens
NOUN
A queen is a female monarch or a woman married to a king.
EXAMPLE The king and queen ruled together.

question questions questioning questioned
NOUN
1 A question is a sentence which asks for information.
EXAMPLE The class asked a lot of questions.

▣ **Similar word:** inquiry

▶ VERB
2 If you question someone, you ask them questions.
EXAMPLE I questioned her about the trip.

3 If you question something, you express doubts about it.
EXAMPLE No one questioned the doctor's decision.

▣ **Similar words:** challenge, dispute

question mark
question marks
NOUN   **ENGLISH**
A question mark is a punctuation mark used to show that a sentence is a question.
EXAMPLE 'What time is it?' ends in a question mark.

quick quicker quickest
ADJECTIVE
1 Quick means moving or doing things with great speed.
EXAMPLE You'll have to be quick.

2 Quick means lasting only a short time.
EXAMPLE She called in for a quick chat.

quiet quieter quietest
ADJECTIVE
1 Something that is quiet makes very little noise.
EXAMPLE The children were very quiet.

▣ **Similar word:** silent

2 A quiet place, time or situation is calm and peaceful.
EXAMPLE They just wanted a quiet evening at home.

▶ NOUN
3 Quiet is silence.
EXAMPLE Ralph asked for complete quiet.

quit quits quitting quit
VERB
If you quit something, you leave it or stop doing it.
EXAMPLE She's trying to quit smoking.

quite
ADVERB
1 Quite means fairly but not very.
EXAMPLE London is quite a long way away.

2 Quite means completely.
EXAMPLE Our position is quite clear.

quote quotes quoting quoted
VERB
If you quote something that someone has written or said, you repeat their words.
EXAMPLE He quoted straight from the textbook.

Qur'an   **RE**
▣ **Said:** kaw-*rahn*
NOUN
The Qur'an is the holy book of Islam.
EXAMPLE He knew whole passages of the Qur'an by heart.

Qur'an is also spelt Koran.

race races racing raced
NOUN

1 A race is a competition to see who is fastest, for example in running or driving.
EXAMPLE They took part in the 1500 metres race.

2 A race is one of the major groups that human beings can be divided into according to their physical features.
EXAMPLE No one should be criticized because of their race or colour.

▶ VERB

3 If you race, you go quickly or take part in a race.
EXAMPLE She has raced against some of the best in the world.

racial
⬛ Said: *ray-shl*

ADJECTIVE
Racial refers to the different races that people belong to.
EXAMPLE The court heard of a racial attack on a teenage girl.

racism   CITIZENSHIP
⬛ Said: *ray-sizm*

NOUN
Racism is unfair treatment of people because of their race or skin colour.
EXAMPLE Thousands of people joined the march against racism.

rack racks
NOUN
A rack is a piece of equipment for holding things or hanging things on.
EXAMPLE He put his case on the luggage rack.

radical
ADJECTIVE
Something radical is very important or basic.
EXAMPLE He suggested a radical change in the law.

radius radii   MATHS
NOUN
The radius of a circle is the length of a line drawn from the centre to the circumference.
EXAMPLE He drew a circle with a radius of six centimetres.

rage rages raging raged
NOUN

1 Rage is strong, uncontrollable anger.
EXAMPLE The boy could not control his rage.

⬛ Similar words: anger, fury

▶ VERB

2 If something rages, it continues with great force or violence.
EXAMPLE The fire raged for more than four hours.

raid raids raiding raided
VERB
When people raid a place, they enter it by force in order to attack it or look for something.
EXAMPLE The police raided the house and arrested a man.

railway railways
NOUN
A railway is a route along which trains travel.
EXAMPLE The road ran beside a railway.

raise raises raising raised
VERB

1 If you raise something, you make it higher.
EXAMPLE He raised his hand.

2 If you raise your voice, you speak more loudly.
EXAMPLE Anne had to raise her voice to be heard.

3 To raise money for a cause means to get people to donate money towards it.
EXAMPLE The event raised lots of money for local charities.

ranch ranches
NOUN
A ranch is a large farm where cattle or horses are reared, especially in the USA.
EXAMPLE He worked on a cattle ranch.

range ranges ranging ranged
NOUN

1 A range is a number of different things of the same kind.
EXAMPLE A wide range of colours is available.

⬛ Similar words: series, variety

MATHS

2 Range is the difference between the highest and lowest values in a set of numbers; it is a single number.
EXAMPLE The range of years from 35 to 40 is 5.

3 The range of something is the maximum distance over which it can reach things or detect things.
EXAMPLE The missile had a range of 2,000 kilometres.

▶ VERB

4 When a set of things ranges between two points, they vary within these points on a scale.
EXAMPLE Prices range from £35 to £65.

A B C D E F G H I J K L M N O P Q R S T U V W X Y Z

A
B
C
D
E
F
G
H
I
J
K
L
M
N
O
P
Q
R
S
T
U
V
W
X
Y
Z

rank ranks ranking ranked
NOUN

1 Someone's rank is their position or grade in an organization.
EXAMPLE He eventually rose to the rank of captain.

2 A rank is a row of people or things.
EXAMPLE There were several people waiting at the taxi rank.

▶ *PLURAL NOUN*
3 The ranks of a group are its members.
EXAMPLE We welcomed five new members to our ranks.

▶ *VERB*
4 If someone or something is ranked at a particular position, they are at that position on a scale.
EXAMPLE He is ranked among the world's top tennis players.

rap raps rapping rapped
NOUN

1 A rap is a quick knock or blow on something.
EXAMPLE There was a sharp rap on the door.

MUSIC

2 Rap is a type of music in which the words are spoken in a rapid, rhythmic way.
EXAMPLE The rap group reached the top of the charts last week.

▶ *VERB*
3 If you rap something or rap on it, you hit it with a series of quick blows.
EXAMPLE She rapped on Simon's door.

rape rapes raping raped
VERB

1 If someone is raped, they are forced to have sex.
EXAMPLE She identified the man who had raped her.

▶ *NOUN*
2 Rape is the crime of forcing someone to have sex.
EXAMPLE Victims of rape find it hard to recover from what has happened to them.

rapid
ADJECTIVE

Something rapid happens or moves very quickly.
EXAMPLE His breathing became more rapid.

rare rarer rarest
ADJECTIVE

1 Rare means not common.
EXAMPLE There is a rare flower growing in the wood.

2 Meat that is rare is cooked very lightly.
EXAMPLE I prefer my steak rare.

rash rashes
ADJECTIVE

1 If you are rash, you do something without thinking carefully about it.
EXAMPLE Don't do anything rash.

▶ *NOUN*
2 A rash is an area of red spots that appear on your skin.
EXAMPLE I noticed a rash on my leg.

rate rates rating rated
NOUN

1 The rate at which something happens is the speed or frequency with which it happens.
EXAMPLE I am amazed at the rate at which hair grows.

2 A rate is the amount of money that is charged for goods or services.
EXAMPLE The shop offered special rates for students.

▶ *PHRASE*
3 If you say 'at this rate' something will happen, you mean it will happen if things continue in the same way.
EXAMPLE At this rate we'll be lucky to get home before nightfall.

▶ *VERB*
4 If you rate something as good or bad, you consider them to be good or bad.
EXAMPLE He was rated as one of England's top young players.

rather
ADVERB

1 Rather means to a fairly large extent.
EXAMPLE We got along rather well.

▣ **Similar words:** quite, relatively

▶ *PHRASE*
2 If you 'would rather' do something, you would prefer to do it.
EXAMPLE Kids would rather play than study.

ratio ratios
MATHS

▣ **Said:** *ray-shee-o*
NOUN

A ratio is a relationship which shows how many times one thing is bigger than another.
EXAMPLE The ratio of boys to girls in the class is 2 to 1.

rave raves raving raved
VERB

1 If someone raves, they talk in an excited and uncontrolled way.
EXAMPLE He started raving about being treated badly.

2 If you rave about something, you talk about it very enthusiastically.
EXAMPLE Rachel raved about the new foods she ate.

▶ *ADJECTIVE*
3 A rave review is a very enthusiastic one.
EXAMPLE The band's new album has received rave reviews.

▶ *NOUN*
4 A rave is a large dance event with electronic music.
EXAMPLE They went to an all-night rave.

react reacts reacting reacted
VERB

1 When you react to something, you behave in a particular way because of it.
EXAMPLE He reacted badly to the news.

SCIENCE

2 If one substance reacts with another, a chemical change takes place.
EXAMPLE Note down how the acid reacts with the alkali.

reaction reactions

NOUN

1 Your reaction to something is what you feel, say, or do because of it.
EXAMPLE He was surprised at her reaction to his remark.

SCIENCE

2 A reaction is a chemical change that takes place when two substances are put together.
EXAMPLE Observe the chemical reaction carefully.

ready

ADJECTIVE

Something is ready if it has reached the required stage for something or is prepared for something.
EXAMPLE Your glasses will be ready in a fortnight.

reality

NOUN

Reality is the real nature of things, rather than the way someone imagines it.
EXAMPLE In reality, he knew she would not be his girlfriend.

■ Similar words: fact, truth

realize realizes realizing realized

VERB

If you realize something, you become aware of it.
EXAMPLE People don't realize how serious the problem is.

Realize is also spelt realise.

really

ADVERB

1 You use the word really to emphasize a statement.
EXAMPLE It is a really good film.

2 You use the word really when you are talking about the true facts about something.
EXAMPLE What was really going on?

rear rears rearing reared

NOUN

1 The rear of something is the part at the back.
EXAMPLE They left by the door at the rear of the building.

▶ *VERB*

2 To rear children or animals means to bring them up.
EXAMPLE I was reared in east Texas.

3 When a horse rears, it rises up so that its front legs are in the air.
EXAMPLE The horse reared and threw off its rider.

reason reasons

NOUN

The reason for something is the fact or situation that explains why it happens.
EXAMPLE There were good reasons for his action.

■ Similar word: cause

reasonable

ADJECTIVE

1 Reasonable means fair and sensible.
EXAMPLE I'm a reasonable man.

2 A reasonable amount is a fairly large amount.
EXAMPLE There were a reasonable number of people there.

3 Something that is reasonable is fairly good, but not very good.
EXAMPLE The weather was reasonable for October.

rebel rebels rebelling rebelled

NOUN

HISTORY

▣ Said: rebl

1 Rebels are people who fight against a political system or any authority.
EXAMPLE There was fierce fighting between rebels and government forces.

▶ *VERB*

▣ Said: reb-*el*

2 To rebel means to reject society's values.
EXAMPLE I rebelled against everything when I was young.

recall recalls recalling recalled

VERB

When you recall something, you remember it.
EXAMPLE She could not recall ever seeing him before.

receive receives receiving received

VERB

When you receive something, it is sent or given to you.
EXAMPLE I received your letter today.

recent

ADJECTIVE

Something recent happened a short time ago.
EXAMPLE She met an old friend on her recent trip to Chile.

recently

ADVERB

Recently means a short time ago.
EXAMPLE He recently celebrated his eightieth birthday.

reckon reckons reckoning reckoned

VERB

If you reckon that something is true, you think it is true.
EXAMPLE I reckon we'll be there by midnight.

recognize recognizes recognizing recognized

VERB

1 If you recognize someone, you realize that you know who they are.
EXAMPLE The shopkeeper recognized me at once.

■ Similar words: identify, know

2 If you recognize something, you accept that it exists or that it is true.
EXAMPLE They have been slow to recognize the problem.

Recognize is also spelt recognise.

recommend recommends recommending recommended

VERB

If you recommend something to someone, you suggest that they try it.
EXAMPLE He recommended the book to all his friends.

A B C D E F G H I J K L M N O P Q  R  S T U  V W X Y Z

record records recording recorded
NOUN

☐ **Said:** re-cord

1 A record is a written account of something.
EXAMPLE The doctor looked at his medical records.

▤ **Similar words:** document, file, register

MUSIC

2 A record is a round, flat piece of plastic on which music has been recorded.
EXAMPLE He bought me one of my favourite records.

3 A record is an achievement which is the best of its type.
EXAMPLE He broke the world record for the high jump.

4 Your record is what is known about your achievements or past activities.
EXAMPLE He had a criminal record.

▶ *VERB*

☐ **Said:** ri-cord

5 If you record information, you write it down so that it can be referred to later.
EXAMPLE He recorded everything in his diary.

▤ **Similar words:** note, register, write down

MUSIC

6 When music or speech is recorded, it is put on tape, record or CD.
EXAMPLE The album was recorded in Ireland.

recover recovers recovering recovered
VERB

1 If you recover from an illness or a bad experience, you get well again or stop being upset by it.
EXAMPLE She is now recovering in hospital.

2 If you recover a lost object or your ability to do something, you get it back.
EXAMPLE Most of the goods were never recovered.

recovery recoveries
NOUN

If a sick person makes a recovery, they become well again.
EXAMPLE He made a remarkable recovery from the accident.

reduce reduces reducing reduced
VERB

To reduce something means to make it smaller in size or amount.
EXAMPLE Exercise reduces the risk of heart disease.

▤ **Similar word:** cut

reduction reductions
NOUN

When there is a reduction in something, it is made smaller.
EXAMPLE The company made dramatic reductions in staff.

refer refers referring referred
VERB

1 If you refer to someone or something, you mention them or describe them.
EXAMPLE He never once referred to his recent troubles.

2 If you refer to a book or other source of information, you look at it in order to find something out.
EXAMPLE He had to keep referring to his textbook.

3 If a person or problem is referred to another person, that person is asked to deal with them.
EXAMPLE I was referred to an ear specialist.

reference references
NOUN

1 A reference to something is a mention of it.
EXAMPLE He made no reference to his old girlfriend.

2 If someone gives you a reference when you apply for a job, they write a letter about your abilities.
EXAMPLE I've given you a marvellous reference.

reflect reflects reflecting reflected
VERB

When something is reflected in a mirror or in water, you can see its image there.
EXAMPLE The boy's grin was reflected in the mirror.

reflection reflection
NOUN

SCIENCE

1 Reflection is when light or sound bounces off an object.
EXAMPLE They observed the reflection of light from the moon.

2 A reflection is an image in a mirror or water.
EXAMPLE He looked at his reflection in the mirror.

reflex angle reflex angles
NOUN

MATHS

A reflex angle is an angle which measures between 180 and 360 degrees.
EXAMPLE The reflex angle measured 240 degrees.

reform reforms
NOUN

HISTORY

A reform is a major change to a law or an institution.
EXAMPLE The health service reforms did not please everyone.

Reformation
NOUN

HISTORY

The Reformation was a sixteenth-century movement against the Catholic church, resulting in the formation of the Protestant church.
EXAMPLE Martin Luther's criticism of the Catholic church began the Reformation.

refraction
NOUN

SCIENCE

Refraction is the bending of light as it passes from one material into another.
EXAMPLE The straw in the glass of lemonade looked bent due to refraction.

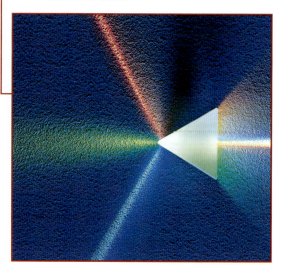

refugee refugees
NOUN
Refugees are people who have been forced to leave their country and live elsewhere.
EXAMPLE Thousands of refugees made their way to the border.

refuse refuses refusing refused
VERB
1 If you refuse to do something, you say or decide firmly that you will not do it.
EXAMPLE He refused to comment after the trial.
2 If you refuse something, you do not allow it or do not accept it.
EXAMPLE He offered me another drink, which I refused.

regard regards regarding regarded
VERB
1 If you regard something in a particular way, you think of it in that way.
EXAMPLE We all regard him as a friend.
▸ PHRASES
2 'Regarding', 'as regards', 'with regard to' and 'in regard to' are all used to indicate what you are referring to.
EXAMPLE As regards my birthday, it will be held in the club.
▸ NOUN
3 Regards means friendly feelings.
EXAMPLE Give my regards to your husband.

region regions
NOUN
GEOGRAPHY
1 A region is a large area of land.
EXAMPLE He was born in a remote region of the country.
Similar words: area, district, territory
▸ PHRASE
2 'In the region of' means roughly.
EXAMPLE The scheme will cost in the region of six million pounds.

register registers registering registered
NOUN
1 A register is a list or record.
EXAMPLE The teacher took the class register to the office.
▸ VERB
2 When something is registered, it is recorded on a list.
EXAMPLE The car was registered in my name.

regret regrets regretting regretted
VERB
1 If you regret something, you wish that it had not happened.
EXAMPLE I hurt him, and I've regretted it ever since.
▸ NOUN
2 Regret is a feeling of sadness or disappointment.
EXAMPLE He feels deep regret about his friend's death.

regular regulars
ADJECTIVE
1 Regular events happen at equal or frequent intervals.
EXAMPLE I try to take regular exercise.
Similar words: even, steady
2 Regular describes something having a well-balanced appearance.
EXAMPLE They were asked to construct a regular geometrical shape.
▸ NOUN
3 People who go to a place often are known as its regulars.
EXAMPLE He knew all the regulars at his local pub.

regulation regulations
NOUN
Regulations are rules.
EXAMPLE The firm told the workers about the new safety regulations.

reign reigns reigning reigned HISTORY
Said: rain
VERB
1 When a king or queen reigns, he or she is the leader of the country.
EXAMPLE Henry II reigned from 1154 to 1189.
▸ NOUN
2 The reign of a king or queen is the period when they are on the throne.
EXAMPLE He was born during the reign of Queen Anne.

reject rejects rejecting rejected
VERB
1 If you reject a proposal or request, you refuse to agree to it.
EXAMPLE The president was correct to reject the offer.
Similar words: decline, refuse, turn down
2 If you are rejected by someone, they tell you that they do not want you.
EXAMPLE As a youngster he was rejected by Leeds United.

relate relates relating related
VERB
1 If you relate to someone, you understand their thoughts and feelings.
EXAMPLE The new teacher related well to the children.
2 If you relate a story, you tell it.
EXAMPLE He related the tale of an Irish drummer-boy.
3 If two things are related, they are connected in some way.
EXAMPLE Crime and poverty are closely related.
4 People who are related belong to the same family.
EXAMPLE We have the same name but we're not related.

relation relations
NOUN
1 If there is a relation between two things, they are connected in some way.
EXAMPLE This book bears no relation to his previous ones.
2 Relations between people are their feelings and behaviour towards each other.
EXAMPLE Relations between the couple had not improved.
3 Your relations are the members of your family.
EXAMPLE We visit our relations at Christmas.

relationship relationships
NOUN

1 The relationship between two people or groups is the way they feel and behave towards each other.
EXAMPLE Their relationship later became strained.

2 A relationship is a close friendship, especially one involving romantic or sexual feelings.
EXAMPLE She is having a relationship with someone else.

3 The relationship between two things is the way in which they are connected.
EXAMPLE There is a clear relationship between poor diet and cancer.

relative relatives
ADJECTIVE

1 You use the word relative when comparing the size or quality of two or more things.
EXAMPLE The commentator compared the relative strengths of the English and German forwards.

▶ *NOUN*

2 Your relatives are the members of your family.
EXAMPLE Get a relative to look after the children.

relatively
ADVERB

Relatively means fairly or quite.
EXAMPLE It's relatively easy.

relax relaxes relaxing relaxed
VERB

1 If you relax, you become calm and less tense.
EXAMPLE I ought to relax and stop worrying.

☐ **Similar words:** rest, take it easy

2 If you relax a rule, you make it less strict.
EXAMPLE He relaxed the rules concerning school uniform.

release releases releasing released
VERB

1 Release means to set free.
EXAMPLE He was released from prison last year.

2 If you release something, you stop holding it.
EXAMPLE Wade released the hand brake.

3 When a new record, film or document is released, it becomes available for people to buy, see or read.
EXAMPLE He is releasing an album of love songs.

▶ *NOUN*

4 The release of someone or something is the act of setting them free or making them available.
EXAMPLE She died three days after her release from hospital.

reliable
ADJECTIVE

Reliable people, things and information can be trusted to do what you want or to be correct.
EXAMPLE Japanese cars are so reliable.

relief
NOUN

1 If you feel relief, you feel glad because something unpleasant is over.
EXAMPLE I breathed a sigh of relief when he left.

2 If something provides relief, it stops or reduces the pain.
EXAMPLE The new pills brought some relief from the pain.

relief map relief maps **GEOGRAPHY**
NOUN

A relief map is a map showing the shape of the hills and valleys.

EXAMPLE The relief map showed the height of the mountains.

religion religions **RE**
NOUN

1 Religion is belief in a god or gods.
EXAMPLE The bishop gave a talk about the importance of religion.

2 A religion is a particular set of religious beliefs.
EXAMPLE The teachings of Jesus are at the heart of the Christian religion.

religious **RE**
ADJECTIVE

1 Religious means to do with religion.
EXAMPLE They had different religious beliefs.

2 Someone who is religious has a strong belief in a god or gods.
EXAMPLE He is a very religious man.

reluctant
ADJECTIVE

If you are reluctant to do something, you do not want to do it.
EXAMPLE Mr Spero was reluctant to ask for help.

rely relies relying relied
VERB

1 If you rely on someone or something, you need them in order to do something.
EXAMPLE She has to rely on money from her parents.

2 If you can rely on someone to do something, you can trust them to do it.
EXAMPLE I know I can rely on you to sort it out.

remain remains remaining remained
VERB

1 If you remain in a particular place or state, you do not move from that place or do not change from that state.
EXAMPLE The three men remained silent.

2 Something that remains continues to exist.
EXAMPLE Other dangers still remain.

▶ *PLURAL NOUN*

3 The remains of something are the parts that are left after a lot of it has been destroyed.
EXAMPLE The remains of the castle are impressive.

remark remarks remarking remarked
VERB

1 If you remark on something, you say something about it.
EXAMPLE Everyone remarked on her new hairstyle.

▶ *NOUN*

2 A remark is something that you say about a thing.
EXAMPLE His remarks were repeated in all the papers.

A B C D E F G H I J K L M N O P Q R S T U V W X Y Z

remarkable
ADJECTIVE
Remarkable means impressive and unexpected.
EXAMPLE Swimming the English Channel is a remarkable achievement.

■ **Similar words:** extraordinary, outstanding, wonderful

remember remembers remembering remembered
VERB
1 If you remember something from the past, you still have an idea of them.
EXAMPLE I remember her very well.

■ **Similar word:** recall

2 If you remember to do something, you do it when you planned to.
EXAMPLE Did you remember to bring the camera?

remind reminds reminding reminded
VERB
1 If someone reminds you of a fact, they say something to make you think about it.
EXAMPLE Remind me to buy a bottle of wine, will you?

2 If someone reminds you of another person, they are similar to that person.
EXAMPLE She reminds me of my grandmother.

remote remoter remotest
ADJECTIVE
1 Remote means far away from where most people live.
EXAMPLE The buses do not go to villages in remote areas.

2 Remote means unlikely.
EXAMPLE The chances of the victims surviving are pretty remote.

remove removes removing removed
VERB
If you remove something from a place, you take it off or away.
EXAMPLE He removed his jacket.

renew renews renewing renewed
VERB
1 If you renew an activity or relationship, you begin it again.
EXAMPLE After the war the two men renewed their friendship.

2 If you renew a licence or a book, you extend the period of time for which it can be used.
EXAMPLE His contract is not being renewed.

rent rents renting rented
VERB
1 If you rent something, you pay the owner a regular sum of money in exchange for being able to use it.
EXAMPLE He sold his house and rented a flat.

2 If you rent something to someone, or if you rent it out, you let them use it in exchange for a regular payment.
EXAMPLE She rented out rooms to students.

▶ NOUN
3 Rent is the amount of money that you pay regularly for the use of land or accommodation.
EXAMPLE How much rent do you pay?

repair repairs repairing repaired
NOUN
1 A repair is something that you do to mend something that is damaged.
EXAMPLE She does her own repairs on the car.

▶ VERB
2 If you repair something that is damaged, you mend it.
EXAMPLE He moved out while the roof was being repaired.

repeat repeats repeating repeated
VERB
1 If you repeat something, you say, write or do it again.
EXAMPLE He kept repeating the question.

▶ NOUN
2 A repeat is something which is done again or happens again.
EXAMPLE There are too many repeats on TV.

replace replaces replacing replaced
VERB
1 When one thing replaces another, the first thing takes the place of the second.
EXAMPLE He replaced the broken exhaust pipe with a new one.

2 If you replace something, you put it back where it was before.
EXAMPLE He replaced the book on the shelf.

replacement replacements
NOUN
The replacement for something is the thing that takes their place.
EXAMPLE Taylor was Adams's replacement in the team.

reply replies replying replied
VERB
1 If you reply to something, you say or write something as an answer to it.
EXAMPLE I've not replied to Lee's letter yet.

▶ NOUN
2 A reply is what you say or write when you answer someone.
EXAMPLE I called her name but there was no reply.

report reports reporting reported
VERB
1 If you report that something has happened, you tell someone about it.
EXAMPLE I have nothing else to report.

2 If you report someone, you make an official complaint about them.
EXAMPLE His ex-wife reported him to the police.

▶ NOUN
3 A report is an account of an event or situation.
EXAMPLE The news report described the plane crash.

■ **Similar words:** account, description

reporter reporters
NOUN
A reporter is someone who writes news articles or broadcasts news reports.
EXAMPLE She is a sports reporter on television.

represent represents representing represented
VERB
1 If someone represents you, they act on your behalf.
EXAMPLE The lawyer representing the victims then spoke.

2 If a sign or symbol represents something, it is accepted as meaning that thing.
EXAMPLE The red lines on the map represent main roads.

representative representatives
CITIZENSHIP
NOUN
A representative is a person who acts on behalf of another person or group of people.
EXAMPLE The trade union representatives met with the manager.

republic republics
CITIZENSHIP
NOUN
A republic is a country which has a president rather than a king or queen.
EXAMPLE France is a republic.

reputation reputations
NOUN
The reputation of something or someone is the opinion that people have of them.
EXAMPLE The college had a good reputation.

request requests requesting requested
VERB
1 If you request something, you ask for it politely or formally.
EXAMPLE She had requested that the door be left open.

▶ NOUN
2 If you make a request for something, you ask for it.
EXAMPLE He ignored my request to put out his cigarette.

require requires requiring required
VERB
If you require something, you need it.
EXAMPLE What qualifications are required?

requirement requirements
NOUN
A requirement is something that you must have or must do.
EXAMPLE Maths is no longer a requirement for many courses.

rescue rescues rescuing rescued
VERB
1 If you rescue someone, you save them from a dangerous or unpleasant situation.
EXAMPLE He rescued her from a horrible life.

▶ NOUN
2 Rescue is the act of saving someone from a dangerous or unpleasant situation.
EXAMPLE The attempted rescue failed miserably.

research researches researching researched
NOUN
1 Research is work that tries to discover facts about something.
EXAMPLE The group will publish its research in two weeks.

▶ VERB
2 To research something is to try to discover facts about it.
EXAMPLE Jay researched the topic on the Internet.

resent resents resenting resented
VERB
If you resent something, you feel bitter and angry about it.
EXAMPLE I resent the way she treats me like a child.

reserve reserves reserving reserved
VERB
1 If something is reserved for a particular person or purpose, it is kept specially for that person or purpose.
EXAMPLE A double room had been reserved for him.

▪ Similar words: put by, save, set aside

▶ NOUN
2 A reserve is a supply of something for future use.
EXAMPLE The country's gold reserves are kept in the Bank of England.

resident residents
NOUN
The residents of a house or area are the people who live there.
EXAMPLE They put up new traffic lights after complaints by local residents.

resign resigns resigning resigned
VERB
1 If you resign from a job, you formally announce that you are leaving it.
EXAMPLE He resigned as chairman a week later.

2 If you resign yourself to an unpleasant situation, you accept it.
EXAMPLE He resigned himself to being unemployed.

resignation resignations
NOUN
A resignation is a formal statement that you plan to leave your job.
EXAMPLE The manager has accepted my resignation.

resist resists resisting resisted
VERB
1 If you resist something, you refuse to accept it and try to prevent it.
EXAMPLE He resisted demands for a public inquiry.

▪ Similar words: fight, oppose

2 If you resist doing something, you stop yourself from doing it.
EXAMPLE She cannot resist giving him advice.

resistance
NOUN

1 Resistance to something is a refusal to accept it.
EXAMPLE His stubborn resistance to anything new made him unpopular at work.

2 Resistance to an attack consists of fighting back.
EXAMPLE The demonstrators offered no resistance.

resolution resolutions
NOUN

1 Resolution is determination.
EXAMPLE She acted with great resolution.

2 If you make a resolution, you decide to try very hard to do something.
EXAMPLE She made a resolution to get fit.

3 The resolution of a problem is the solving of it.
EXAMPLE They hoped for a peaceful resolution to the crisis.

resolve resolves resolving resolved
VERB

1 If you resolve a problem, you find a solution to it.
EXAMPLE We must find a way of resolving these problems.

2 If you resolve to do something, you make a firm decision to do it.
EXAMPLE He resolved to wait until she called him.

resort resorts resorting resorted
VERB

1 If you resort to a course of action, you do it.
EXAMPLE People who resort to drugs sometimes end up in jail.

▸ *NOUN*
2 A resort is a place where people spend their holidays.
EXAMPLE They went to a ski resort for their holiday.

▸ *PHRASE*
3 If you do something 'as a last resort', you do it because you can find no other way of solving a problem.
EXAMPLE As a last resort, they can sleep here.

resource resources
NOUN

1 The resources of an organization or person are the money or skills they have.
EXAMPLE They used all their resources to solve the problem.

GEOGRAPHY

2 Resources are a country's source of wealth, such as land, oil and people.
EXAMPLE The United States has a wide variety of resources.

respect respects respecting respected
VERB

1 If you respect someone, you have a good opinion of their character or ideas.
EXAMPLE He needs the advice of people he respects.

2 If you respect someone's rights or wishes, you avoid doing things that they would dislike or regard as wrong.
EXAMPLE I respected her wishes and remained silent.

▸ *NOUN*
3 If you have respect for someone, you have a good opinion of their character or ideas.
EXAMPLE I have great respect for him as a person.

▸ *PHRASE*
4 You can say 'in this respect' and 'in many respects' to show that what you are saying applies to a particular thing or number of things.
EXAMPLE In many respects, nothing has changed.

respiration
NOUN

SCIENCE

Respiration is the process of breathing.
EXAMPLE When you exercise your rate of respiration increases.

respond responds responding responded
VERB

When you respond to something, you react to it by doing or saying something.
EXAMPLE Please respond to this letter immediately.

response responses
NOUN

Your response to something is your reaction or reply to it.
EXAMPLE There has been no response to his request.

responsibility responsibilities
NOUN

CITIZENSHIP

1 A responsibility is something which you are expected or trusted to do.
EXAMPLE Citizens have a responsibility to keep the law of the land.

2 If you accept responsibility for something, you agree that you were to blame for it.
EXAMPLE Jasmine accepted responsibility for the accident.

responsible
ADJECTIVE

1 If you are responsible for something that has happened, it is your fault.
EXAMPLE Who's responsible for this mess?

▣ **Similar word:** liable

2 If you are responsible for something, it is your duty to deal with it.
EXAMPLE The children were responsible for cleaning their own rooms.

restaurant restaurants

▣ **Said:** *rest*-ront
NOUN
A restaurant is a place where you can buy and eat a meal.
EXAMPLE They celebrated her birthday at an Italian restaurant.

restore restores restoring restored
VERB

To restore something means to cause it to exist again or to return to its previous state.
EXAMPLE The army was brought in to restore peace.

restrict restricts restricting restricted
VERB

1 If you restrict something, you put a limit on it.
EXAMPLE **They put up parking prices to restrict the number of cars entering the city.**

2 To restrict someone's movements or actions means to prevent them from moving or acting freely.
EXAMPLE **His injury restricts his movement.**

restriction restrictions
NOUN

A restriction is a rule or situation that limits what you can do.
EXAMPLE **We need greater restrictions on tobacco advertising.**

result results resulting resulted
NOUN

1 The result of an action is the situation that is caused by it.
EXAMPLE **The disaster was the result of a single careless act.**

Similar words: consequence, outcome

2 The result of a contest, calculation or exam is the final score, figures or marks at the end of it.
EXAMPLE **The exam results were posted on the board.**

SCIENCE

3 The results of an experiment are the measurements or findings.
EXAMPLE **He listed the results in a table.**

▸ VERB

4 If something results in a particular event, it causes that event to happen.
EXAMPLE **Half of all road accidents result in head injuries.**

resume resumes resuming resumed
Said: riz-*yoom*

VERB

If you resume an activity, you begin it again.
EXAMPLE **The search for the missing teenager resumed early today.**

retain retains retaining retained
VERB

To retain something means to keep it.
EXAMPLE **The athlete retained his world title.**

retire retires retiring retired
VERB

When older people retire, they leave their job and stop working.
EXAMPLE **Gladys retired at the age of 68.**

retirement
NOUN

Retirement is the time when someone retires, or the period after they have retired.
EXAMPLE **She bought a house for her retirement.**

retreat retreats retreating retreated
VERB

To retreat means to move away from something.
EXAMPLE **The dog retreated to the kitchen.**

return returns returning returned
VERB

1 To return means to go back to a place or to a particular condition.
EXAMPLE **When do you plan to return to Britain?**

2 If you return something to someone, you give it back to them.
EXAMPLE **He returned her passport.**

▸ NOUN

3 Your return is your arrival back at a place or at a former condition.
EXAMPLE **He has been ill since his return from Berlin.**

▸ PHRASE

4 If you do something 'in return' for what someone has done for you, you do it because of what they did.
EXAMPLE **There's little I can do for him in return.**

reveal reveals revealing revealed
VERB

If you reveal something, you uncover it.
EXAMPLE **They revealed all the details of the plan.**

reverse reverses reversing reversed
VERB

1 When someone reverses a process or decision, they change it to its opposite.
EXAMPLE **They won't reverse the decision to increase prices.**

2 When you reverse a car, you drive it backwards.
EXAMPLE **She reversed into the garage.**

▸ NOUN

3 The reverse is the opposite of what has been said or done.
EXAMPLE **It's not difficult – quite the reverse.**

review reviews reviewing reviewed
NOUN

1 A review is an article or a talk on television or radio, giving an opinion of a new book, play or film.
EXAMPLE **The review praised her new book.**

▸ VERB

2 When someone reviews a book, play or film, they give an account expressing their opinion of it.
EXAMPLE **Both films will be reviewed next week.**

3 If you review a situation or system, you examine it to see whether changes are needed.
EXAMPLE **The government will review the situation in June.**

revolution revolutions
HISTORY
NOUN

1 A revolution is an attempt by a large group of people to change their country's political system, using force.
EXAMPLE **She wrote a history of the French Revolution.**

2 A revolution is an important change in an area of human activity.
EXAMPLE **The Industrial Revolution transformed the nature of work.**

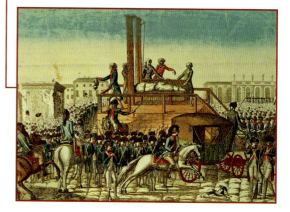

revolutionary revolutionaries
ADJECTIVE
1 Revolutionary describes anything involving great changes.
EXAMPLE He discovered a revolutionary new cure for backache.

▸ NOUN   **HISTORY**
2 A revolutionary is a person who takes part in a revolution.
EXAMPLE The revolutionaries soon surrendered.

reward rewards rewarding rewarded
NOUN
1 A reward is something you are given because you have done something good.
EXAMPLE She received a reward for bravery.

▸ VERB
2 If you reward someone, you give them a reward.
EXAMPLE He was rewarded with a smile.

rhyme rhymes rhyming rhymed   **ENGLISH**
VERB
If two words rhyme they have a similar sound.
EXAMPLE 'Toy' rhymes with 'boy'.

rhythm rhythms   **MUSIC**
Said: ri-thum

NOUN
Rhythm is a regular pattern of sound.
EXAMPLE The rhythm was perfect for dancing.

rib ribs
NOUN
Your ribs are the curved bones that go from your spine to your chest.
EXAMPLE He was suffering from a broken rib.

rig rigs rigging rigged
VERB
1 If someone rigs a contest, they dishonestly arrange for a particular person to succeed.
EXAMPLE She accused her opponents of rigging the vote.

▸ NOUN
2 A rig is a large structure used for extracting oil or gas from the ground or the sea bed.
EXAMPLE He worked on an oil rig.

right rights
NOUN
1 Right is used to refer to behaviour which is morally correct.
EXAMPLE At least he knew right from wrong.

2 If you have a right to do something, you are entitled to do it.
EXAMPLE People have the right to read whatever they want.

▸ PLURAL NOUN   **CITIZENSHIP**
3 Rights are how we may expect to be treated as members of a community.
EXAMPLE I have certain rights as a British citizen.

▸ ADJECTIVE OR ADVERB
4 Right means correct.
EXAMPLE That clock never tells the right time.

5 Right means on or towards the right of something.
EXAMPLE Turn right at the corner.

▸ ADJECTIVE
6 Right means the best or most suitable.
EXAMPLE She's the right person for the job.

▣ Similar words: proper, suitable

▸ ADVERB
7 Saying right emphasizes the exact position or time of something.
EXAMPLE I'm right here.

right angle right angles   **MATHS**
NOUN
A right angle is an angle which measures 90 degrees.
EXAMPLE A square has four right angles.

riot riots rioting rioted
NOUN
1 When there is a riot, a crowd of people behave violently in a public place.
EXAMPLE Several policemen were injured in the riots.

▸ VERB
2 To riot is to behave violently in a public place.
EXAMPLE They rioted in protest against the government.

risk risks risking risked
NOUN
1 Risk means a possibility of something bad happening.
EXAMPLE There's a small risk that he may be injured.

▸ VERB
2 If you risk something, you take a chance on it.
EXAMPLE If he doesn't play today, he risks losing his place in the team.

rival rivals
NOUN
Someone's rival is the person they are competing with.
EXAMPLE He is well ahead of his nearest rival.

▣ Similar word: opponent

role roles
NOUN
1 The role of someone is their position or function in a situation.
EXAMPLE He played a major role in getting the two sides to meet.

DRAMA
2 An actor's role is the character that he or she plays.
EXAMPLE He gave her a leading role in his film.

romantic
ADJECTIVE
Romantic means connected with love, especially intense or pure love.
EXAMPLE He arranged a romantic dinner for two.

root roots
NOUN
1 The roots of a thing are the parts that grow underground.
EXAMPLE He tripped over the roots of an apple tree.

R

A B C D E F G H I J K L M N O P Q R S T U V W X Y Z

2 You can refer to the place or culture that you come from as your roots.
EXAMPLE I am proud of my Brazilian roots.

3 The root of a problem is the thing that caused it.
EXAMPLE We got to the root of the problem.

rough rougher roughest
📖 Said: ruff

ADJECTIVE

1 Rough means uneven and not smooth.
EXAMPLE His hands were hard and rough

2 Rough means using too much force.
EXAMPLE Don't be so rough or you'll break it.

3 Rough means dangerous or violent.
EXAMPLE They lived in a rough part of town.

4 Rough means approximate.
EXAMPLE At a rough guess, it is five miles away.

routine routines

ADJECTIVE

1 Routine activities are done regularly.
EXAMPLE He had some routine medical tests.

▸ *NOUN*

2 Routine is the usual way or order in which you do things.
EXAMPLE Their daily routine included a three-mile walk.

row rows rowing rowed
📖 Said: rhymes with *snow*

NOUN

1 A row of people or things is several of them arranged in a line.
EXAMPLE He approached the row of cottages.

▸ *VERB*

2 When you row a boat, you use oars to make it move through the water.
EXAMPLE The boatman refused to row him back.

row rows rowing rowed
📖 Said: rhymes with *now*

NOUN

1 A row is a serious argument.
EXAMPLE We had a terrible row about money.

2 A row is a big and ugly noise.
EXAMPLE Our little van made an awful row.

▸ *VERB*

3 If people row, they have a noisy argument.
EXAMPLE He often rowed with his girlfriend.

royal
HISTORY

ADJECTIVE

Royal means belonging to or involving a queen, a king or a member of their family.
EXAMPLE Do you like the royal family?

ruin ruins ruining ruined

VERB

1 If you ruin something, you destroy or spoil it completely.
EXAMPLE He has ruined his chances of ever being her friend.

▸ *NOUN*

2 A ruin or the ruins of something refers to the parts that are left after it has been badly damaged.
EXAMPLE It was splendid once, but it is a ruin now.

rule rules ruling ruled

NOUN

1 Rules are instructions which tell you what you are allowed to do.
EXAMPLE The rules of cricket are many and complex.

📗 Similar words: law, regulation

▸ *VERB*   HISTORY

2 To rule means to control the affairs of a country.
EXAMPLE In 1998 Britain was ruled by a Labour government.

▸ *PHRASE*

3 'As a rule' means usually or generally.
EXAMPLE As a rule, she eats dinner with us.

4 If you 'rule out' an idea or course of action, you reject it.
EXAMPLE Murder cannot be ruled out.

rumour rumours

NOUN

A rumour is a piece of information that people are talking about, which may or may not be true.
EXAMPLE There are rumours that he is about to resign.

📗 Similar words: gossip, story

rural
GEOGRAPHY

ADJECTIVE

Rural means to do with the countryside.
EXAMPLE Rural areas can be quite cut off from public services.

rush rushes rushing rushed

VERB

1 If you rush somewhere you go there quickly.
EXAMPLE She was rushed to hospital in an ambulance.

2 If you rush something you do it too quickly.
EXAMPLE Don't rush your homework.

▸ *NOUN*

3 A rush is a situation in which you need to go somewhere or do something very quickly.
EXAMPLE It was a real rush to get here on time.

Russian Russians

ADJECTIVE

1 Russian means to do with Russia.
EXAMPLE The Russian Revolution was in 1917.

▸ *NOUN*

2 A Russian is someone who comes from Russia.
EXAMPLE Russians are proud of their country.

3 Russian is the main language spoken in Russia.
EXAMPLE Gail studied Russian at university.

rust

NOUN

Rust is a brown substance that forms on iron or steel when it comes into contact with water.
EXAMPLE The car was covered in rust.

Ss Ss Ss

sacrifice · sacrifices sacrificing sacrificed
Said: *sak-riff-ice*

VERB
If you sacrifice something valuable or important, you give it up.
EXAMPLE He sacrificed his marriage for his career.

safety
NOUN
Safety is the state of being free from harm or danger.
EXAMPLE Wear a seatbelt for your own safety.

saint · saints
RE
NOUN
A saint is a person who has been honoured by the Christian church because of their holy life.
EXAMPLE The pilgrims entered the shrine of the saint.

salary · salaries
NOUN
A salary is a regular monthly payment to an employee.
EXAMPLE She earns a huge salary.

salt · salts
SCIENCE
NOUN
A salt is a substance formed when an acid reacts with a base.
EXAMPLE The reaction between the acid and base formed a salt.

satellite · satellites
NOUN
1 A satellite is a spacecraft sent into orbit around the Earth.
EXAMPLE The satellite gathered information about the atmosphere of the Earth.
SCIENCE
2 A satellite is an object in space which moves around a planet or star.
EXAMPLE The Earth is a satellite of the sun.

satire · satires
ENGLISH
NOUN
A satire is a piece of writing intended to poke fun at something.
EXAMPLE The story is a satire on political life.

sauce · sauces
NOUN
Sauce is a liquid eaten with food to give it more flavour.
EXAMPLE John likes tomato sauce with his pasta.

scale · scales
NOUN
1 The scale of something is its size or extent.
EXAMPLE The aid programme is small in scale.

2 The scale of a map or model is the relationship between the size of something in the map or model and its size in the real world.
EXAMPLE The plan had a scale of 1:10,000.
MUSIC

3 A scale is a series of notes that goes up or down.
EXAMPLE The piano piece used only three notes in the scale.

▸ *PLURAL NOUN*
4 Scales are a piece of equipment used for weighing things or people.
EXAMPLE I step on the scales every morning.

scan · scans scanning scanned
VERB
1 If you scan something, you look at all of it carefully.
EXAMPLE I scanned the advertisements in the newspaper.

2 If a machine scans something, it examines it with a beam of light or X-rays.
EXAMPLE Our luggage was scanned at the airport.

▸ *NOUN*
3 A scan is an examination of part of the body with X-ray or laser equipment.
EXAMPLE He had a brain scan after the accident.

scene · scenes
NOUN
DRAMA
1 A scene is part of a play or film in which a series of events happen in one place.
EXAMPLE I enjoyed the opening scenes of the play best.

2 A scene is an area of activity.
EXAMPLE Manchester is famous for its music scene.

schedule · schedules
Said: *shed-yool*

NOUN
A schedule is a plan which gives a list of events or tasks, together with the times at which each thing should be done.
EXAMPLE I have a full schedule this week.

A B C D E F G H I J K L M N O P Q R S T U V W X Y Z

139

A B C D E F G H I J K L M N O P Q R **S** T U V W X Y Z

science sciences   SCIENCE
NOUN
Science is the study of the nature; also the knowledge obtained from this study.
EXAMPLE She has a great interest in science.

scientist scientists
NOUN
A scientist is someone who has studied science and does work connected with it.
EXAMPLE Scientists are working on a cure for cancer.

Scottish
ADJECTIVE
Scottish means to do with Scotland.
EXAMPLE He lived in the Scottish highlands.

screen screens screening screened
NOUN
1 A screen is a flat vertical surface on which a picture is shown.
EXAMPLE The film was shown on a large screen.

2 A screen is a panel used to separate different parts of a room or to protect something.
EXAMPLE There was a screen around his bed.

scripture scriptures   RE
NOUN
Scripture is the sacred writings of a religion.
EXAMPLE The Bible is the Christian scripture.

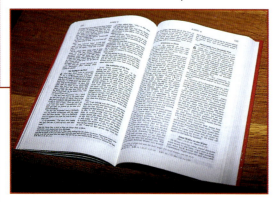

sculpture sculptures   ART
NOUN
1 A sculpture is a work of art made by carving or shaping stone, clay or other materials.
EXAMPLE She made a sculpture of a fox.

2 Sculpture is the art of making sculptures.
EXAMPLE She went to a sculpture class every Saturday.

seal seals sealing sealed
1 A seal is a piece of wax or another means of closing a container securely.
EXAMPLE The seal of the carton was broken.

2 A seal is a large animal which lives partly on land and partly in the sea.
EXAMPLE They spotted several seals by the rocks.

▶ VERB
3 If you seal an opening, you cover it securely.
EXAMPLE She sealed the jar to keep the food fresh.

search searches searching searched
VERB
1 If you search for something, you look for it in several places.

EXAMPLE Police are searching for a missing child.

▶ NOUN
2 A search is an attempt to find something.
EXAMPLE I found my purse after a long search.

search engine search engines   ICT
NOUN
A search engine is a program which looks up information on the computer or the Internet.
EXAMPLE The search engine allowed him to find the information very quickly.

season seasons seasoning seasoned
NOUN
1 The seasons are spring, summer, autumn and winter.
EXAMPLE Autumn is my favourite season.

2 A season is a period of the year when something usually happens.
EXAMPLE I hate the football season.

▶ VERB
3 If you season food, you add salt, pepper, herbs or spices to it.
EXAMPLE The chef seasoned the dish with parsley.

secret secrets
ADJECTIVE
1 Something that is secret is told to only a small number of people.
EXAMPLE The boys held a secret meeting.

▶ NOUN
2 A secret is a fact told to only a small number of people.
EXAMPLE I'll tell you my plan if you can keep it a secret.

secretary secretaries
NOUN
A secretary is a person employed by an organization to keep records and do office work.
EXAMPLE Ask the secretary to arrange an appointment.

section sections
NOUN
A section of something is one of the parts it is divided into.
EXAMPLE The new section of the motorway will open soon.

secure
ADJECTIVE
1 If a place is secure, it is tightly locked or well protected.
EXAMPLE We will make our house as secure as possible.

2 If an object is secure, it is firmly fixed in place.
EXAMPLE These shelves seem quite secure.

3 If you feel secure, you feel safe and confident.
EXAMPLE She felt secure when she was with him.

sensible
ADJECTIVE
Sensible means showing good sense and judgement.
EXAMPLE It would be sensible to leave.

sensitive
ADJECTIVE
1 If you are sensitive to other people's feelings, you understand them.
EXAMPLE He was always a sensitive and caring man.

2 If you are sensitive about something, you are easily upset about it.
EXAMPLE He was sensitive about his height.

sentence sentences   ENGLISH
NOUN
1 A sentence is a group of words which makes a statement, question or command.
EXAMPLE Try to write using complete sentences.

Sentences begin with a capital letter, and end with a full stop, a question mark or an exclamation mark: 'The child was asleep.'

CITIZENSHIP
2 In a law court, a sentence is a punishment given to someone who has been found guilty.
EXAMPLE He was given a prison sentence for robbery.

separate separates separating separated
ADJECTIVE
1 If something is separate from something else, the two things are not connected.
EXAMPLE My brother and I have separate rooms.

▶ VERB
2 To separate people or things means to cause them to be apart from each other.
EXAMPLE I separated the girls for the rest of the lesson.

sequence sequences
NOUN
The sequence is the order in which things are arranged.
EXAMPLE Do it in the right sequence.

series
NOUN
1 A series of things is a number of them coming one after the other.
EXAMPLE There was a series of loud explosions.

2 A radio or television series is a set of programmes with the same title.
EXAMPLE There is a new drama series starting tonight.

serious
ADJECTIVE
Serious means very bad and worrying.
EXAMPLE Crime is a very serious problem here.

seriously
ADVERB
1 You say seriously to emphasize that you mean what you say.
EXAMPLE Seriously, though, something must be done.

▶ PHRASE
2 If you 'take something seriously', you regard it as important.
EXAMPLE I hope you are taking what I said seriously.

service services   RE
NOUN
A service is a religious ceremony.
EXAMPLE There were two services on Sunday morning.

settle settles settling settled
VERB
1 To settle an argument means to put an end to it.
EXAMPLE We are trying to settle our differences.

▶ PHRASE
2 When someone 'settles down', they start living a quiet life in one place.
EXAMPLE I'd like to settle down and have a family.

3 To 'settle down' means to become quiet or calm.
EXAMPLE The children have settled down now.

settlement settlements   GEOGRAPHY
NOUN
A settlement is a place, such as a village or a town, where people live.
EXAMPLE The settlement dated back to Roman times.

severe
ADJECTIVE
Severe means extremely bad or unpleasant.
EXAMPLE The boy had severe stomach pains.

sex sexes
NOUN
The sex of a person or animal is whether they are male or female.
EXAMPLE She did not get the job because of her sex.

shelter shelters sheltering sheltered
NOUN
1 A shelter is a small building made to protect people from bad weather or danger.
EXAMPLE Greg reached the bus shelter first.

2 Shelter means protection from bad weather or danger.
EXAMPLE The refugees were given food and shelter.

▶ VERB
3 If you shelter in a place, you stay there and are safe.
EXAMPLE I saw a man sheltering in a doorway.

shortage shortages
NOUN
If there is a shortage of something, there is not enough of it.
EXAMPLE Vietnam is suffering from a food shortage.

should
VERB
You use should to say that something ought to happen.
EXAMPLE Wade should have done better.

shoulder shoulders
NOUN
Your shoulders are the parts of your body between your neck and the tops of your arms.
EXAMPLE He looked back over his shoulder.

sigh sighs sighing sighed
VERB
When you sigh, you let out a deep breath.
EXAMPLE She sighed when she remembered the crash.

sign signs signing signed
NOUN
1 A sign is a mark or symbol which has a particular meaning.
EXAMPLE The equation needed a plus sign.

A B C D E F G H I J K L M N O P Q R **S** T U V W X Y Z

2 A sign is a movement or gesture with a particular meaning.
EXAMPLE His wave was a sign to move on.

▸ VERB

3 If you sign a document, you write your name on it.
EXAMPLE He signed the death certificate.

▸ PHRASE

4 If you 'sign up' for a job or course, you agree to do it by signing a contract.
EXAMPLE He had signed up for a driving course.

signal signals
NOUN

1 A signal is a gesture or sound intended to give a message to someone.
EXAMPLE He raised his hand as the signal to stop.

2 A railway signal is a piece of equipment beside the track which tells train drivers when to stop or go.
EXAMPLE The train crashed when the signal did not work.

significant
ADJECTIVE
Significant means large or important.
EXAMPLE A significant number of people can't read.

Sikh Sikhs   RE
🔊 Said: seek
NOUN
A Sikh is a person who believes in Sikhism, an Indian religion which separated from Hinduism in the sixteenth century and which teaches that there is only one God.
EXAMPLE They saw Sikhs worshipping at the Golden Temple.

silence
NOUN
Silence is complete quietness.
EXAMPLE They stood in silence for a while.

similar
ADJECTIVE
If one thing is similar to another, they are like each other.
EXAMPLE The accident was similar to one that happened before.

Be careful when deciding whether to use 'similar' or 'same'. 'Similar' means 'alike but not identical', and 'same' means 'identical'.

simile similes   ENGLISH
NOUN
A simile is an expression in which something is described as being similar to something else.
EXAMPLE 'She ran as fast as a deer' is a simile.

simple simpler simplest
ADJECTIVE

1 Something that is simple is easy to understand or do.
EXAMPLE I can do simple maths.

2 Simple also means plain in style.
EXAMPLE She wore a simple coat.

single singles
ADJECTIVE

1 Single means only one and not more.
EXAMPLE A single shot was fired.

2 People who are single are not married.
EXAMPLE When I was single I had no worries.

3 A single bed or bedroom is for one person.
EXAMPLE I reserved a single room at the hotel.

▸ NOUN   MUSIC

4 A single is a recording of one or two short pieces of music on a small record, CD or cassette.
EXAMPLE Many of the group's singles were hits.

site sites
NOUN
A site is a piece of ground where a building is or where a particular thing happens.
EXAMPLE Building sites are dangerous places.

ski skis skiing skied
NOUN

1 Skis are long pieces of wood, metal or plastic which help you move easily on snow.
EXAMPLE I hired a pair of skis.

▸ VERB

2 When you ski, you move on snow wearing skis.
EXAMPLE They skied down the mountain.

slight slighter slightest
ADJECTIVE

1 Slight means small in amount or degree.
EXAMPLE There was a slight dent in the car.

2 A slight person has a slim body.
EXAMPLE She is smaller and slighter than Christine.

slightly
ADVERB
Slightly means to some degree only.
EXAMPLE We bought a slightly larger house.

social   CITIZENSHIP
ADJECTIVE

1 Social is to do with society or life within a society.
EXAMPLE They were from similar social backgrounds.

2 Social is to do with leisure activities which involve meeting other people.
EXAMPLE We should organize more social events.

society societies   CITIZENSHIP
NOUN

1 Society is the people in a particular country or region.
EXAMPLE Crime is a major problem in society.

2 A society is an organization for people who have the same interest or aim.
EXAMPLE We are starting a literature society.

software   ICT
NOUN
Computer programs are known as software.
EXAMPLE He used the new software on his computer.

soldier soldiers
NOUN
A soldier is a person in an army.
EXAMPLE **Soldiers are being sent into the area.**

solicitor solicitors
NOUN
A solicitor is a lawyer who gives legal advice and prepares legal documents and cases.
EXAMPLE **If you are arrested you can phone a solicitor.**

solid
ADJECTIVE
A solid substance or object is hard or firm.
EXAMPLE **The baby is already eating solid food.**

soliloquy soliloquies   **DRAMA**
▢ **Said:** sol-*ill*-ok-wee
NOUN
A soliloquy is a speech made by an actor who is alone on the stage.
EXAMPLE **Hamlet's soliloquy begins 'To be or not to be'.**

solution solutions
NOUN
1 A solution is a way of dealing with a problem or difficult situation.
EXAMPLE **They looked for a peaceful solution to the conflict.**

2 The solution to a riddle or a puzzle is the answer.
EXAMPLE **The solution can be found on page 8.**
SCIENCE

3 A solution is a liquid in which a solid substance has been dissolved.
EXAMPLE **They heated the solution and noted when it changed colour.**

solve solves solving solved
VERB
If you solve a problem or a question, you find a solution or answer to it.
EXAMPLE **Henry solved the puzzle in fifteen minutes.**

◼ **Similar words:** resolve, work out

someone
PRONOUN
You use someone to refer to a person without saying exactly who you mean.
EXAMPLE **I need someone to help me.**

'Someone' and 'somebody' mean the same thing.

sometimes
ADVERB
Sometimes means occasionally.
EXAMPLE **We sometimes play cards together.**

soul souls
NOUN
1 A person's soul is the spiritual part of them.
EXAMPLE **They prayed for the souls of the dead.**

2 Soul also means a person's mind, character and feelings.
EXAMPLE **I put my heart and soul into the job.**

sour
ADJECTIVE
If something is sour, it has a sharp, acid taste.
EXAMPLE **The milk tastes sour.**

source sources
NOUN
The source of something is the person, place or thing that it comes from.
EXAMPLE **Knowledge is the source of his confidence.**

Spanish
ADJECTIVE
1 Spanish means to do with Spain.
EXAMPLE **Granada is a Spanish town.**

▶ NOUN
2 Spanish is the main language spoken in Spain.
EXAMPLE **They chattered in Spanish.**

special
ADJECTIVE
Special means different from normal, often more important or better.
EXAMPLE **Pete is a special friend of his.**

specialist specialists
NOUN
A specialist is someone who has a particular skill or who knows a lot about a particular subject.
EXAMPLE **Manjit was a skin specialist.**

specialize specializes specializing specialized
VERB
If you specialize in something, you know a lot about it and spend a lot of time on it.
EXAMPLE **We visited a shop specializing in video games.**

Specialize is also spelt specialise.

species   **SCIENCE**
▢ **Said:** *spee*-shees
NOUN
A species is a group of plants or animals of the same type.
EXAMPLE **Friesians and Jerseys are different species of cow.**

specification specifications   **DESIGN**
NOUN
A specification is a description of materials and work that is to be carried out.
EXAMPLE **The specification of the project was clearly set out.**

spectacular
ADJECTIVE
Spectacular means very impressive or dramatic.
EXAMPLE **The show was a spectacular success.**

◼ **Similar word:** impressive

spectrum spectrums spectra   **SCIENCE**
NOUN
A spectrum is the whole range of colours.
EXAMPLE **A rainbow shows the colours in a spectrum.**

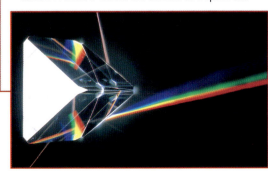

speech marks `ENGLISH`
NOUN

Speech marks are punctuation marks which show which words in a sentence have been spoken.
EXAMPLE The words 'Good morning' are enclosed in speech marks.

spell spells spelling spelt spelled
VERB

1 When you spell a word, you name or write its letters in order.
EXAMPLE She spelt her name out for him.

▸ *NOUN*

2 A spell of something is a short period of it.
EXAMPLE We had a spell of good weather.

3 A spell is a word or sequence of words used to perform magic.
EXAMPLE The witches chanted a spell.

spirit spirits
NOUN

1 Your spirit is the part of you that is connected with your deepest thoughts and feelings.
EXAMPLE Marian still has a youthful spirit.

2 A spirit is a ghost or supernatural being.
EXAMPLE The woods are haunted by evil spirits.

3 Spirit is liveliness, energy and self-confidence.
EXAMPLE I admired her spirit.

spiritual `RE`
ADJECTIVE

Spiritual refers to people's thoughts and beliefs, including their religious beliefs.
EXAMPLE He was concerned for the spiritual health of his workers.

spread spreads spreading spread
VERB

1 If you spread something out, you open it out or arrange it so that it can be seen or used easily.
EXAMPLE He spread the map out on his knees.

2 If you spread a substance on a surface, you put a thin layer on the surface.
EXAMPLE She spread marmalade on her toast.

3 If something spreads, it gradually reaches or affects more people.
EXAMPLE The disease spread quickly.

spreadsheet spreadsheets `ICT`
NOUN

A spreadsheet is a computer program used for entering and arranging numbers.
EXAMPLE The spreadsheet showed how the profits had fallen.

	A1	×✓	Investment Type		
	A	B	C	D	E
1	Investment Type	Investment Name	Date of Purchase	No. of Shares	Price Per Share
2	Ranch	Flying D	22/3/95	1	########
3	Stocks	Apple Stock	29/3/95	1110	£ 45.00
4	Rocks	Diamonds	15/4/95	25	£ 350.00
5	Gold Coins	Maple Leaf	12/6/95	150	£ 380.00
6	Stocks	ABC Stock	1/7/95	1000	£ 45.50
7					
8					
9					

squad squads
NOUN

A squad is a small group chosen to do something.
EXAMPLE The England manager picked his squad.

square squares `MATHS`
NOUN

1 A square is a shape with four equal sides and four right angles.
EXAMPLE She drew a square on the paper.

2 In a town, a square is an open place bordered by buildings or streets.
EXAMPLE The square was full of children playing.

squeeze squeezes squeezing squeezed
VERB

When you squeeze something, you press it firmly from two sides.
EXAMPLE She paused to squeeze my hand.

stable stables
ADJECTIVE

1 Stable means not likely to change or move.
EXAMPLE The price of bread has been stable for months.

▸ *NOUN*

2 A stable is a building in which horses are kept.
EXAMPLE The horses were led back to their stable.

stain stains
NOUN

A stain is a mark on something which is difficult to remove.
EXAMPLE She had a dark stain on her dress.

stake stakes staking staked
PHRASE

1 If something is 'at stake', it might be lost or damaged if something else is not successful.
EXAMPLE The whole future of the company was at stake.

▸ *VERB*

2 If you say you would stake something, such as money or your life, on a result, you mean you would risk it.
EXAMPLE He is prepared to stake his career on this.

stanza stanzas `ENGLISH`
NOUN

A stanza is a verse of a poem.
EXAMPLE The poem was written in four stanzas.

stare stares staring stared
VERB

1 If you stare at something, you look at it for a long time.
EXAMPLE He kept staring at the photograph.

▸ *NOUN*

2 A stare is a long fixed look at something.
EXAMPLE Dominic gave him a long, cold stare.

state states stating stated
NOUN

1 The state of something is its condition or its circumstances.
EXAMPLE The room was in a terrible state.

2 Countries are sometimes referred to as states.
EXAMPLE Luxembourg is a small European state.

3 Some countries are divided into regions called states.
EXAMPLE The State of Vermont is in north-eastern USA.

▸ *VERB*

4 If you state something, you say it or write it, especially in a formal way.
EXAMPLE Please state your name and address.

statement statements
NOUN
A statement is something you say or write which gives information.
EXAMPLE She made a formal statement to the police.

station stations stationing stationed
NOUN
1 A station is a building by a railway line where trains stop for passengers.
EXAMPLE I'm going to get out at the next station.
2 A station is a place where some buses or coaches start their journeys.
EXAMPLE The bus pulled out of the station.
3 A radio or television station is a particular radio or television company.
EXAMPLE She turned to a music station on the car radio.
▶ *VERB*
4 Someone who is stationed somewhere is sent there to work or do a particular job.
EXAMPLE Her husband was stationed in Vienna.

statistic statistics
NOUN
Statistics are facts obtained by analysing information which is expressed in numbers.
EXAMPLE They published the latest statistics about the economy.

status
☐ **Said:** *stay*-tuss
NOUN
A person's status is their position and importance in society.
EXAMPLE He gained the status of national hero.

stave staves   MUSIC
NOUN
A stave is the five lines on which you write music.
EXAMPLE Chris wrote three notes on the stave.

still life still lives   ART
NOUN
A still life is a picture of a group of objects which have been arranged together.
EXAMPLE He drew a still life of fruit in a bowl.

stomach stomachs   SCIENCE
NOUN
Your stomach is the organ inside your body where food is digested.
EXAMPLE I woke up with a pain in my stomach.

straight straighter straightest
ADJECTIVE OR ADVERB
1 Straight means continuing in the same direction without curving or bending.
EXAMPLE Amy stared straight ahead of her.
▶ *ADVERB*
2 Straight means immediately and directly.
EXAMPLE We will go straight to the hotel.

strange stranger strangest
ADJECTIVE
1 Strange means unusual or unexpected.
EXAMPLE I had a strange dream last night.
■ **Similar words:** curious, odd
2 Strange means not known, seen or experienced before.

EXAMPLE She was all alone in a strange country.
■ **Similar word:** new

strength strengths
NOUN
1 Your strength is your physical energy.
EXAMPLE He pulled with all his strength.
2 Someone's strengths are their good qualities and abilities.
EXAMPLE His generosity was his greatest strength.
3 The strength of an object is how well it can stand rough treatment.
EXAMPLE He checked the strength of the rope.

strengthen strengthens strengthening strengthened
VERB
1 To strengthen something means to give it more power, influence or support.
EXAMPLE The incident strengthened their friendship.
2 To strengthen an object means to make it stronger.
EXAMPLE The exercises strengthened his spine.

stretch stretches stretching stretched
VERB
1 Something that stretches over an area covers the whole of that area.
EXAMPLE Forests stretched the length of the valley.
2 When you stretch, you hold out part of your body as far as you can.
EXAMPLE He stretched out a hand.
3 To stretch something soft or elastic means to pull it to make it longer or bigger.
EXAMPLE You'll stretch your jumper if you do that.

strike strikes striking struck
NOUN
1 If there is a strike, people stop working as a protest.
EXAMPLE Staff at the hospital went on strike.
▶ *VERB*
2 To strike something means to hit it.
EXAMPLE She struck him across the mouth.
3 If an illness, disaster or enemy strikes, it suddenly affects or attacks someone.
EXAMPLE A powerful earthquake struck Sicily.

strings   MUSIC
NOUN
Strings is the term given to the stringed instruments in an orchestra.
EXAMPLE The strings then played the melody.

A B C D E F G H I J K L M N O P Q R **S** T U V W X Y Z

structure structures
NOUN
The structure of something is the way it is made, built or organized.
EXAMPLE **The structure of the brain is very complicated.**

struggle struggles struggling struggled
VERB
1 If you struggle to do something, you try hard to do it.
EXAMPLE **Bernard struggled to explain.**

2 When people struggle, they resist being held.
EXAMPLE **I struggled, but could not get free.**

▶ *NOUN*
3 Something that is a struggle is difficult to achieve.
EXAMPLE **Chandra was only allowed back to school after a long struggle.**

student students
NOUN
A student is a person studying at a university, college or school.
EXAMPLE **Lisa is a music student.**

studio studios
NOUN   **ART**
1 A studio is a room where an artist or craftsman works.
EXAMPLE **Most of her hats are made at a studio in New York.**

2 A studio is a room containing special equipment where records, films or radio or television programmes are made.
EXAMPLE **He visited a television studio.**

study studies studying studied
VERB
1 If you study a particular subject, you spend time learning about it.
EXAMPLE **She went on to study history and politics.**

2 If you study something, you look at it carefully.
EXAMPLE **He studied the map in silence.**

subject subjects
NOUN
1 The subject of writing or a conversation is the thing or person being discussed.
EXAMPLE **What is the subject of the lecture?**

2 A subject is an area of study.
EXAMPLE **Biology was my favourite subject at school.**

3 The subjects of a country are the people who live there.
EXAMPLE **The victims were all British subjects.**

ENGLISH

4 The subject of a sentence is the person or thing performing the action of the sentence.
EXAMPLE **In the sentence 'Lisa threw the ball', the subject is 'Lisa'.**

substance substances   **SCIENCE**
NOUN
A substance is anything that is a solid, a powder, a liquid or a paste.
EXAMPLE **It was a sticky black substance.**

📗 **Similar words:** material, stuff

substitute substitutes substituting substituted
VERB
1 To substitute one thing for another means to use it instead of the other thing.
EXAMPLE **We substituted margarine for butter.**

📗 **Similar words:** exchange, replace

▶ *NOUN*
2 If one thing is a substitute for another, it is used instead of it or put in its place.
EXAMPLE **Jones came on as a substitute in the second half.**

📗 **Similar words:** alternative, replacement

succeed succeeds succeeding succeeded
VERB
To succeed means to achieve the result you want.
EXAMPLE **He was determined to succeed as a writer.**

📗 **Similar words:** be successful, do well, make it

success successes
NOUN
1 Success is the achievement of something you have been trying to do.
EXAMPLE **The cast were amazed at the play's success.**

2 Someone who is a success has achieved an important position or made a lot of money.
EXAMPLE **If you want to be a success, you will have to work harder.**

successful
ADJECTIVE
Someone or something that is successful achieves the result that was intended.
EXAMPLE **Javed became a successful lawyer.**

sudden
ADJECTIVE
Sudden means happening quickly and unexpectedly.
EXAMPLE **She gave a sudden cry.**

suddenly
ADVERB
Suddenly means quickly and unexpectedly.
EXAMPLE **The door opened suddenly.**

suffer suffers suffering suffered
VERB
If someone suffers something, they are badly affected by it.
EXAMPLE **The poor have suffered most from the cuts.**

sufficient
ADJECTIVE
If a supply or quantity is sufficient for a purpose, there is enough of it available.
EXAMPLE **There was sufficient food and shelter for everyone.**

suffix suffixes
NOUN
A suffix is a group of letters which is added to the end of a word to form a new word.
EXAMPLE '-ology' and '-itis' are both suffixes.

suggest suggests suggesting suggested
VERB
1 If you suggest a plan or idea to someone, you ask them to consider doing it.
EXAMPLE I suggested we walk to the park.

■ Similar words: propose, recommend

2 If something suggests a particular thought or impression, it makes you think in that way or gives you that impression.
EXAMPLE Nothing you say suggests he is ill.

■ Similar words: hint, imply

suggestion suggestions
NOUN
A suggestion is a plan or idea which is mentioned as a possibility for someone to consider.
EXAMPLE Jim made some suggestions for improvements.

■ Similar words: proposal, recommendation.

suicide
NOUN
People who commit suicide deliberately kill themselves.
EXAMPLE He had committed suicide by taking an overdose of drugs.

suitable
ADJECTIVE
Suitable means right or acceptable for a particular purpose or occasion.
EXAMPLE Many roads are not suitable for cycling.

■ Similar word: appropriate

summarize summarizes summarizing summarized
EXAM TERM
VERB
To summarize means to mention the key points of a subject.
EXAMPLE Summarize Hitler's foreign policy.

Summarize is also spelt summarise.

summit summits
NOUN
1 The summit of a mountain is its top.
EXAMPLE They approached the summit of Mount Cosna.

2 A summit is a meeting between leaders of different countries to discuss important matters.
EXAMPLE A summit of Central Asian leaders was held in Kabul.

superb
ADJECTIVE
Superb means very good indeed.
EXAMPLE The shop had a superb selection of local cheeses.

superior
ADJECTIVE
Superior means better or of higher quality.
EXAMPLE It is worth paying more for superior quality coffee.

support supports supporting supported
VERB
1 If you support someone, you agree with their aims and want them to succeed.
EXAMPLE He thanked everyone who had supported him during the campaign.

2 If something supports an object, it is underneath it and holding it up.
EXAMPLE Thick wooden posts supported the ceiling.

▶ NOUN
3 If you give support to someone, you are kind and helpful to them.
EXAMPLE He thanked his wife for her constant support.

supporter supporters
NOUN
A supporter is someone who supports a person or activity.
EXAMPLE England supporters filled the stadium.

suppose supposes supposing supposed
VERB
1 If you suppose that something is the case, you think that it is likely.
EXAMPLE I suppose that you are busy tonight?

▶ PHRASE
2 If you are 'supposed to' do something, you should do it.
EXAMPLE You are supposed to report it to the police.

surface surfaces
NOUN
The surface of something is the top or outside area of it.
EXAMPLE The surface of the diamond was scratched.

surgery surgeries
NOUN
Surgery is medical treatment involving cutting open part of a person's body.
EXAMPLE He needed emergency surgery for his injuries.

surprise surprises surprising surprised
NOUN
1 A surprise is an unexpected event.
EXAMPLE His success came as a great surprise.

2 Surprise is the feeling caused when something unexpected happens.
EXAMPLE They all looked at her in surprise.

▶ VERB
3 If something surprises you, it gives you a feeling of surprise.
EXAMPLE The way they reacted to the news surprised me.

surrender surrenders surrendering surrendered

HISTORY

VERB

To surrender means to stop fighting and agree that the other side has won.

EXAMPLE He surrendered to the authorities after three weeks.

surround surrounds surrounding surrounded

VERB

To surround someone or something means to be situated all around them.

EXAMPLE The house is surrounded by a high fence.

survive survives surviving survived

VERB

To survive means to recover from great danger or difficulties.

EXAMPLE One sailor had survived the shipwreck.

suspect suspects suspecting suspected

VERB

☐ **Said:** sus-*pect*

1 If you suspect something, you think that it is likely.
EXAMPLE I suspected that they were right.

2 If you suspect someone of doing something wrong, you think that they have done it.
EXAMPLE He suspected Tom of being a thief.

▶ *NOUN*

☐ **Said:** *sus*-pect

3 A suspect is someone who is thought to be guilty of a crime.
EXAMPLE The most obvious suspect was her boyfriend.

suspend suspends suspending suspended

VERB

1 If something is suspended, it is hanging from a high place.
EXAMPLE A television set was suspended above the bar.

2 To suspend an activity or event means to delay it or stop it for a while.
EXAMPLE Lessons were suspended for the day.

suspicion suspicions

NOUN

1 Suspicion is the feeling of not trusting someone or something.
EXAMPLE He looked at his workmates with suspicion.

2 Suspicion is a feeling that something is likely to happen or is probably true.
EXAMPLE He had the suspicion that more could have been achieved.

sustainable

GEOGRAPHY

ADJECTIVE

A resource, such as oil or gas, is sustainable if it can be made use of, while keeping the amount available at a steady level.

EXAMPLE The wood they used on their fire was sustainable.

switch switches switching switched

NOUN

1 A switch is a small control for an electrical device or machine.
EXAMPLE She flicked the light switch.

▶ *VERB*

2 To switch to a different task or topic means to change to it.
EXAMPLE Jack switched from Mathematics to Biology.

symbol symbols

NOUN

A symbol is a shape, design or idea which is used to represent something.

EXAMPLE There are many religious symbols, such as the cross and the star of David.

☐ **Similar word:** sign

sympathy

NOUN

Sympathy is kindness and understanding towards someone who is in difficulties.

EXAMPLE She received no sympathy from her parents.

☐ **Similar word:** pity

synonym synonyms

ENGLISH

☐ **Said:** sin-u-nim

NOUN

If two words have the same or very similar meanings they are synonyms.

EXAMPLE 'Fast' and 'quick' are synonyms.

system systems

NOUN

1 A system is an organized way of doing or arranging something.
EXAMPLE She developed a system for dealing with complaints.

☐ **Similar words:** method, procedure, routine

TECHNOLOGY

2 A system is a group of parts that work together to perform a task.
EXAMPLE The computer system includes a CD-ROM.

A B C D E F G H I J K L M N O P Q R **S** T U V W X Y Z

Tt Tt Tt

table tables
NOUN
1 A table is a piece of furniture with a flat top supported by one or more legs.
EXAMPLE The loaf of bread was on the kitchen table.

2 A table is a set of facts or figures arranged in rows or columns.
EXAMPLE The headmaster looked at the table of exam results.

tackle tackles tackling tackled
VERB
1 If you tackle a difficult task, you start dealing with it seriously.
EXAMPLE We need to tackle this matter at once.

■ **Similar words:** deal with

2 If you tackle someone in a game such as rugby, you try to get the ball away from them.
EXAMPLE He was tackled before he reached the try line.

▶ NOUN
3 A tackle in sport is an attempt to get the ball away from your opponent.
EXAMPLE What a dangerous tackle!

tactic tactics
NOUN
Tactics are the methods you use to achieve something.
EXAMPLE The team used defensive tactics to win the match.

tale tales
NOUN
A tale is a story.
EXAMPLE She told tales of magic and adventure.

talent talents
NOUN
Talent is the natural ability to do something well.
EXAMPLE She was a player with lots of talent.

■ **Similar word:** ability

tank tanks
NOUN
1 A tank is a large container for storing liquid or gas.
EXAMPLE The petrol tank held eleven gallons.

2 A tank is an armoured vehicle which moves on tracks and has guns or rockets.
EXAMPLE The army sent in its tanks.

tap taps tapping tapped
NOUN
1 A tap is a device that you turn to control the flow of liquid or gas from a pipe or container.
EXAMPLE Someone left the tap running.

2 A tap is the action of hitting something lightly; also the sound that this action makes.
EXAMPLE She gave him a little tap on the arm.

▶ VERB
3 If you tap something or tap on it, you hit it lightly.
EXAMPLE I tapped him on the shoulder.

tape tapes taping taped
NOUN
1 Tape is plastic ribbon covered with a magnetic substance and used to record sounds, pictures and computer information.
EXAMPLE The students were interviewed on tape.

2 A tape is a cassette with magnetic tape wound round it.
EXAMPLE We listened to an old Beatles tape.

3 Tape is a long, thin strip of fabric that is used for binding or fastening.
EXAMPLE Use the tapes to tie the curtains back.

4 Tape is a strip of sticky plastic which you use for sticking things together.
EXAMPLE She used a piece of tape to mend her glasses.

▶ VERB
5 If you tape sounds or television pictures, you record them using a tape recorder or a video recorder.
EXAMPLE I want to tape this programme.

6 To tape means to fasten things together using tape.
EXAMPLE He taped the list to the fridge door.

target targets
NOUN
1 A target is something which you aim at when firing a weapon.
EXAMPLE The children fired arrows at a target in the garden.

2 Your target is a result that you are trying to achieve.
EXAMPLE Her target was 100 metres in 10 seconds.

A B C D E F G H I J K L M N O P Q R S T U V W X Y Z

A B C D E F G H I J K L M N O P Q R S **T** U V W X Y Z

task tasks
NOUN
A task is a job which has to be done.
EXAMPLE My task was to collect the wood.
◼ Similar words: duty, job

taste tastes tasting tasted
NOUN
1 Your sense of taste is your ability to recognize the flavour of things in your mouth.
EXAMPLE I lost my sense of taste when I was ill.

2 The taste of something is its flavour.
EXAMPLE I don't like the taste of fish.

3 A person's taste is their choice in the things they like to buy or have around them.
EXAMPLE He has great taste in music.

▶ PHRASE
4 If you have a 'taste for' something, you enjoy it.
EXAMPLE She has a taste for dancing.

▶ VERB
5 To taste something means to be aware of its flavour.
EXAMPLE I could hardly taste the meat.

6 If food or drink tastes of something, it has that flavour.
EXAMPLE This pizza tastes delicious.

tax taxes taxing taxed   CITIZENSHIP
NOUN
1 Tax is an amount of money that people have to pay to the government so that it can provide public services.
EXAMPLE The more you earn the more income tax you have to pay.

▶ VERB
2 If a sum of money is taxed, a certain amount of it has to be paid to the government.
EXAMPLE Everything you earn is taxed.

3 If a person or company is taxed, they have to pay a certain amount of their income to the government.
EXAMPLE The government intends to tax the rich more.

teach teaches teaching taught
VERB
1 To teach someone means to give them information so that they know about it or know how to do it.
EXAMPLE My mother taught me how to cook.
◼ Similar words: educate, instruct, train

2 To teach a subject means to help students learn about that subject.
EXAMPLE I taught history for many years.

teacher teachers
NOUN
Someone who teaches at a school, college or university is called a teacher.
EXAMPLE She liked her chemistry teacher.

team teams
NOUN
A team is a group of people who play together against another group in a sport or game.
EXAMPLE The New Zealand rugby team is very talented.

tear tears tearing tore torn
NOUN
1 Tears are the drops of liquid that come out of your eyes when you cry.
EXAMPLE Tears ran down his face.

2 A tear is a hole that has been made in something.
EXAMPLE There was a tear in the curtain.
◼ Similar words: hole, rip

▶ VERB
3 If you tear something, you damage it by making a hole in it.
EXAMPLE She tore her dress on the railing.

4 If you tear something from somewhere, you remove it roughly.
EXAMPLE He tore the tie from his neck.

When tear means 'drop of liquid' (sense 1) it rhymes with 'fear'. For all the other senses it rhymes with 'hair'.

technical   TECHNOLOGY
ADJECTIVE
Technical means to do with machines, processes and materials used in industry, transport and communications.
EXAMPLE Certain technical problems have to be solved.

technique techniques
NOUN
1 A particular way of doing something is called a technique.
EXAMPLE Modern techniques for making cars involve computers.

2 Technique is skill in an activity which is developed through training.
EXAMPLE Good high jumping technique takes years to perfect.

technology   TECHNOLOGY
NOUN
Technology refers to practical things which are the result of knowledge about science.
EXAMPLE Recent advances in space technology are astonishing.

teenager teenagers
NOUN
Someone who is between thirteen and nineteen years old is a teenager.
EXAMPLE As a teenager he went to the local high school.

telephone telephones telephoning telephoned
NOUN
1 A telephone is a piece of electrical equipment for talking directly to someone.
EXAMPLE He answered the telephone gruffly.

▶ VERB
2 If you telephone someone, you speak to them using a telephone.
EXAMPLE Peter telephoned his sister to thank her.

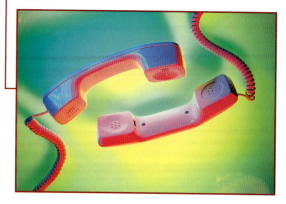

television televisions
NOUN
A television is a piece of electronic equipment which provides pictures and sounds.
EXAMPLE I turned on the television.

temper
NOUN
1 If someone has a temper, they become angry very easily.
EXAMPLE I hope he can control his temper.

2 Your temper is the mood you are in.
EXAMPLE I started the day in a bad temper.

▶ PHRASE
3 If you 'lose your temper', you become very angry.
EXAMPLE He lost his temper and smashed a window.

temperature temperatures
NOUN
1 The temperature of something is how hot or cold it is.
EXAMPLE There was a sudden drop in temperature.

2 Your temperature is how hot or cold your body is.
EXAMPLE His temperature continued to rise.

temple temples · RE
NOUN
A temple is a building used for the worship of a god.
EXAMPLE They visited a local Hindu temple.

temporary
ADJECTIVE
If something is temporary it lasts for only a short time.
EXAMPLE His job here is only temporary.

tempt tempts tempting tempted
VERB
1 If you tempt someone, you try to persuade them to do something by offering them something they want.
EXAMPLE He tempted her to stay by offering her a higher wage.

2 If you are tempted to do something, you want to do it.
EXAMPLE I'm tempted to sell my house.

tend tends tending tended
VERB
1 If something tends to happen, it happens usually or often.
EXAMPLE I tend to wake up early.

2 If you tend someone or something, you look after them.
EXAMPLE He tends the flower beds.

tendency tendencies
NOUN
Tendency is the way someone usually behaves.
EXAMPLE He has a tendency to be too careful.

tense tenser tensest; tenses tensing tensed
ADJECTIVE
1 If you are tense, you are nervous and cannot relax.
EXAMPLE I have never seen him so tense.

◼ Similar words: anxious, nervous

2 If your body is tense, your muscles are tight.
EXAMPLE A bath can relax tense muscles.

▶ VERB
3 If you tense, your muscles become tight and stiff.
EXAMPLE Jane tensed when I told her the bad news.

▶ NOUN · ENGLISH
4 The tense of a verb shows whether you are talking about the past, present or future.
EXAMPLE In English you must use the correct tense.

tension tensions
NOUN
Tension is the feeling of nervousness or worry that you have when something dangerous or important is happening.
EXAMPLE The tension between the two countries increased.

tenth tenths
ADJECTIVE
1 The tenth item in a series is the one counted as number ten.
EXAMPLE He came tenth in the race.

▶ NOUN · MATHS
2 A tenth is one of ten equal parts.
EXAMPLE She ate a tenth of the cake.

term terms
NOUN
1 A term is a name or word used for a particular thing.
EXAMPLE The medical term for short-sightedness is myopia.

2 A term is a fixed period of time.
EXAMPLE He was given a seven-year term in prison.

▶ PLURAL NOUN
3 The terms of an agreement are the conditions that have been accepted by the people involved in it.
EXAMPLE They would not surrender on any terms.

▶ PHRASE
4 If you 'come to terms with' something difficult or unpleasant, you learn to accept it.
EXAMPLE James never came to terms with her death.

terrible
ADJECTIVE
1 Terrible means serious and unpleasant.
EXAMPLE He suffered from a terrible illness.

2 Terrible means very bad or of poor quality.
EXAMPLE The barber gave him a terrible haircut.

territory territories · HISTORY
NOUN
The territory of a country is the land that it controls.
EXAMPLE The city was in Russian territory.

A
B
C
D
E
F
G
H
I
J
K
L
M
N
O
P
Q
R
S
T
U
V
W
X
Y
Z

terror terrors
NOUN
Terror is great fear or panic.
EXAMPLE I was shaking with terror.

text texts
NOUN
1 Text is any written material.
EXAMPLE The disk stores thousands of pages of text.

2 A text is a book or other piece of writing used at a school or college.
EXAMPLE I studied many texts in my English class.

textile textiles   TECHNOLOGY
NOUN
A textile is a fabric made by the process of weaving, knitting or bonding.
EXAMPLE Some modern textiles are both light and hard-wearing.

theatre theatres   DRAMA
Said: *theer*-ter
NOUN
A theatre is a building where plays and other entertainments are performed on a stage.
EXAMPLE We went to the theatre on Saturday.

their
ADJECTIVE
You use the word their to refer to something that belongs or relates to the group of people or things that you are talking about.
EXAMPLE Trees lose their leaves in autumn.

Be careful not to confuse 'their' with 'there'.

theme themes
NOUN
A theme is a main idea in a piece of music or writing, a film or a painting.
EXAMPLE The main theme of the book was the horror of war.

themselves
PRONOUN
You use themselves to refer to people or things that have already been mentioned.
EXAMPLE They were talking among themselves.

there
ADVERB
There means in, at or to a place that has already been mentioned, or that you are looking at.
EXAMPLE I like America and I will go there again.

Be careful not to confuse 'there' with 'their'. A good way to remember that 'there' is connected to the idea of place is by remembering the spelling of two other place words, 'here' and 'where'.

therefore
ADVERB
Therefore means as a result.
EXAMPLE This bottle is bigger and therefore more expensive.

thing things
NOUN
1 You use thing instead of another word when you can't be more exact.
EXAMPLE What is that thing?

2 A thing is an object, rather than a living being.
EXAMPLE Babies are people, not things!

Similar words: article, object

▸ PLURAL NOUN
3 Your things are your clothes or possessions.
EXAMPLE I'll get my things and we'll go.

think thinks thinking thought
VERB
1 If you think something, you have the opinion that it is true.
EXAMPLE I think she's got a boyfriend.

▸ PHRASE
2 To 'think about' something means to consider it.
EXAMPLE I'll need to think about that.

3 If you 'think of' something, you remember it or it comes into your mind.
EXAMPLE Nobody could think of anything to say.

third thirds
ADJECTIVE
1 The third item in a series is the one counted as number three.
EXAMPLE She came third in the test.

▸ NOUN   MATHS
2 A third means one of three equal parts.
EXAMPLE She ate a third of the packet of biscuits.

thorough
Said: *thur*-ruh
ADJECTIVE
Thorough describes something which is done very carefully and completely.
EXAMPLE The doctor gave the boy a thorough examination.

though
Said: rhymes with *show*
CONJUNCTION
1 Though is used when you are saying something which contrasts with something else.
EXAMPLE I ran off, though I didn't get very far.

▸ PHRASE
2 'As though' is used to say what seems to be happening, or to compare two situations.
EXAMPLE It looks as though you were right.

threat threats
NOUN
1 A threat is a statement that someone will harm you, especially if you do not do what they want.
EXAMPLE He received death threats.

2 A threat is anything that seems likely to harm you.
EXAMPLE Nuclear weapons are a major threat to the planet.

threaten threatens threatening threatened
VERB

1 If you threaten to harm someone or threaten to do something unpleasant, you say that you will do it.
EXAMPLE He threatened me with a knife.

2 If something threatens a person or thing, it is likely to harm them.
EXAMPLE Smoking threatens your health.

throat throats
NOUN

Your throat is the back of your mouth and the top part of the tubes inside your neck.
EXAMPLE I have a sore throat.

through
☐ **Said:** threw

PREPOSITION

1 Through means from one side of something to the other.
EXAMPLE They took a path through the woods.

2 Through means because of.
EXAMPLE He was exhausted through lack of sleep.

3 Through means during.
EXAMPLE He has to work through the summer.

throughout
PREPOSITION

Throughout is another word for during.
EXAMPLE I stayed awake throughout the night.

throw throws throwing threw thrown
VERB

1 When you throw something you make it move through the air.
EXAMPLE He was throwing a ball against a wall.

■ **Similar words:** chuck, fling, hurl

2 If you throw yourself somewhere, you move there suddenly and with force.
EXAMPLE We threw ourselves on the ground.

ticket tickets
NOUN

A ticket is a piece of paper or card which shows that you have paid for a journey or entrance.
EXAMPLE He bought a ticket for the match.

tide tides
NOUN

The tide is the regular change in the level of the sea on the shore.
EXAMPLE The tide is going out.

tight tighter tightest
ADJECTIVE

1 Tight describes anything fitting closely.
EXAMPLE The shoes are too tight.

▶ *ADVERB*

2 Tight means held firmly and securely.
EXAMPLE He held me tight.

tiny tinier tiniest
ADJECTIVE

Tiny means extremely small.
EXAMPLE The bedroom is tiny.

■ **Similar word:** minute

tired
ADJECTIVE

If you are tired, you feel you want to rest or sleep.
EXAMPLE I'm too tired to go out.

tissue tissues
☐ **Said:** *tiss*-yoo

NOUN

A tissue is a small piece of soft paper that you use as a handkerchief.
EXAMPLE Because she had a cold, she bought a box of tissues.

title titles
NOUN

1 Title is the word to describe the name of a book, play or piece of music.
EXAMPLE The title of this book is 'Word Bank'.

2 Title is also a word that describes someone's rank or job.
EXAMPLE My official title is Design Manager.

together
ADVERB

1 If people do something together, they do it with each other.
EXAMPLE They all live together in a flat.

2 If two things happen together, they happen at the same time.
EXAMPLE 'Yes,' they said together.

3 If things or people are together, they are very near to each other.
EXAMPLE The trees are close together.

tolerance   **CITIZENSHIP**
NOUN

Tolerance is the acceptance of other people's values.
EXAMPLE She wanted her children to show tolerance to those of other faiths.

tomorrow
ADVERB OR NOUN

Tomorrow means the day after today.
EXAMPLE The results will be announced tomorrow.

ton tons
NOUN

A ton is a unit of weight equal to 2240 pounds or about 1016 kilograms.
EXAMPLE Hundreds of tons of oil have spilled into the sea.

tone tones
NOUN   **MUSIC**

1 The tone of a sound is the kind of sound it has.
EXAMPLE The clear tone of the bell could be heard for miles.

2 Someone's tone is a quality in their voice which shows what they are thinking or feeling.
EXAMPLE Her tone suggested that she was getting impatient.

                                    ART
3 A tone is a different shade of the same colour.

A B C D E F G H I J K L M N O P Q R S **T** U V W X Y Z

EXAMPLE **The room was decorated in two tones of green.**

tonight
ADVERB OR NOUN
Tonight is the evening or night that will come at the end of today.
EXAMPLE **What are you doing tonight?**

tonne *tonnes*   **SCIENCE**
🔊 Said: tun
NOUN
A tonne is a unit of weight equal to 1000 kilograms.
EXAMPLE **The lorry weighed 1.15 tonnes.**

too
ADVERB
1 Too means also or as well.
EXAMPLE **She too was there.**
2 You use the word too to indicate that there is more of something than is needed.
EXAMPLE **The tea was too hot to drink.**

tool *tools*   **TECHNOLOGY**
NOUN
A tool is any hand-held instrument or piece of equipment that you use to help you do a particular kind of work.
EXAMPLE **The tools he used to make the box were a hammer and a saw.**

torture *tortures torturing tortured*
NOUN
1 Torture is great pain that is inflicted on someone to punish them or get information from them.
EXAMPLE **The instruments of torture were all around the room.**
▸ *VERB*
2 If someone tortures another person, they inflict great pain to punish them or get information from them.
EXAMPLE **The prisoner was tortured to death.**

Tory *Tories*   **CITIZENSHIP**
NOUN
In Britain, a Tory is a member or supporter of the Conservative Party.
EXAMPLE **The Tory government lasted for eighteen years.**

total *totals totalling totalled*   **MATHS**
NOUN
1 The total is the number you get when you add several numbers together.
EXAMPLE **The meal cost a total of twenty pounds.**
▣ Similar words: sum, whole
▸ *VERB*
2 If several numbers total a certain figure, that is the figure you get when all the numbers are added together.
EXAMPLE **Their debts totalled over 300,000 dollars.**
▸ *ADJECTIVE*
3 Total means complete.
EXAMPLE **Their attempt was a total failure.**

touch *touches touching touched*
VERB
1 If you touch something, you make physical contact with it.
EXAMPLE **I touched his arm.**
▸ *NOUN*
2 Your sense of touch is your ability to tell what something is like by touching it.

EXAMPLE **The water was cold to the touch.**
▸ *PHRASE*
3 If you are 'in touch' with someone, you are in contact with them.
EXAMPLE **I'll be in touch soon.**

tough *tougher toughest*
🔊 Said: tuff
ADJECTIVE
1 A tough person or thing is strong and able to put up with hardship or bad treatment.
EXAMPLE **He is tough enough to do the job.**
▣ Similar word: strong
2 Tough also means difficult or full of hardship.
EXAMPLE **She had a tough childhood.**
3 Tough actions are strict and firm.
EXAMPLE **The government brought in tough measures against crime.**

tour *tours touring toured*
NOUN
1 A tour is a long journey during which you visit several places.
EXAMPLE **They went on a tour of Spain.**
2 A tour is a short trip round a place or building.
EXAMPLE **There are daily tours of the castle.**
▸ *VERB*
3 If you tour a place, you go on a journey or a trip round it.
EXAMPLE **He toured Europe for three months.**

tourist *tourists*
NOUN
A person who visits places for pleasure or interest is called a tourist.
EXAMPLE **London has many foreign tourists.**

towards
PREPOSITION
1 Towards means in the direction of.
EXAMPLE **He turned towards the door.**
2 Towards means about or involving.
EXAMPLE **My feelings towards Susan have changed.**

tower *towers towering towered*
NOUN
A tower is a tall, narrow building, sometimes attached to a larger building such as a castle or church.
EXAMPLE **The tower could be seen for miles.**

trace traces tracing traced
VERB

1 If you trace something, you find it after looking for it.
EXAMPLE Police are trying to trace the owner of the car.

EXAM TERM

2 To trace means to give an account of the development of something.
EXAMPLE Trace the rise of the cotton industry in Lancashire.

▶ **NOUN**

3 A trace is a sign which shows you that someone or something has been there.
EXAMPLE No trace of his father has been found.

track tracks
NOUN

1 A track is a narrow road or path.
EXAMPLE They climbed a mountain track.

2 A track is a strip of ground with rails on it that a train travels along.
EXAMPLE Someone fell on to the tracks.

3 A track is a piece of ground on which horses, cars or athletes race.
EXAMPLE We watched the horses go round the track.

trade trades trading traded **GEOGRAPHY**
NOUN

1 Trade is the activity of buying, selling or exchanging goods or services between people or countries.
EXAMPLE He worked in the building trade.

Similar word: business

▶ **VERB**

2 When people or countries trade, they buy, sell or exchange goods or services.
EXAMPLE The two countries have stopped trading with each other.

tradition traditions
NOUN

A tradition is a custom or belief which has existed for a long time.
EXAMPLE It's a tradition for our family to gather at Christmas.

Similar words: convention, custom

traditional
ADJECTIVE

Something traditional has existed for a long time without changing.
EXAMPLE It is traditional in Britain to celebrate the New Year.

traffic
NOUN

Traffic is the movement of vehicles or people along a route.
EXAMPLE There was heavy traffic on the road.

tragedy tragedies
💬 Said: traj-id-ee
NOUN

1 A tragedy is an event or situation that is disastrous or very sad.
EXAMPLE She suffered a personal tragedy.

DRAMA

2 A tragedy is a serious story or play, which usually ends with the death of the main character.
EXAMPLE Macbeth is one of Shakespeare's tragedies.

trail trails trailing trailed
NOUN

1 A trail is a rough path across open or wooded land.
EXAMPLE We set out on the trail again.

2 A trail is a series of marks or other signs left by someone or something as they move along.
EXAMPLE He left a trail of mud behind him.

▶ **VERB**

3 If you trail something or if it trails, it drags along behind you as you move, or it hangs down loosely.
EXAMPLE She trailed her fingers through the water.

train trains training trained
NOUN

1 A train is a number of carriages or trucks which are pulled by a railway engine.
EXAMPLE They took a high-speed train to London.

▶ **VERB**

2 If you train, you learn how to do a particular job.
EXAMPLE She trained to be an actress.

3 If you train for a sports match or a race, you prepare for it by doing exercises.
EXAMPLE I'm training for the London marathon.

transfer transfers transferring transferred
VERB

If you transfer something from one place to another, you move it there.
EXAMPLE They transferred the money to a Swiss bank.

transport
NOUN

1 Vehicles that you travel in are referred to as transport.
EXAMPLE Have you got your own transport?

2 Transport is the moving of goods or people from one place to another.
EXAMPLE The transport of equipment is now complete.

trap traps trapping trapped
NOUN

1 A trap is a piece of equipment or a hole used to catch animals or birds.
EXAMPLE The rabbit had been caught in a trap.

▶ **VERB**

2 If you trap animals, you catch them using a trap.
EXAMPLE The locals often trapped and killed the wildlife.

3 If you are trapped somewhere, you cannot move or escape.
EXAMPLE People were trapped in the building by the fire.

travel travels travelling travelled
VERB

1 To travel is to go from one place to another.
EXAMPLE We have travelled hundreds of miles to get here.

Similar words: go, journey

A B C D E F G H I J K L M N O P Q R S **T** U V W X Y Z

155

A B C D E F G H I J K L M N O P Q R S **T** U V W X Y Z

▶ *PLURAL NOUN*

2 Someone's travels are the journeys that they make to places.
EXAMPLE Have you heard about my travels in the Himalayas?

treat treats treating treated
VERB

1 If you treat someone or something in a particular way, you behave that way towards them.
EXAMPLE Stop treating me like a child.

2 When a doctor treats a patient or an illness, he or she gives them medical care and attention.
EXAMPLE The boy was treated for a leg injury.

▶ *NOUN*

3 A treat is a special present or occasion given to someone.
EXAMPLE For my birthday treat he took me to the theatre.

treatment treatments
NOUN

1 Treatment is medical attention given to a sick or injured person or animal.
EXAMPLE She is receiving treatment for cuts.

2 Your treatment of someone is the way you behave towards them.
EXAMPLE We don't want any special treatment.

treason   **HISTORY**
NOUN

Treason is when someone plans something against the interests of their country.
EXAMPLE Guy Fawkes was put to death for treason after he plotted to blow up the Houses of Parliament.

treaty treaties   **HISTORY**
NOUN

A treaty is a written agreement between countries to do something or to help each other.
EXAMPLE The Treaty of Versailles was drawn up after the First World War.

tremendous
ADJECTIVE

Tremendous means large, impressive or very good.
EXAMPLE It was a tremendous performance.

trend trends
NOUN

A trend is a change towards doing or being something different.
EXAMPLE There is now a trend towards healthier eating.

trial trials
NOUN   **CITIZENSHIP**

1 A trial is the legal process in which a judge and jury decide whether a person is guilty of a crime.
EXAMPLE They saw a murder trial on their visit to the court.

2 A trial is an experiment in which something is tested.
EXAMPLE Trials of the drug start next month.

trick tricks tricking tricked
VERB

1 If someone tricks you, they deceive you.
EXAMPLE His family tricked him into leaving home.

▶ *NOUN*

2 A trick is an action done to deceive someone.
EXAMPLE He will use any trick to get what he wants.

3 Tricks are clever or skilful actions which are done in order to entertain people.
EXAMPLE The magician performed an amazing trick.

trigger triggers
NOUN

A trigger is the small lever on a gun which is pulled in order to fire it.
EXAMPLE Don't pull the trigger!

trouble troubles troubling troubled
NOUN

1 Troubles are difficulties or problems.
EXAMPLE Try to forget your troubles.

■ Similar words: difficulty, problem

2 If there is trouble, people are arguing or fighting.
EXAMPLE There was more trouble after the match.

▶ *VERB*

3 If something troubles you, it makes you feel worried or anxious.
EXAMPLE He was troubled by the change in his son's behaviour.

true truer truest
ADJECTIVE

1 If something is true it is based on facts.
EXAMPLE The film is based on a true story.

■ Similar words: accurate, correct

2 True is used to describe things or people that are genuine.
EXAMPLE She was a true friend.

▶ *PHRASE*

3 If something 'comes true', it happens.
EXAMPLE I hope your wish comes true.

trust trusts trusting trusted
VERB

1 If you trust someone, you believe that they are honest and will not harm you.
EXAMPLE I simply don't trust him.

2 If you trust someone to do something, you believe they will do it.

EXAMPLE Can I trust you to meet the deadline?

▶ NOUN
3 Trust is the responsibility you are given to deal with or look after important or secret things.
EXAMPLE You have betrayed their trust.

truth
NOUN
The truth is the facts about something.
EXAMPLE I know she was telling the truth.

■ **Similar words:** fact, reality

tube tubes
NOUN
1 A tube is a long, hollow object like a pipe.
EXAMPLE In hospital, he was fed by a tube that entered his nose.

2 A tube is a long, thin container.
EXAMPLE He bought a tube of toothpaste.

tunnel tunnels tunnelling tunnelled
NOUN
A tunnel is a long underground passage.
EXAMPLE The Channel Tunnel connects England and France.

turn turns turning turned
VERB
1 When you turn something or when it turns, it moves so that it faces in a different direction or is in a different position.
EXAMPLE She turned the chair to face the door.

▶ NOUN
2 A turn is an act of turning something so that it faces in a different direction.
EXAMPLE Take a right turn at the lights.

3 If it is your turn to do something, you have the right, chance or duty to do it.
EXAMPLE It's my turn to cook tonight.

■ **Similar words:** chance, go

▶ PHRASE
4 When something 'turns into' something else, it becomes something different.
EXAMPLE A hobby can be turned into a career.

5 'In turn' is used to refer to people, things or actions that are in sequence one after the other.
EXAMPLE She spoke to each student in turn.

6 If you 'turn down' someone's request or offer, you refuse or reject it.
EXAMPLE This job is too good to turn down.

7 When you 'turn on' a piece of equipment or a supply of something, you cause heat, sound or water to be produced.
EXAMPLE They turned the lights on.

8 If you 'turn over' something, you move it so that the top part faces downwards.
EXAMPLE Could you turn the tape over, please?

twin twins
NOUN
1 If two people are twins, they have the same mother and were born on the same day.
EXAMPLE Are you both twins?

▶ ADJECTIVE
2 Twin is used to describe two similar things that are close together or happen together.
EXAMPLE It is a building with twin towers.

twist twists twisting twisted
VERB
1 When you twist something, you turn the two ends in opposite directions.
EXAMPLE She twisted the lid off the bottle.

2 When something twists or is twisted, it moves or bends into a strange shape.
EXAMPLE The photograph showed the twisted wreckage of the train.

type types typing typed
NOUN
1 A type of something is a group of those things that have the same qualities.
EXAMPLE What type of dog should we get?

▶ VERB
2 If you type something, you use a typewriter or word processor to write it.
EXAMPLE I'll type the letter so it's neater.

typical
ADJECTIVE
If something is typical it behaves in a usual or expected way.
EXAMPLE It's typical of him to be late.

■ **Similar words:** characteristic, usual

Uu Vv Uu

ultimate
ADJECTIVE
1 Ultimate means final or eventual.
EXAMPLE Winning the World Cup is their ultimate goal.

2 Ultimate means highest or most significant.
EXAMPLE My ultimate aim is to write a novel.

understand understands understanding understood
VERB
1 If you understand what someone says, you know what they mean.
EXAMPLE I understand you completely.

2 If you understand a situation, you know what is happening and why.
EXAMPLE You are too young to understand what is going on.

understanding
NOUN
1 If you have an understanding of something, you have some knowledge about it.
EXAMPLE I have a basic understanding of computers.

▶ ADJECTIVE
2 Understanding means kind and sympathetic.
EXAMPLE They will need to be patient and understanding.

unemployment   CITIZENSHIP
NOUN
Unemployment is the state of being without a job.
EXAMPLE We now have the highest rate of unemployment for five years.

unexpected
ADJECTIVE
Unexpected means surprising.
EXAMPLE His death was totally unexpected.

unfortunate
ADJECTIVE
Unfortunate means unlucky.
EXAMPLE Some unfortunate people were injured in the crash.

unfortunately
ADVERB
You can say unfortunately to show that you are sorry about what you are saying.
EXAMPLE Unfortunately, I can't stay for long.

unhappy unhappier unhappiest
ADJECTIVE
1 Unhappy means sad and depressed.
EXAMPLE I was very unhappy when I lost my job.

2 Unhappy means not pleased or satisfied.
EXAMPLE I am unhappy at being left out.

union unions   CITIZENSHIP
NOUN
A union is an organization of workers which aims to improve the working conditions of its members.
EXAMPLE She is thinking of joining a union.

unique
◻ Said: yoo-neek
ADJECTIVE
1 Something that is unique is the only one of its kind.
EXAMPLE Each person's fingerprint is unique.

2 If something is unique to one person or thing, it is to do with that person or thing only.
EXAMPLE Some trees are unique to the Canary Islands.

Something is either 'unique' or 'not unique', so you should avoid saying things like 'rather unique' or 'very unique'.

unit units
NOUN
1 A unit is a single complete thing.
EXAMPLE The support of the family unit is important for children.

2 A unit is a group of people who work together at a particular job.
EXAMPLE The police sent in its Rapid Response Unit.

unite unites uniting united
VERB
If a number of people unite, they join together and act as a group.
EXAMPLE The other parties united to defeat the government.

United Kingdom
NOUN
The United Kingdom is Great Britain and Northern Ireland.
EXAMPLE It was her first visit to the United Kingdom.

United Kingdom

United Nations

NOUN

The United Nations is an organization which tries to encourage peace and co-operation between countries.

EXAMPLE **A spokesman from the United Nations then came forward.**

United States of America

NOUN

The United States of America is a country in the continent of North America.

EXAMPLE **Petrol is cheaper in the United States of America.**

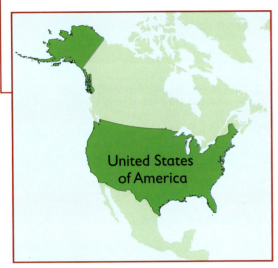

United States of America

universe

NOUN

The universe is the whole of space, including all the stars and planets.

EXAMPLE **There are millions of stars in the universe.**

university universities

NOUN

A university is a place where students study for degrees.

EXAMPLE **He spent three years at university.**

unknown

ADJECTIVE

If something is unknown, people do not know about it or have not heard of it.

EXAMPLE **An unknown number of people were hurt.**

unlikely

ADJECTIVE

If something is unlikely, it is probably not true or probably will not happen.

EXAMPLE **It is unlikely that he'll arrive today.**

unusual

ADJECTIVE

Something that is unusual does not happen very often.

EXAMPLE **It's very unusual for him to make a mistake.**

urban   GEOGRAPHY

ADJECTIVE

Urban means to do with towns or cities.

EXAMPLE **Urban areas can be very crowded and noisy.**

urge urges urging urged

NOUN

1 An urge is a strong wish to do something.

EXAMPLE **He had an urge to take revenge.**

▶ VERB

2 If you urge someone to do something, you try hard to persuade them to do it.

EXAMPLE **He urged her to come to Ireland.**

urgent

ADJECTIVE

Urgent means needing to be dealt with as soon as possible.

EXAMPLE **The unit sent an urgent request for reinforcements.**

urine   SCIENCE

NOUN

Said: *yoor*-rin

Urine is the waste liquid that you get rid of when you go to the toilet.

EXAMPLE **Urine is tested for traces of glucose to find out if a person is diabetic.**

used

VERB

1 Something that used to be done or used to be true was done or was true in the past.

EXAMPLE **People used to come and visit him every day.**

▶ PHRASE

2 If you are 'used to' something, you are familiar with it and have often experienced it.

EXAMPLE **I'm used to having very little sleep.**

▶ ADJECTIVE

3 A used object has had a previous owner.

EXAMPLE **The garage sold used cars.**

useful

ADJECTIVE

If something is useful, you can use it in order to do something or to help you in some way.

EXAMPLE **That is useful information.**

usual

ADJECTIVE

1 Usual describes something that happens or is done or used most often.

EXAMPLE **My father took his usual seat by the fire.**

▶ PHRASE

2 If something happens 'as usual', it normally happens or happens in the way that it normally does.

EXAMPLE **As usual, when he was nervous he started to shake.**

usually

ADVERB

If something usually happens, it is the thing that most often happens in a particular situation.

EXAMPLE **We usually eat in here.**

utensil utensils   TECHNOLOGY

Said: *yoo-ten*-sul

NOUN

A utensil is a hand-held instrument that you use to help you do a particular kind of work, especially cooking.

EXAMPLE **They put the kitchen utensils back in the drawer.**

A B C D E F G H I J K L M N O P Q R S T **U** V W X Y Z

vacuum vacuums
SCIENCE

📖 **Said:** *vak*-yoom

NOUN

A vacuum is a space containing no matter.

EXAMPLE They sucked out the air from the jar to produce a vacuum.

valley valleys
GEOGRAPHY

NOUN

A valley is a stretch of land between hills.

EXAMPLE The Martindale Valley is much visited by walkers.

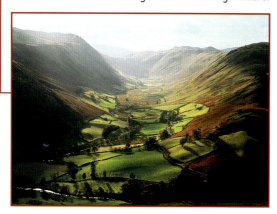

valuable valuables

ADJECTIVE

1 Something that is valuable has great value.

EXAMPLE My grandfather left me a valuable watch in his will.

▬ **Similar word:** expensive

▶ *PLURAL NOUN*

2 Valuables are things that you own which cost a lot of money.

EXAMPLE Keep your valuables in a safe place.

value values valuing valued

NOUN

1 The value of something is its importance or usefulness.

EXAMPLE The spy had information of great value.

2 The value of something is the amount of money that it is worth.

EXAMPLE The value of the company rose to £5 million.

3 Our values are our beliefs about what is right.

EXAMPLE Becky questioned her mother's values.

▶ *VERB*

4 If you value something, you think it is important.

EXAMPLE I value my free time.

variety varieties

NOUN

1 If something has variety, it consists of things which are not all the same.

EXAMPLE I like to have variety in my life.

2 A variety of things is a number of different kinds of them.

EXAMPLE The paper has a wide variety of readers.

▬ **Similar words:** mixture, range

3 A variety of something is a type of it.

EXAMPLE King Edwards are a variety of potato.

various

ADJECTIVE

Various means of several different types.

EXAMPLE The forest has trees of various sorts.

vary varies varying varied

VERB

1 If things vary, they change.

EXAMPLE Weather patterns vary greatly.

2 If you vary something, you introduce changes in it.

EXAMPLE Vary your routes as much as possible.

vegetable vegetables

NOUN

Vegetables are plants which can be eaten, such as carrots.

EXAMPLE Eat plenty of fresh vegetables.

vehicle vehicles

📖 **Said:** *vee*-ik-kl

NOUN

A vehicle is a machine, often with an engine, used for moving people or goods.

EXAMPLE The army vehicles rumbled through the village.

velocity velocities
SCIENCE

NOUN

Velocity is speed in a particular direction.

EXAMPLE They calculated the velocity of the car after 15 seconds.

venue venues

📖 **Said:** *ven*-yoo

NOUN

The venue for an event is the place where it will happen.

EXAMPLE Where is the venue for this birthday party?

verb verbs
ENGLISH

NOUN

A verb is a word that describes an action or a state of being.

EXAMPLE 'Has', 'go' and 'run' are all verbs.

Some verbs indicate events that happen: 'Kathryn visits the dentist.' Other verbs indicate the way things are: 'Kathryn has one sister.'

verse verses
ENGLISH

NOUN

1 In poetry, verse is another word for stanza.

EXAMPLE The poem had four verses.

2 Verse is another word for poetry.
EXAMPLE She preferred writing in verse, not prose.

version versions
NOUN
A version of something is a different form of it.
EXAMPLE My computer is a cheaper version of yours.

vertical
ADJECTIVE
Something which is vertical points up.
EXAMPLE He drew a vertical line down the page.

vet vets
NOUN
A vet is a doctor for animals.
EXAMPLE I must take the dog to the vet.

veteran veterans
NOUN
1 A veteran is someone who has served in the armed forces, particularly during a war.
EXAMPLE My cousin is a veteran of the Gulf War.

2 A veteran is someone who has been involved in a particular activity for a long time.
EXAMPLE Tony Benn is a veteran of British politics.

victim victims
NOUN
A victim is someone who has been harmed or injured by someone or something.
EXAMPLE She was a victim of road rage.

victory victories
NOUN
Victory is success in a battle or competition.
EXAMPLE The game ended in a victory for Manchester United.

■ **Similar word:** win

video videos videoing videoed
NOUN
1 Video is the recording and showing of films and events using a video recorder, tape and a television set.
EXAMPLE They watched the race on video.

2 A video is a video recorder.
EXAMPLE Set the video for 8 o'clock.

▶ *VERB*
3 If you video something, you record it on tape to watch later.
EXAMPLE I'll video that programme for you.

view views viewing viewed
NOUN
1 A view is a belief or an opinion.
EXAMPLE His political views were well known.

2 A view is everything you can see from a particular place.
EXAMPLE The new building spoiled the view from my window.

■ **Similar word:** scene

▶ *VERB*
3 If you view something in a particular way, you think of it in that way.
EXAMPLE They viewed me with dislike.

village villages GEOGRAPHY
NOUN
A village is a collection of houses and other buildings in the countryside.
EXAMPLE There are some beautiful villages in the Cotswolds.

violence
NOUN
Violence is a physical activity which is meant to harm people.
EXAMPLE Twenty people were killed in the violence.

violent
ADJECTIVE
If someone or something is violent, it is likely to cause physical harm.
EXAMPLE The police warned that he was a violent criminal.

virtual
🔲 **Said:** *vur-tyool*
ADJECTIVE
Virtual means that something is so nearly true it can be seen as completely true.
EXAMPLE The country is in a virtual state of war.

virtually
ADVERB
Virtually means almost.
EXAMPLE It is virtually impossible to do it all in a day.

virus viruses
🔲 **Said:** *vie-russ*
NOUN SCIENCE
1 A virus is a kind of germ which can cause disease.
EXAMPLE The flu virus is dangerous for old people.

ICT
2 A virus is a program which damages the information stored in a computer system.
EXAMPLE Check the disk for viruses.

visible
ADJECTIVE
If something is visible it can be seen.
EXAMPLE The island is visible from the beach.

vision visions
NOUN
1 Vision is the ability to see clearly.
EXAMPLE The illness can cause loss of vision.

2 Your vision of something is what you imagine it might be like.
EXAMPLE My vision of the future is bleak.

A B C D E F G H I J K L M N O P Q R S T U **V** W X Y Z

A B C D E F G H I J K L M N O P Q R S T U **V** W X Y Z

vital
ADJECTIVE
Vital means necessary or very important.
EXAMPLE The messenger had some vital information.

⊟ **Similar words:** essential, necessary

vitamin vitamins SCIENCE
NOUN
Vitamins are substances in food which you need in order to remain healthy.
EXAMPLE Vitamin C is an important part of our diet.

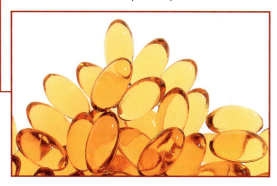

vocabulary vocabularies
NOUN
1 The vocabulary of a language is all the words in it.
EXAMPLE The German vocabulary is vast.
2 Someone's vocabulary is all the words they know in a particular language.
EXAMPLE She has a wide vocabulary for a child of that age.

voice voices
NOUN
Your voice is what you hear when you speak or sing.
EXAMPLE She has a lovely voice.

volt volts SCIENCE
NOUN
A volt is a unit of the force of an electric current.
EXAMPLE It was a 3 volt battery.

volume volumes MATHS
NOUN
1 The volume of something is the amount of it that there is, or the space it occupies.
EXAMPLE Can you work out the volume of the box?
2 The volume of a radio, TV or record player is how loud it is.
EXAMPLE He turned down the volume.
3 A volume is a book, or one of a series of books.
EXAMPLE The first volume of his diaries was published last year.

voluntary
ADJECTIVE
Something is voluntary if you are not forced to do it.
EXAMPLE These classes are voluntary.

volunteer volunteers volunteering volunteered
NOUN
1 A volunteer is someone who does work for which they are not paid.
EXAMPLE She worked as a volunteer for Greenpeace.

▶ VERB
2 If you volunteer to do something, you offer to do it willingly.
EXAMPLE James volunteered to clean the kitchen.

vote votes voting voted CITIZENSHIP
VERB
1 If you vote for someone, you choose them to be a leader.
EXAMPLE Millions of South Africans voted for Nelson Mandela.

▶ NOUN
2 A person's vote is their chance to elect a leader.
EXAMPLE When the votes have been counted, the winner will be announced.

vowel vowels ENGLISH
NOUN
The vowels are the letters a, e, i, o and u.
EXAMPLE There are two vowels in the word 'tractor'.

vulnerable
ADJECTIVE
Vulnerable means weak and without protection.
EXAMPLE Old people can be very vulnerable.

⊟ **Similar word:** weak

wage wages waging waged
NOUN
1 Someone's wages are the payment they receive each week for the work they do.
EXAMPLE His wages have gone up.

▶ VERB
2 If a person or country wages a campaign or war, they start it and carry it on over a period of time.
EXAMPLE Rebels have been waging a campaign against the government.

wait waits waiting waited
VERB
1 If you wait, you spend time before something happens.
EXAMPLE I had to wait a week for the results.

▶ NOUN
2 A wait is a period of time before something happens.
EXAMPLE You'll have a long wait for a bus.

wake wakes waking woke woken
VERB
To wake means to become conscious, or to make someone conscious, after being asleep.
EXAMPLE She woke to find her mother in her room.

walk walks walking walked
VERB
1 When you walk, you move along by putting one foot in front of the other.
EXAMPLE The baby had just learnt to walk.

▶ NOUN
2 A walk is a journey made by walking.
EXAMPLE The hotel is a short walk from the station.

wall walls
NOUN
1 A wall is one of the vertical sides of a building or room.
EXAMPLE Ben covered his bedroom walls with posters.

2 A wall is a vertical structure made of stone or brick that surrounds or divides an area of land.
EXAMPLE Frances climbed the garden wall.

want wants wanting wanted
VERB
1 If you want something, you feel a desire or a need for it.
EXAMPLE Do you want a drink?

2 If someone is wanted by the police, the police are searching for them.
EXAMPLE John was wanted for fraud.

war wars
NOUN

HISTORY

1 War is a period of fighting between countries.
EXAMPLE The Second World War ended in 1945.

2 A war is a competition between groups of people, or a campaign against something.
EXAMPLE She was a great fighter in the war against drugs.

ward wards
NOUN
A ward is a room in a hospital which has beds for several people.
EXAMPLE The emergency ward was very busy.

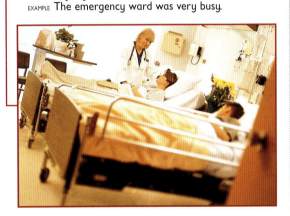

warm warmer warmest; warms warming warmed
ADJECTIVE
1 Something that is warm has some heat, or is made of material that will give you heat.
EXAMPLE It's not very warm today, is it?

2 Warm means friendly.
EXAMPLE He liked her warm smile.

▶ VERB
3 To warm means to heat something gently.
EXAMPLE He warmed his hands by the fire.

warn warns warning warned
VERB
1 If you warn someone about a problem or danger, you tell them about it.
EXAMPLE They warned him of the dangers of sailing alone.

2 If you warn someone not to do something, you advise them not to do it.
EXAMPLE Mrs Blunt warned me not to interfere.

warning warnings
NOUN
A warning is something which is said or written to tell people of a possible problem or danger.
EXAMPLE The soldiers opened fire without warning.

wash washes washing washed
VERB
1 If you wash something, you clean it with water and soap.
EXAMPLE He had to wash the mud out of his hair.

A B C D E F G H I J K L M N O P Q R S T U V **W** X Y Z

▸ *NOUN*
2 If you have a wash, you clean yourself using soap and water.
EXAMPLE **She had a wash and changed her clothes.**

▸ *PHRASE*
3 If something is 'washed up' on land, it is carried there by a river or the sea.
EXAMPLE **A body had been washed up on the beach.**

waste *wastes wasting wasted*
VERB
1 To waste something means to use too much of it on something.
EXAMPLE **I don't want to waste money on a hotel.**

2 If you waste an opportunity, you do not take advantage of it .
EXAMPLE **He wasted his chance to score.**

▸ *NOUN*
3 If something is a waste of time, money or energy, it is not important or necessary.
EXAMPLE **It's a waste of time complaining about it.**

4 Waste is material that has been used and is no longer wanted.
EXAMPLE **How should we dispose of all our waste?**

watch *watches watching watched*
NOUN
1 A watch is a small clock which you wear on your wrist.
EXAMPLE **He was given a gold watch.**

▸ *VERB*
2 If you watch something, you look at it or pay attention to it.
EXAMPLE **They were watching television.**

▸ *PHRASE*
3 If you 'watch out' for something, you pay attention so that you notice it.
EXAMPLE **Watch out for more special offers next week.**

water *waters watering watered*
NOUN
1 Water is a clear liquid which falls from clouds as rain.
EXAMPLE **Fetch me a glass of water.**

▸ *VERB*
2 If you water a plant, you pour water into the soil around it.
EXAMPLE **He forgot to water the flowers.**

3 If your eyes or mouth water, they produce liquid.
EXAMPLE **The smell of dinner made his mouth water.**

wave *waves waving waved*
VERB
1 If you wave something, you hold it up and move it from side to side.
EXAMPLE **People lined the streets waving flags.**

▸ *NOUN*
2 A wave is the action of waving your hand.
EXAMPLE **She gave them a wave from the window.**

3 A wave is a ridge of water on the surface of the sea, caused by winds or tides.
EXAMPLE **The waves broke on the shore.**

SCIENCE

4 Some types of energy, such as light and sound, travel in the form of waves.
EXAMPLE **An electric field generates electromagnetic waves.**

way *ways*
NOUN
1 A way of doing something is the method that you use in order to do it.
EXAMPLE **That's an excellent way of cooking chicken.**

2 The way in which you do something is the manner in which you do it.
EXAMPLE **I like the way he speaks.**

3 The way to a particular place is the route that you take in order to get there.
EXAMPLE **Is this the way in?**

▸ *PLURAL NOUN*
4 The ways of a person or group are their customs or their usual behaviour.
EXAMPLE **Their ways are certainly different from ours.**

▸ *PHRASE*
5 You use way in expressions such as 'a little way' or 'a long way' to say how far away something is.
EXAMPLE **Christmas is still a long way away.**

weak *weaker weakest*
ADJECTIVE
1 If something is weak, they do not have much strength or energy.
EXAMPLE **He was weak from lack of sleep.**

2 Weak means not very determined.
EXAMPLE **He was a weak man who wouldn't speak out.**

weaken *weakens weakening weakened*
VERB
If someone weakens something, they make it less strong or certain.
EXAMPLE **Tom has been weakened by his illness.**

wealth
NOUN
Wealth is a large amount of money or property which someone owns.
EXAMPLE **His own wealth grew and grew.**

You cannot talk about more than one 'wealths'.

weapon *weapons*
NOUN
A weapon is an object used to kill or hurt people, such as a gun, knife or missile.
EXAMPLE **Several countries now have nuclear weapons.**

wear *wears wearing wore worn*
VERB
1 When you wear clothes, jewellery or make-up, you have them on your body or face.
EXAMPLE **He was wearing a brown uniform.**

▸ *PHRASE*
2 If a feeling 'wears off', it gradually disappears.
EXAMPLE **After an hour the pain wore off.**

3 When something 'wears out' or when you wear it out, it is used so much that it becomes thin or weak.

EXAMPLE He wore out his shoes walking around the city.

4 If something wears you out, they make you very tired.
EXAMPLE The kids wore him out.

weather
GEOGRAPHY

NOUN
The weather is the condition in the atmosphere at a particular time.
EXAMPLE The weather today is surprisingly mild.

wedding weddings
NOUN
A wedding is a marriage ceremony.
EXAMPLE I would like a traditional wedding.

Wednesday Wednesdays
NOUN
Wednesday is the day between Tuesday and Thursday.

week weeks
NOUN
1 A week is a period of seven days.
EXAMPLE I had a letter from my mother last week.

2 A week is the number of hours you spend at work during a week.
EXAMPLE He works a 35-hour week.

weekend weekends
NOUN
A weekend is Saturday and Sunday.
EXAMPLE I'll see you at the weekend.

weekly
ADJECTIVE OR ADVERB
Weekly refers to something that happens or appears once a week.
EXAMPLE The group meets weekly.

weigh weighs weighing weighed
□ Said: way
VERB
1 If someone or something weighs a particular amount, that is how heavy they are.
EXAMPLE He weighs 60 kilograms.

2 If you weigh something, you measure how heavy it is.
EXAMPLE Weigh your parcels before you post them.

▶ PHRASE
3 To weigh something down means to stop it moving easily because of its weight.
EXAMPLE He was weighed down by his heavy bag.

weight weights
□ Said: wayt
NOUN
1 The weight of someone or something is how heavy they are.
EXAMPLE What is your height and weight?

2 Weights are metal objects which weigh a known amount.
EXAMPLE I was in the gym lifting weights.

welcome welcomes welcoming welcomed
VERB
1 If you welcome someone, you greet them in a friendly way.
EXAMPLE Welcome to Washington.

2 If you welcome something, you approve of it and support it.
EXAMPLE He welcomed the decision.

▶ NOUN
3 A welcome is a greeting to a visitor.
EXAMPLE He's sure to receive a warm welcome.

▶ ADJECTIVE
4 If someone is welcome somewhere, they will be accepted there in a friendly way.
EXAMPLE New members are always welcome.

5 A welcome action or decision is one that you approve of and support.
EXAMPLE This was certainly a welcome change.

welfare
NOUN
1 The welfare of a person or group is their general state of health and comfort.
EXAMPLE I am concerned for his welfare.

2 Welfare services are provided to help with people's living conditions and financial problems.
EXAMPLE They proposed changes to the welfare system.

well better best; wells
ADVERB
1 Well means in a good, skilful or pleasing way.
EXAMPLE We treat our employees well.

2 Well means thoroughly and completely.
EXAMPLE I don't know her very well.

▶ PHRASE
3 'As well' means also.
EXAMPLE I'm hurt as well.

▶ ADJECTIVE
4 If you are well, you are healthy.
EXAMPLE I'm not very well today.

▶ NOUN
5 A well is a hole drilled in the ground from which water, oil or gas is obtained.
EXAMPLE She went to fetch some water from the well.

well-known
ADJECTIVE
Well-known means famous or known to many people.
EXAMPLE Charles Dickens is a well-known writer.

Welsh
ADJECTIVE
1 Welsh means to do with Wales.
EXAMPLE He lived in the Welsh valleys.

▶ NOUN
2 Welsh is a language spoken in some parts of Wales.
EXAMPLE He is learning Welsh.

western westerns
ADJECTIVE

1 Western means in or from the west.
EXAMPLE He never left western Europe.

▸ *NOUN*
2 A western is a book or film about life in the west of America in the nineteenth century.
EXAMPLE He played a cowboy in a western.

wet wetter wettest; wets wetting wetted
ADJECTIVE

1 If something is wet, it is covered in water or another liquid.
EXAMPLE My hair was still wet.

2 If the weather is wet, it is raining.
EXAMPLE It was very wet and windy that day.

3 If something such as paint or cement is wet, it is not yet dry.
EXAMPLE Mind the wet paint on the walls.

▸ *VERB*
4 To wet something means to put water or some other liquid on it.
EXAMPLE For the best results, wet the hair first.

what
PRONOUN

1 You use what in questions when you are asking for information.
EXAMPLE What time is it?

2 You use what to refer to something that is unknown or that has not been described.
EXAMPLE I don't know what you mean.

▸ *ADJECTIVE*
3 You use what to show that you are talking about the whole of an amount.
EXAMPLE They had to use what money they had.

4 You use what to express your opinion of something.
EXAMPLE What a terrible thing to do!

whatever
PRONOUN

1 You use whatever to refer to anything or everything of a particular type.
EXAMPLE He said he would do whatever he could.

▸ *CONJUNCTION*
2 You use whatever when you do not know precisely what something is.
EXAMPLE Whatever it is, I don't like it.

3 You use whatever to say that something is the case in all circumstances.
EXAMPLE Whatever happens, you have to behave properly.

▸ *ADVERB*
4 You use whatever to emphasize a negative statement or a question.
EXAMPLE You have no proof whatever.

wheel wheels
NOUN

1 A wheel is a circular object which is fixed underneath vehicles so that they can move along.
EXAMPLE The car's wheels needed adjusting.

2 The wheel of a car is its steering wheel.
EXAMPLE My dad was at the wheel of his van.

when
ADVERB

1 You use when to ask what time something happened or will happen.
EXAMPLE When are you leaving?

▸ *CONJUNCTION*
2 You use when to refer to the time at which something happens.
EXAMPLE I met him when I was sixteen.

3 You use when to state the reason for an opinion or question.
EXAMPLE How did you pass the exam when you hadn't studied for it?

whenever
CONJUNCTION

Whenever means at any time, or every time that something happens.
EXAMPLE Avoid fried food whenever possible.

where
ADVERB

1 You use where to ask about the place something is in, or the place it is coming from or going to.
EXAMPLE Where is Philip?

▸ *CONJUNCTION*
2 You use where to refer to the place in which something is situated or happening.
EXAMPLE I don't know where we are.

whereas
CONJUNCTION

You use whereas to introduce a comment which contrasts with the other part of the sentence.
EXAMPLE Her eyes are blue, whereas mine are brown.

whether
CONJUNCTION

You use whether when you are talking about a choice between two or more alternatives.
EXAMPLE They have two weeks to decide whether or not to buy it.

which
ADJECTIVE OR PRONOUN

1 You use which to ask about two or more alternatives or to refer to a choice between alternatives.
EXAMPLE Which room are you in?

▸ *PRONOUN*
2 You use which at the beginning of a clause in order to give more information about it.
EXAMPLE Soldiers opened fire on a car which failed to stop.

while
CONJUNCTION

1 If something happens while something else is happening, the two things happen at the same time.
EXAMPLE I look after the children while she works.

2 You use the word while to introduce something which contrasts with another part of the sentence.
EXAMPLE The first two services are free, while the third costs £10.

▸ NOUN
3 A while is a period of time.
EXAMPLE They walked on in silence for a while.

whip whips whipping whipped
NOUN

1 A whip is a thin piece of leather or rope attached to a handle, which is used for hitting people or animals.
EXAMPLE He held a leather whip.

▸ VERB
2 To whip means to hit with a whip.
EXAMPLE He was whipping the horse too hard.

whisper whispers whispering whispered
VERB

If you whisper something, you say it very quietly.
EXAMPLE He whispered the message to David.

white whiter whitest; whites
NOUN OR ADJECTIVE

1 White is the lightest possible colour.
EXAMPLE He had nice white teeth.

▸ ADJECTIVE
2 Someone who is white has a pale skin and is of European origin.
EXAMPLE He was white, with short brown hair.

▸ NOUN
3 The white of an egg is the clear liquid surrounding the yolk.
EXAMPLE It was a pudding made from egg whites and sugar.

who
PRONOUN OR CONJUNCTION

1 You use the word who when you are asking or talking about someone's identity.
EXAMPLE Who's there?

▸ PRONOUN
2 You use the word who at the beginning of a clause in order to specify the person you are talking about or to give more information about them.
EXAMPLE There's the man who took my bag!

whole
NOUN OR ADJECTIVE

1 The whole of something is all of it.
EXAMPLE We spent the whole summer there.

▸ PHRASE
2 You say 'on the whole' to show that what you are saying is true only in a general sense.
EXAMPLE On the whole, I'm in favour of it.

▸ ADJECTIVE
3 Whole means in one piece and not broken or damaged.
EXAMPLE He swallowed it whole.

whom
PRONOUN OR CONJUNCTION

Whom is used instead of who in formal English when it is the object of a verb or preposition.
EXAMPLE They are free to appoint whom they like.

whose
PRONOUN

You use whose to ask or talk about who something belongs to.
EXAMPLE Whose CD is this?

Don't confuse 'whose' with 'who's'. 'Whose' is used to show possession or belonging: 'Whose bag is this?' 'Who's' stands for 'who is'.

wide wider widest
ADJECTIVE

1 Something that is wide measures a large distance from one side to the other.
EXAMPLE The wreckage was scattered over a wide area.

▸ ADVERB
2 If you open or spread something wide, you open it as far as you can.
EXAMPLE Open your mouth wide.

widespread
ADJECTIVE

Something that is widespread exists or happens over a large area or to a great extent.
EXAMPLE Protesters complained about the widespread use of chemicals in farming.

wife wives
NOUN

A man's wife is the woman he is married to.
EXAMPLE His wife is a teacher.

wild wilder wildest
ADJECTIVE

1 Wild means living or growing in natural surroundings and not looked after by people.
EXAMPLE Wolves roam forests and other wild areas.

2 Wild behaviour is excited or uncontrolled.
EXAMPLE As George came on stage, they went wild.

will wills willing willed
VERB

1 If you will something to happen, you try to make it happen by thinking hard.
EXAMPLE I looked at the phone, willing it to ring.

▸ NOUN
2 Will is the determination to do something.
EXAMPLE He lost his will to live.

3 A will is a legal document stating what you want to happen to your money and property when you die.

A
B
C
D
E
F
G
H
I
J
K
L
M
N
O
P
Q
R
S
T
U
V
W
X
Y
Z

EXAMPLE He left the house to his grandson in his will.

willing
ADJECTIVE
If you are willing to do something, you will do it if someone wants you to.
EXAMPLE They are now willing to take part.

wind winds
NOUN
1 A wind is a current of air moving across the earth's surface.
EXAMPLE There was a strong wind blowing.
2 Wind is gas in your stomach, which produces discomfort.
EXAMPLE The food he had eaten gave him wind.

wind winds winding wound
VERB
1 If a road or river winds somewhere, it twists and turns in that direction.
EXAMPLE The road winds uphill for another mile.
2 When you wind something round something else, you wrap it round it several times.
EXAMPLE She wound the bandage round his knee.
3 When you wind a device such as a watch, you turn a key or handle several times in order to make it work.
EXAMPLE I'd forgotten to wind my watch.

wine wines
NOUN
Wine is an alcoholic drink, usually made from grapes.
EXAMPLE She enjoyed a glass of wine with her meal.

wing wings
NOUN
1 The wings of a bird or insect are the two parts of its body that it uses for flying.
EXAMPLE The bird flapped its wings furiously.
2 The wings of an aircraft are the long, flat parts on each side that support it while it is flying.
EXAMPLE He had a seat beside the wing.

winner winners
NOUN
The winner of a prize, race or competition is the person or thing that wins it.
EXAMPLE The winner was a horse called Last Town.

wipe wipes wiping wiped
VERB
If you wipe something, you rub its surface to remove dirt or liquid from it.
EXAMPLE She wiped her hands on a towel.

wire wires
NOUN
Wire is a thin piece of metal that is used to fasten things or to carry electric current.
EXAMPLE The electrician joined the wires carefully.

wise wiser wisest
ADJECTIVE
Someone who is wise uses their experience and knowledge to make sensible decisions.
EXAMPLE He was wise not to go out during the storm.

wish wishes wishing wished
NOUN
1 A wish is a desire for something.
EXAMPLE It was her wish to be a doctor.
▶ VERB
2 If you wish to do something, you want to do it.
EXAMPLE If you wish to leave a message, speak after the tone.

witch witches
NOUN
A witch is a woman who claims to have magic powers.
EXAMPLE They read a fairy tale about an evil witch.

within
PREPOSITION OR ADVERB
1 Within means in or inside.
EXAMPLE A man appeared from within the building.
2 Within means before a period of time has passed.
EXAMPLE You must write back within fourteen days.

without
PREPOSITION
Without means not having, doing or feeling a particular thing.
EXAMPLE He looked younger without his glasses.

witness witnesses
NOUN
A witness to an accident or crime is someone who saw it.
EXAMPLE There were no witnesses to the crime.

wonder wonders wondering wondered
VERB
If you wonder about something, you try to guess or understand more about it.
EXAMPLE I wonder what the noise was.

wonderful
ADJECTIVE
If something is wonderful it is very good.
EXAMPLE It's wonderful to see you.

woodwind   MUSIC
NOUN
Woodwind is the group of instruments (not including brass instruments) that make sound by being blown.
EXAMPLE The oboe is in the woodwind section of the orchestra.

word words
NOUN
1 A word is a single unit of language in speech or writing.
EXAMPLE She crossed out the word 'handsome'.

2 If you have a word with someone, you have a short conversation with them.
EXAMPLE Could I have a word with you?

3 If you give someone your word, you promise to do something.
EXAMPLE He gave me his word that he would come.

word process word processes
word processing word processed ICT
VERB
If you word process you use the computer to produce and print a piece of writing.
EXAMPLE She word processed her homework.

word processor
word processors ICT
NOUN
A word processor is an electronic machine which is used to produce pieces of writing.
EXAMPLE I like to write stories on the word processor.

world
NOUN
The world is the planet that we live on.
EXAMPLE I'd like to travel around the world.

World Wide Web ICT
NOUN
The World Wide Web is a massive library of information which can be reached through the Internet.
EXAMPLE The company advertised on the World Wide Web.

worried
ADJECTIVE
Worried means anxious.
EXAMPLE I'm worried about losing my passport.

worry worries worrying worried
VERB
To worry means to feel anxious.
EXAMPLE I worry about her constantly.

worship worships worshipping
worshipped RE
VERB
To worship is to praise God.
EXAMPLE The family liked to worship together.

worth
PREPOSITION
1 If something is worth a sum of money, it has that value.
EXAMPLE They bought a house worth £200,000.

2 If something is worth doing, it is so good or enjoyable that it deserves to be done.
EXAMPLE It cost a lot but it was worth it.

▸ NOUN
3 Worth is the amount of something that you can buy for a particular sum of money.
EXAMPLE He put five pound's worth of petrol into his car.

would
VERB
1 You use would to say what someone thought was going to happen.
EXAMPLE We were sure it would be a success.

2 You use would when you are referring to the result of a possible situation.
EXAMPLE It would be fun to try.

3 You use would when you are referring to someone's willingness to do something.
EXAMPLE She said she would help me.

4 You use would in polite questions.
EXAMPLE Would you like a drink?

wound wounds wounding wounded
NOUN
A wound is an injury to your body, especially a cut or hole caused by a weapon.
EXAMPLE The soldier died from his wounds.

wrap wraps wrapping wrapped
VERB
If you wrap something or wrap it up, you fold paper or cloth around it to cover it.
EXAMPLE Carrie was wrapping up the family's presents.

wrong
ADJECTIVE
1 Wrong means unsatisfactory or not working properly.
EXAMPLE There was something wrong with the car.

2 Wrong means bad or immoral.
EXAMPLE She was wrong to leave her child alone.

▸ NOUN
3 Wrong means actions that are bad or immoral.
EXAMPLE She was old enough to know the difference between right and wrong.

A B C D E F G H I J K L M N O P Q R S T U V **W** X Y Z

A B C D E F G H I J K L M N O P Q R S T U V W X Y Z

X-ray X-rays

NOUN

An X-ray is a stream of powerful rays which is used by doctors to examine the bones or organs inside a person's body.

EXAMPLE The X-ray showed that my arm was broken.

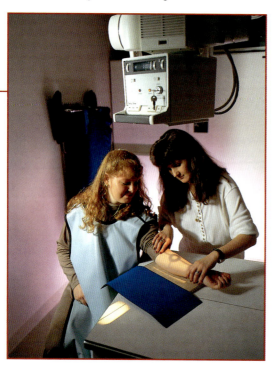

Yy Yy Yy

yacht yachts
📢 **Said:** yot
NOUN
A yacht is a boat used for racing or for pleasure trips.
EXAMPLE **They entered the round-the-world yacht race.**

yard yards
NOUN
1 A yard is a unit of length equal to 36 inches or about 91.4 centimetres.
EXAMPLE **The shop is just a few yards from my house.**

2 A yard is an area next to a building, often with a wall around it.
EXAMPLE **I saw him standing in the yard.**

yesterday
ADVERB OR NOUN
Yesterday is the day before today.
EXAMPLE **What did you do yesterday?**

yet
ADVERB
1 Yet means up to the present time.
EXAMPLE **I haven't decided yet.**

▶ *CONJUNCTION*
2 You can use yet to introduce a fact which is surprising.
EXAMPLE **He isn't a smoker, yet he always carries a lighter.**

yolk yolks
📢 **Said:** yoke
NOUN
The yolk of an egg is the yellow part in the middle.
EXAMPLE **Beat three egg yolks into the mixture.**

young younger youngest
ADJECTIVE
1 Young means not very old and not yet mature.
EXAMPLE **David is such a young child.**

▶ *PLURAL NOUN*
2 The young of an animal are its babies.
EXAMPLE **The hen may not be able to feed its young.**

your
ADJECTIVE
Your means to do with you.
EXAMPLE **I put them on your desk.**

yours
PRONOUN
1 Yours refers to something to do with you.
EXAMPLE **His hair is longer than yours.**

2 People write 'Yours sincerely' or 'Yours faithfully' at the end of a letter before they sign their name.
EXAMPLE **Yours sincerely, Ray Peacock.**

yourself yourselves
PRONOUN
1 You use yourself to refer to the person that you are speaking or writing about.
EXAMPLE **Help yourselves to food.**

2 Yourself is used to emphasize the word you.
EXAMPLE **Why can't you do it yourself?**

youth youths
NOUN
1 Someone's youth is the period of their life before they are fully adult.
EXAMPLE **In my youth I wanted to be a pilot.**

2 A youth is a young man.
EXAMPLE **They were helped by a group of youths.**

A B C D E F G H I J K L M N O P Q R S T U V W X **Y** Z

zero zeros

NOUN

MATHS

1 Zero is the number 0.

EXAMPLE Five minus five makes zero.

SCIENCE

2 Zero is freezing point.

EXAMPLE The temperature fell to ten degrees below zero.

▸ *ADJECTIVE*

3 Zero means none or nil.

EXAMPLE His chances are zero.

zone zones

GEOGRAPHY

NOUN

A zone is an area which has particular features.

EXAMPLE The two countries are in different time zones.

A B C D E F G H I J K L M N O P Q R S T U V W X Y Z